MW00946917

Marius' Mules VIII

Sons of Taranis

by S. J. A. Turney

1st Edition

"Marius' Mules: nickname acquired by the legions after the general Marius made it standard practice for the soldier to carry all of his kit about his person."

*For all my loyal readers, still
with me after eight years of
Fronto's troubles. Thank you all
from the bottom of my heart*

I would like to thank those people who helped bring Marius' Mules 8 to completion and make it a readable tome. That's Jenny and Lilian for their initial editing, my beautiful wife Tracey for her support and love, my two wonderful kids for endless procrastinating interruptions. My top cadre Leni, Barry, Paul, Robin, Alun & Stu for beta reading and catching the really dubious typos and issues.

Thanks also to Garry and Dave for the cover work and innumerable other fab folk for their support (you all know who you are, and so do I.)

Cover photos by Hannah Haynes, courtesy of Paul and Garry of the Deva Victrix Legio XX. Visit http://www.romantoursuk.com/ to see their excellent work.

Cover design by Dave Slaney.

Many thanks to the above for their skill and generosity.

All internal maps are copyright the author of this work.

DARKNESS

on the

DELTA

by

G. E. Johnson

Copyright © 2018 G. E. Johnson

All rights reserved. This book or any portion thereof may not be reproduced or used in any manner whatsoever without the expressed written permission of the author except for the use of brief quotations in a book review.

Printed in the United States of America

First Printing 2018

ISBN-13   978-1986624015

ISBN-10   1986624013

Portions of religious liturgy taken from the Book of Common Prayer® (According to the use of the Episcopal Church) © 1986 by the Church Pension Fund

Book cover from an original piece of artwork by Carolina Asbill Kile, used by artist's permission

Special Thanks to:

Melody Cleaver Dowlearn for giving me the courage to put fingers on the keyboard to see what full story was waiting to come alive

Patty Burt for being the midwife in the birth of this novel, its infancy, its growth, and for invaluable feedback on each chapter as it developed

Lisa Couch for total dedication to her job as a beta reader and the invaluable feedback she provided to make me believe this was a worthwhile undertaking

Nicole Waggoner and Roger Geiger, valued educational colleagues and published authors, for their guidance and inspiration in both writing and publishing

Neil and Barbara Melillo for critiques that helped fill in gaps and timelines to give greater clarity and reality to the overall book

To the people in the Mississippi Delta (both living and deceased) who helped shape my career in education, forming the foundation of this endeavor, but who are too many to name (but hopefully you know if you are included here)

Holy Trinity by the Lake Episcopal Church for the spiritual guidance that helped me reconcile so much of my past through unequivocal love and opportunities to serve others

Frances Farmer for her strength beyond measure to conquer cancer and share in whatever success may come from this lifelong dream of writing a book

Marty Symes, Al J. Neiburg, and Jerry Livingston (all now deceased) for giving the world a song that so completely pictures Delta life at the end of the day

INTRODUCTION

This story has waited over forty years to be told. The vast majority of it is factual with a sparse amount of fiction injected to tie events into a reasonable timeline. Some names have been altered completely, although some characters bear their true names or a variation similar enough to be recognized. Some characters are a combination of personalities, and some are entirely fictional.

Admittedly, I have not been kind to everyone in my portrayal of them. I have dealt with them somewhat harshly, just as the Delta itself deals harshly with many of us trapped in a culture that cannot surrender its generational attitudes of distrust and suspicion, anger and hate, race and divisions.

Nevertheless, this is a story that patiently stood in the wings, letting an educational career take the spotlight, but waiting to come onstage and recite its lines with sorrowful empathy and compassionate understanding. It is the story of a teacher learning some hard lessons but still being able to find joy, even in the shackles of Delta living, where we are challenged daily to embrace the discomforting humidity of separation that comes with both life and death and with race.

1 Welcome to the Delta

Itta Bena, MS 1966

The cicadas were in full volume clatter-buzzing in the heat of the midday Delta sun. Standing on the bridge that crosses Blue Lake in Berclair just outside of Itta Bena, I was startled to see a gun-toting stranger approaching me at a clip that was both determined and mission-minded. My first encounter with John Sylvester Hamilton, though friendly, was somewhat at the heart of it confrontational as a challenge to whether I truly "belonged" in his part of the Great State of Mississippi. As I had stood marveling at the blueness of the lake, he approached me with a .22 rifle in his hand.

"Hey, man! Whatcha doin'?" he asked. He was my age and height with blonde hair and brown eyes, wearing jeans and a denim shirt that had seen better years for sure. He wore a dirty, sweaty ballcap with a Staplcotton logo. And he carried a rifle as if it were part of his everyday attire. He seemed everything that I wasn't except for being another fourteen year old boy like me.

"Just admiring the view and wishing I had a fishing pole with me," I replied, but still keeping an eye on that rifle he carried.

"Aw, then you muss be new 'round here. Everybody knows you ain't gonna catch nothin' in Blue Lake. All the fish are choked out from them water hy-cents." He pronounced hyacinths as two syllables instead of three. "Best you can hope for in Blue Lake is to pop a few turtles like I plan to do with my rifle here. I'm John Sylvester. So what's your name, stranger?"

"Bern," I said.

"Bern what?" he asked.

"Just Bern. That's all."

"Just Bern?" he asked, a pinch of disdain in his tone. "What the hell kinda name is that? Yo folks Yankees or sumpin? Don't they know folks round here have two first names? You met James Harold and his two sisters Doris Fay and Sara Beth, right? They live right across the bridge there in that gray house?"

"Yes, but I also met Dimple and Trixie and their brother named Brother that live on this side of the bridge in the brick house."

"Aw, crap, boy! Don't be gettin' smart wid me. Them ain't they real names. Thems just they nicknames; but anyway, usually round here only the niggers have just one first name. So I guess I'll have to call you "Just Bern" since you ain't no nigger. Where'd yo folks get a name like that anyways? Is it short for Bernard, like a St. Bernard? Yo folks name you after a dog?"

"Well, hell no! I'm named after my grandfather Bernard Elijah Gresham who started our family business down in Jackson during the Depression. How did you get a double name like John Sylvester? Were you named after a cartoon cat?"

He grinned at the comeback. "Naw, I uz named for my granddaddy, too. His name was Elmer Sylvester Hamilton. He uz a cotton farmer in these parts who took over runnin' the farm after his daddy, my great granddaddy, Sylvester Moses, got drunk and fell into the Yazoo River and drowned when he uz settin' out trot lines. Damn fool, if you ask me, but he uz kin, so the name lives on. So how long you gonna be around here this summa?"

3

"I'll be here visiting almost all summer long, staying with my aunt while my mom and dad close up their Jackson office and get everything moved up here to Greenwood to open up for business. So I guess we might as well make a peace pact here and now if we're going to be friends living this close, but you can't keep calling me 'Just Bern' like you said. People will be making fun of me before they even have a chance to get to know me."

"Aw, doan you worry bout dat. Kids round here know how I am, just funnin' all the time. And it's just part of Delta ways to make fun of people we don't know anyway. What kind of bidness yo folks run?"

"They are both ACLU civil rights lawyers."

"Aw, shit!" He spit out the words as if he had choked on a gnat in his mouth, which I later learned happened often in the Delta.

"Yep, why do you think I suggested a peace pact up front?"

"Well, Just Bern, you best not be tellin' folks that unless you have to. It might not go well for ya in makin' friends."

Just as he said that, with lightning fast reflexes he raised the rifle and fired at a box turtle that broke the surface near the edge of an overgrowth of mallows. I tried not to flinch, but I know I did. Thank goodness he didn't seem to notice. Reacting in a startled way over a dead turtle didn't seem like a good idea, but killing an animal just for the fun of killing was disconcerting to me. I'd heard too many stories of whites terrorizing and even killing blacks "just for fun." Popping turtles just seemed an awfully strange and savage way to wile away the summer heat, but it was best just to continue the present conversation.

"I'm not too worried about any backlash," I assured him. "I doubt the Delta is so different from Jackson."

"You just a damn fool, ain't cha boy? Here you are up here in the heart of Citizens Council country and doan even know why you need to keep your trap shut! But you'll learn it quick enough, I'm fraid. I can watch your back some, but you gotta get smarter a lot quicker to stay outta trouble round here. I may not can always hep ya."

"I'm sure it'll all work out. Jackson isn't all that liberal on civil rights either. I've learned to lose friends and even had one spit on me once while calling me a nigger lover."

"Why?"

"Because I stuck up for a little black girl being shoved around by a group of white kids just for trying to buy a popsicle from THEIR ice cream truck."

"Did you kick his ass for doing that, or did you pussy up? Which was it, Just Bern?"

"I kicked his ass and told him don't ever call me that again, like I'm telling you don't call me 'Just Bern' again." I gave a look that said I believed I could kick his ass, too, though secretly I doubted it. I was good at bluffing my way out of a lot of confrontations though.

"Whoa, now Sally! I ain't lookin' for no fight wit choo. I uz just checkin' you out to see if you're thick enough for what's surely comin' to ya when folks find out what kind of work yo folks do and where you stand with they influence."

"Don't worry too much about me, John Sylvester. My folks had the foresight to get me into karate at a young age. I'm no black belt or nothing, but I can handle myself ok."

That's when he fell out in a guffaw, holding his stomach from laughing so hard. "Hahahahaha! Black belt! Funny - you just might need a BLACK belt one day to defend a black nigger---or yo self."

"No, it ain't funny! And I don't like hearing you use that slur for colored folks either. I've got to be honest with you up front here if we're going to be friends and hang out. I don't want that kind of thing rubbing off on me from hearing it so much every day."

"I gotcha, Jus....I hear ya, Bern. I'll try, but you better get used to it. You're gonna hear it everywhere you go round here. Folks doan mean nothin' by it really. It's just a word they use. They try to soften it sometimes by sayin' niggra, to be polite, but it's just a word."

"No, it isn't! I guess one day you'll learn it's not **just a word**. It carries a heavy burden with lots of pain."

"What the shit do you know about their burden? What the shit do you know about OUR burden livin' with 'em? Delta niggers are different from Jackson niggers. You'll find that out, and I bet within a week you'll be tellin' me how right I am. You watch and see. Watch and see."

2 Summer Ain't As Fun As It Used to Be

Greenwood 1968

In our two years together in school and hanging out, sharing fun and mischief, John Sylvester and I had grown quite fond on one another. Even though we often called one another some pretty derogatory names, we knew it was all in jest and served to solidify our confidence on each other's loyalty and friendship.

We were quite different in temperament though. He was always a jokester who took life simply as a game, and I was far too serious for my age. When conflicts in ideology arose between us, I still knew at heart John Sylvester was no bona fide racist; he was just a rule follower when it came to daily living in this area of the world. He would never torment or terrorize another human being "just for fun" or because he felt entitled to do so for his own entertainment. He was just a product of the Delta air.

The dust of the Delta got into your nostrils, and the smell lingered like the smoke of cigars on your clothes. The taste of the heat hung on the lips like the hot kiss of a secret lover. The land and its "traditions" just seemed to soak into your skin as smoothly as your grandmother's White Shoulders hand cream. It just became part of your being if you lived there long enough, and John Sylvester had been there from birth. He had lived there long enough to know the PAST was the PRESENT, and the Present was lived to ensure the Future didn't change either of those. It was a sacred covenant I could never understand. I simply could never grasp how the Past could be so precious when so much of it was ugly enough to choke the air out of you like an alcohol bath.

Because of my parents' work and my being a juvenile news junkie, I was well acquainted with the dangers of engagement in civil rights activities. While I often heard my parents discuss the murderous anger among whites in the state and heard of new lynchings and beatings and unjustified arrests, we were never allowed to discuss such matters at the dinner table. It would be just too unseemly and impolite to talk such matters at supper even if they were a daily staple in our news.

My parents and I were living in Jackson that hot June day in 1963 when Byron de la Beckwith gunned down Medgar Evers in his own driveway, with the man's family inside the house to come out and find him bleeding to death and taking his last breath. Looking back on it now, even the eleven year old boy that I was could hardly fathom such indifference toward another person and a family. No one reporting the news on the TV seemed appalled or disgusted. They just read the words and then moved on to the weather.

Hearing about the killing and the manhunt through Jackson for the assassin, words of my Baptismal Covenant ran through my mind, and I could remember hearing that elderly Episcopal priest asking me two key questions.

Will you seek and serve Christ in all persons, loving your neighbor as yourself? (I will, with God's help.)

Will you strive for justice and peace among all people, and respect the dignity of every human being? (I will, with God's help.)

What a shock to my belief system to find out "DeLay" (as everyone in Greenwood called him) was also an Episcopalian! I guess he just didn't take his baptismal vows so seriously since back then blacks weren't really considered "human beings" in Mississippi. And as murderous fate taught us during Freedom Summer the following June of '64, civil rights workers from up North deserved the same treatment of dismissal. The "Mississippi Way" was just kill them and be done with them. No all-white, all-male jury would convict anyone for doing their duty to preserve our way of life. Mississippi was special and protective. Mississippi was holy. Mississippi was sweetly hospitable, but she also believed in justifiable homicide.

Once I moved to the Delta though, John Sylvester taught me the Delta Way was even more restricted in boundaries of the races. When April rolled around and the TV news exploded with disbelief that MLK had been assassinated in Memphis, few whites in the Delta shed tears or felt any outrage. Consensus in town said it was just one less nigger to cause trouble, one less nigger to have to keep tabs on, one less nigger, period, and one less was always seen as a good thing.

That Assassination Thursday, my family had just sat down for supper when Walter Cronkite started off the CBS Evening News saying Martin Luther King, Jr. had been shot to death, a bullet through his throat, as he stood on the balcony of the Lorraine Motel in Memphis, a mere two hour drive away from our house. My father, a very reverential type of man, did what he normally would do during difficult times. He told us to bow our heads, we held hands around the table, and in unison we said words from our prayer book: Lord, have mercy. Christ, have mercy. Lord, have mercy.

I did not see John Sylvester at school the next morning, but it was not unusual for him to play hooky on Fridays, especially now that his father had recently helped him get an old rattle trap truck so he could cruise Greenwood streets and whistle at girls. I was glad we had not made plans for Friday night. I was not in an overly talkative mood and was not very interested in a Friday night foray up and down Park Avenue for the rest of the night.

Saturday morning though he came around at 5:00 all hyped up for the fishing trip we had planned earlier in the week. I had all but forgotten those plans, and I really didn't relish the idea of going out to Matthews Brake and side-stepping baby alligators just to catch a few gars. I could tell he was about to go off into a big huff when I wasn't dressed and had tackle all ready. So I lied to him and said I had been sick last night and had gone to bed early. I quickly gathered my rod and tackle box and climbed in the old truck with bad shocks to bounce down the road.

The morning was a cool 82 degrees with a slight breeze. We would have to be off the lake by 10:00 though if we didn't want to burn to a crisp. I suggested we fish Roebuck Lake instead there in Itta Bena to save travel time and to get on the water faster. Aside from that suggestion, on the way out to the lake I was still quite sullen and uncommunicative for the most part.

"What's wrong wit choo, man?" he asked in a perturbed tone of voice. He just couldn't understand how anyone could be in a bad mood if they were going fishing!

"I'm just upset and don't feel like hanging out."

"You upset? What cha mean? You still got a stomach ache or sumpin'?"

"No, John Sylvester, you damn goober. Haven't you been watching the news?" I went off in a tirade, yelling at him. "This country is going to hell in a handbasket with all these civil rights killings. We can't just keep letting this happen over and over and letting killers walk the street afterwards like it never happened. We can't keep slapping them on the back and putting up signs around town that say WELCOME HOME when a mistrial is declared --like the one that hung across the Yazoo River bridge in Greenwood when Beckwith murdered Evers and walked away as free as the day he killed him. It's wrong, John Sylvester, it's just plain damn wrong!"

"Oh, so you's upset about that nigger being shot up in Memphis? Plenty folks round here are glad to see him gone so maybe things can settle down some. He kept things too stirred up for his own good. Some say he deserved killin' and got what was comin' to him since he wouldn't give up them crazy ideas, thinkin' niggers are ever gonna be equal with us!"

"Dammit, John Sylvester! How can you repeat such horse shit like that? Where do you get such ideas?"

"It's just the South. Just the Delta. Just the way things are. Things MIGHT change some, but it's gonna be a slow ride and it ain't gonna be in our lifetime, buddy boy. Not if Delta folks have a breath in 'em. We can't just up and welcome such a differnt way of livin' just because THEY want it to be differnt. People in hell want ice water, too, but you know how that goes for 'em."

"Just shut up! Just shut the hell up! I know you ain't that damn ignorant, and I don't want to hear that crap comin' out of your mouth! Let's just get this damn boat in the water and fish, Sylvester Pussy. I don't want to hear anymore jabber from your stupid mouth! This is crazy. The country is just fuckin' crazy!"

"Aw right then, St. Bernard, but I'm just tryin' to hep you make sense of the crazy. You gotta understand though that what you call crazy round here, most Delta folks just call it normal."

"Shut up and fish!"

It wasn't long after that conversation that John Sylvester came by in his rat trap truck to ask if I had heard the news out of California—Bobby Kennedy had been shot.

"Yessiree, Bob. It's June again!!" he said, in truth too gleefully for my liking.

I remember I just sat there on the edge of the couch, staring at the floor. I didn't turn on the TV as I normally would have. I just didn't want to hear it, didn't want to talk about it, didn't want to believe it. But there it was. Another fine human being.....lost to the nation, lost to those who still needed a hero, lost to dreams for something different. One by one taken out, as surely dead as if the Mafia had put out a hit on each and every one of them. Just for TALKING equality. I stared out the living room window at a dust devil racing down a turnrow in the field across the road, sucking up and rescattering the dust like the Grand Master of the KKK scatters fear in some and hope in others, but the hatred never dissipates even though the dust devil does.

"Whassa matta, Bernie boy? Didn't cha hear me? Ain't cha gonna turn on the TV and get cha a shot of news? No pun intended. Well, maybe...."

"Shut up, John Sylvester!! Just shut the hell up!"

"Aw, ca'mon, man. At least it didn't happen here in the Delta or even the South. It was fuckin' Cali-forn-I-A! That should make you feel some betta about it."

"Oh, for sure. I feel so much better knowing that!" I retorted with as much sarcasm as I could muster.

"Ca'mon, I'll buy ya an ice cream. Then we can go drivin' out on some gravel roads and kick up some dust. I need some fun."

"You can't just wipe away killing like that with a fuckin' ice cream cone! You don't even have a driver's license, you dick!"

"Hey, in the Delta, we don't need no stinkin' license!" he said, shaking his head side to side with a smirk on his face. "Get up, you mopin' prissy girl. Pull up your britches and let's go raise some hell."

"Seems to me there's been enough hell raising of late. Summer just gets harder every year, it seems."

"Yep, it must be the heat. People get they blood up so much quicker in summa. That's why we need that ice cream."

"Are you EVER serious about anything?"

"Nope. The world turns, the beat goes on, watcha gonna do?"

"I guess so, but I sure as hell hate June. Nothing good ever seems to happen in June down South, for sure."

"Oh, you uz just a pessimist prick. You'll get over it if you stay here long enough."

"And how long does that take?"

"Till you get use to da killing, and it doan phase ya anymore."

I whispered under my breath, "Lord, have mercy. Christ, have mercy. Lord, have mercy."

3 Switcheroo and Thelma Too

Greenwood, MS   May 1969

"What? No! What? Are you serious? How can you do this to me? I have friends here, and it will be my senior year. This is just a bunch of bullshit!!"

I had never spoken to my parents that way, but I was beside myself with anger over their news that we were moving back to Jackson in two weeks. It surprised them as much as I surprised myself, but the decision had been made and there was no going back. They felt they could help more with the desegregation of the schools around the state if they were working out of Jackson where they would have more contacts and resources.

"We've just got a ton of court appearances and adjudications this coming year, and we need to be working those cases to our utmost ability. We lose hours and hours driving up and down the road from here to Jackson. We will have so much more time to work the cases if we are there already and not on the road." They said this to me as if I would say, "Oh, sure, Mommy and Daddy, I understand now."

"So that's it, huh?   You care more about the schooling of black kids than for your own son?" I couldn't believe the venom coming out of my mouth. I had never hated my parents, but this news drove me into a rage such as I had never before experienced. Sure, during my earlier teen years we had had troublesome times, but I never doubted their love for me or their commitment to desegregation. I just never expected one to trump the other. I turned my back on them and walked away, down the hall into my room, and hit the wall with my fist as hard as I dared. It hurt like hell, but it felt good to hit something to release the most intense frustration I had ever felt.

After a half hour of huffing and puffing and stomping around in my room, my mother appeared at my door. "Do I need to go buy you a pair of red three inch high heels?" she asked in all seriousness.

I knew what she meant. She had told all three of us kids many times that when anger overtakes us, we need to step back, put on some red spiked heels and walk it off. Walking the rough gravel roads of anger, broken trusts, or heartaches in spiked heels meant we would we be forced to slow the rush to action, to do something rash and regrettable around the next bend. If we could just slow down and breathe, our words of disgust or ill will could not arrive with full force. Our decision or conclusion would come to us with a clearer head and a lighter heart more willing to make peace with whatever disappointment or disillusion distracted us from our true, loving selves.

Despite the fact that I knew what was right – that I needed to apologize to both my parents – I was still mad and unwilling to acquiesce, and my answer to her let her know the war was still raging. In the most sarcastic tone I could muster, I replied, "Yes, Mother, why don't you do just that! Go get me a pair of your silly ass high heels, and while you and Dad are at it, why don't you both just go to hell and take a toothbrush with you!" While I was ashamed of myself for talking to her that way, I did it anyway. I would deal with the regret and apologies later, but not right now.

"Well, I guess I better go pack a suitcase for that trip to hell then," she said as she turned her back and prissed away. I hated her at that moment for her cool collectedness, but it was that calm way of moving through life and the courtrooms unflustered that made her the perfect advocate for the oppressed and under-served in the face of brutality and vehement hatred.

I sulked for a week and stayed away from home for most of that time. I rarely exchanged even minimal pleasantries with my parents, and my little brother, Will, kept looking at me as if I were a stranger. I guess, in fact, I was a stranger in my house because no one, not even myself, recognized "this" Bern who seethed with hostility and anger. Admittedly, I didn't like myself much that week, and John Sylvester fed that fire.

"Your folks is just assholes!" he would say each and every time I mentioned them or the moving situation. "I tell you what, Big Boy. I been thinkin'. Why not ask yo folks if you can stay out here in Itta Bena for the rest of the summa wit cho Ain't Thelma like that summa we first met up? And maybe if you behave yo silly ass, yo Ain't Thelma jest might ask 'em to let you stay through next school year and finish up here. Whaddaya think of dat plan?"

I swear! Sometimes the boy was brilliant! I felt certain my parents would go for the summer plan if Aunt Thelma was amenable to it. The rest would be up to me to convince my aunt that having a young man around would be a help to her, especially if that young man happens to be a good boy who is never in any trouble and could do all the outside chores around her place. I needed to convince her that she could depend on me. If I could wheedle my way into the deepest recesses of Aunt Thelma's heart, it just might work. I decided I needed to talk to Aunt Thelma first though, because if she balked or was uncertain or unwilling to take me in for the summer, the rest was moot. So John Sylvester and I set our plan in motion and paid Aunt Thelma a visit.

There was always a chocolate pie or bread pudding on the counter of her kitchen. She wasn't a great cook when it came to regular meals, but she could bake like nobody's business. The roly-poly figure attested to that. As soon as we arrived, Aunt Thelma herded us straight into the kitchen where she was in the process of putting the caramel icing on a cake.

"Here. Sit, sit, sit," she said. "What'r you boys doing out here in the country today? You been popping turtles on Bear Creek?"

"No ma'am," I said. We were just out slinging some gravel and were close by, so we thought we'd stop in."

"And I am so delighted! Here, let me pour you some good cold milk, and we will slice this caramel cake just as soon as the icing cools."

"Boy, that sounds great!" exclaimed John Sylvester. The boy had a sweet tooth like no one else I knew, so anytime there was a sweet dessert nearby, he was in it.

"So, your momma and daddy doin' ok these days? It's been a couple of weeks since I last talked with 'em. They like Greenwood it seems."

"Yes, ma'am, they do like it, but there's a problem with them having to travel so much back and forth to Jackson. There's a bunch of new cases it seems taking up more time than usual."

"Well, don't let their busyness let you get into trouble. You know what they say---idle hands, the devil, that bit. You know what I'm saying?"

"Yes, ma'am. I know. That's kind of why I wanted to talk to you." As we sat and ate sweet caramel cake and drank our milk, John Sylvester and I laid out our plan for helping her out during the summer and helping me stay in Leflore County.

God, I could not have loved Aunt Thelma more than when I left her house after that drop by. She didn't hesitate one second and said, "Well, sure, you can, Honey, if your parents will let you. Have you mentioned this to them?" My sin was exposed.

"No, ma'am, I haven't yet. It made no sense to me to talk to them until I knew your answer first."

"Well, I don't want my brother thinking I went behind his back by agreeing to this; so when you talk to them, you might just keep this visit in the dark. I don't want no hurt feelings. If they agree, they'll call me and ask. I'll just pretend I haven't heard this before. It won't exactly be like lying to them, you know. If they don't ask, we won't volunteer the information that this was discussed with each other first. Understood?"

"Oh, yes, ma'am. Absolutely! I'll talk to them tonight after supper. They might call then if they don't nix the plan as soon as it comes out of my mouth. I haven't exactly been on good ground with them since they first told me about the move back to Jackson. I've got some crow to eat first before popping the question to them."

"Well, you know they're very forgiving people, and they love you. I'm sure they understand you just needed some time to work out the problem and come to grips with it. It'll be ok, I'm sure. You just watch your words and mind your manners." I hoped she was right as rain.

All through supper that evening, I was antsy and eager to jump into the proposal, but I knew the timing had to be right, and I had some "making up" to do first. So I was cheerful and polite, helping set the table and taking out the trash. I was the old Bern they knew. It did not go unnoticed, even by Will.

"What's got you so happy now, Bern? You been mad for days now," he commented. I wanted to shush him, lest he ruin my timing, but I just gave him a glance that said, "I'll tell you soon enough." Little did I know--the best laid plans of mice and men.

As soon as supper was finished, Dad announced we were all four going for a short drive. Mom seemed to know what was going on, but Will and I certainly did not. Dad took us downtown to a used car lot and got out to walk around like he was shopping for a vehicle. On the lot, set off from the other cars, was a bright orange Plymouth Fury III with a black vinyl top. Lord, what a beauty of a machine she was! Dad saw me eyeing her and asked, "She's something, isn't she?"

Then you could have knocked me into next week when he said, "I've been waiting for my oldest son to return home, the Bern we know and love instead of some jackass that's been living with us for over a week and done nothing to help with packing." He reached in his pocket and pulled out a key ring with 3 keys on it and handed it to me! "She's yours," he said, just like that.   No further explanation. "She's yours." I looked at the three keys and could tell one key was for the ignition, one for the trunk, and the third looked like a house key.

"That's the key to your Aunt Thelma's house," Mom volunteered. "Your father and I have been talking with her about letting you stay the summer with her while we go on down to Jackson, get the office ready, get the new house ready, and check out your new high school. You will stay with Aunt Thelma for the summer, and then we will come help you move your things right before school starts. We thought with us gone and all, it would be a good idea if you had your own transportation so as not to burden your aunt when you want to go out and meet up with friends and such. We bought it the day of the big fight, but when things blew up at supper we decided the timing wasn't right. We've just been waiting for those high heels to take effect on that anger."

I literally yelled out loud to the heavens, "THANKS BE TO GOD!!!! AND FOR AUNT THELMA!!!" I thought to myself, "That sly fox! Aunt Thelma knew all along my parents' plan and never let on one bit!" Then my shame --for such ugly behavior toward the very people who love me most --washed over me as if Enid Dam had taken down its own spillway. I hung my head. I cried. I was barely audible when I said, "I. am. So. So. Sorry."

"We know, son. We know this is going to be hard on you for your senior year. We know how unfair it must feel. But it IS for the greater good, and I know you know that." My father then wrapped me in his arms and let me cry out my shame, sobbing almost uncontrollably with my head burrowed into his chest, right there in downtown Greenwood, in a used car parking lot, in front of my little brother, in front of my mother, in front of God and in front of myself. And I didn't care.

I deserved every ounce of the shame, but as my father frequently reminded us kids when things got sideways, "I forgive you, Bern. We live and learn. You know, our words can sometimes be like toddlers, sticking close by and selfishly demanding unwarranted attention. Then they grow up a little and stop wanting to play in our own front yards. Our words have great power, and they travel far and wide. That is why we should be so careful when they want to cross the street, go around the corner, hike through the woods, hitchhike to the next town, or bed down under the stars in a deep desert canyon. We have to be careful where and how we loose them onto the world and the people around us. That's why it's important to put some good shoes on them like those red high heels for anger. Now let's crank up that beauty and get her home."

"Hey, Dad?"

"Yes, son?"

"I think I'll name her Thelma. What do you think?"

We all four burst into laughter. I kissed my mom and apologized for cussing at her. It was good to laugh and it felt even more delicious than caramel cake to be whole with my family again.

4 **Delta Ghosts**

Itta Bena, MS   Summer of 1969

The summer passed quickly in terms of Delta time, which usually went by at the pace of a turtle crossing a tar pit. Daytime hours moved as slowly as the people who moved about gasping in the Delta heat and high humidity, their perspiration stains ever present on their clothing and always unattractive, but at least even the prettiest and most handsome had to live with the shame like everyone else.

Greenwood did not offer much summer activity for high school guys, so like everyone else, John Sylvester and I ran up and down the streets of Greenwood practically every evening, burning gas and looking for some female conversation and fun. Now that I had Thelma, literally THE coolest car in the entire Delta, we found girls eager to talk to us and ride the night away in our company. Park Avenue was our main drag through town, and the Sonic drive-in was the primary hangout and pick-up spot.

Our main objective was to find some fun-loving, friendly girls willing to leave town and ride around out in the country. If the girls were also pretty, that was just a bonus. Dozens of gravel roads offered plenty of choice spots for some privacy with no distractions. We had a favorite spot not far from a rickety, dilapidated bridge that crossed the Tallahatchie where we would go for some "parking" with the more adventurous girls, which were usually easy to spot, wearing hot pants and halter tops. Somehow John Sylvester usually managed to get his hands on some beer or Boone's Farm. "Delta girls like drinkin' men," he would say.

Wanting to ingratiate myself and be no problem for Aunt Thelma, I rarely stayed out later than 11:00. But then there was that one night when time meant nothing, when the girls, Mary Ellen and Suzie, were not the least bit eager to go home, and neither were we, considering what they were offering.

The heat as always was too suffocating to tolerate without the air conditioner, so whenever we were out parking with girls, I turned off the headlights, but we always had to leave the engine and A/C running. That particular night we were parked out near Berclair and Blue Lake, and Mary Ellen was a great kisser. I especially liked the way she rubbed her nails up and down my back when kissing me. I liked the way she nibbled my neck and ears while telling me what she wanted me to do next. The hum of the engine and the air conditioner lulled us into a sweet, sexy fog. The dim dashboard lights cast a glow on her skin and a glint in her eyes that told me she wanted me to remember her beyond just these few late hours. If I played my cards right, there would be more trips to the bridge with Mary Ellen.

Lost in the euphoria of bare legs and sweet kisses, next thing I knew it is 1:30 a.m. I still needed to drive back into Greenwood to get the girls home, get John Sylvester home, and get myself home to Aunt Thelma. By the time I was headed down the winding gravel road to her house, it was almost 2:30 a.m. As young men are apt to do when running late on overtime, I sped like there was no tomorrow, slinging gravel at every tight turn, kicking dust twenty feet in the air, cursing myself for my poor timing. I couldn't really say I thought I had made a bad decision, given the rewards of the time spent, but the timing surely was going to cause a problem.

Then as luck would have it, about a mile and a half from Aunt Thelma's house, I lost control in the tightest curve with lots of loose gravel and put my big, beautiful honey of a car straight into the four foot ditch of the bog that ran along the left side of the road! Spin tires as I might, there was no getting Thelma loose from the sucking mud and brackish water of that devilish ditch. I debated just spending the rest of the night in the car and walking home at daybreak, but heavy rain was in the forecast starting at dawn, and I feared the ditch filling up with more water and Thelma being engulfed in mud up past the axle. I needed to get home and get some help to extract her. So I decided to walk that mile and half home, in the dark, at 3 a.m., with no flashlight and very little moonlight.

I was completely unprepared for this mission, wearing thin soled shoes sure to leave my feet achy and bruised from every rock I walked over. I admit there was a good amount of fear and trepidation also. Walking a lonely, deserted gravel road past midnight in the dark Delta surely was not for the faint of heart. There were feral hogs that roamed the fields at night that could kill you in seconds. There were water moccasins, silent and deadly, slithering along the edge of the road. There were big dogs at the ready to attack any stranger walking past their owners' houses. But the worst could be the truck driving drunken good ol' boys who just might take a notion to chase you down like a rabbit rather than offer you a lift home. Being a fairly reasonable young man though, I convinced myself I was being stupid and overly imaginative; so I mustered up enough gumption to "race walk" home, figuring I could get there in the next forty minutes or so, maybe.

I failed to consider the low light of the moon for guidance though, and about a quarter mile from the car I tripped and went down hard in the gravel, skinning up both hands and my knees, tearing a hole in my favorite pair of pants, and spraining one wrist. "Dammit to hell," I yelled into the night as I just sat there in the middle of the road. I considered going back to the car, but just as I started to stand up, I heard it.... A tractor motor cranked and running, clear as a bell, the sound unmistakable.

I scanned the cotton fields off to my right, looking for tractor lights, looking for motion. There was nothing but darkness. A vast amount of nothing – just the steady hum of the motor somewhere out there in the black dark. It creeped me out like nothing ever scared me before in my life, especially when the crickets and tree frogs suddenly stopped their evening tirades and serenades. The silent nature and eeriness of it dried out my mouth, and my heart began thundering like a neighbor with a house fire pounding on your door at midnight, frantic for help. I don't know why it scared me so much; it just had that palpable unnaturalness about it. That's when I remembered my father always telling us that our words have power.

As I stood in the middle of road almost frozen in fear at the spooky nothingness and blackness of the motor's sound, the word "courage" came to me, stood in front of me with arms crossed, tapping its foot, smirking, and with pursed lips it said, "Get going, chump! You've done harder things than this. You've known scarier things than this. You're just spooking yourself. Stop standing there and get moving!"

It's funny how ideas like that creep into our psyches, but one thing I've noticed is that each time my friend words cropped up, like my mother would say---they always had on the perfect shoes needed for the job, whether work boots, dancing shoes, house slippers, or running shoes to help us race toward our dreams or run from our fears --and from ghosts in the darkness of a Delta cotton field way past midnight.

I finally made it home, tired and sore. As I approached the long gravel drive toward the old farm house, every light was on, and the yard was awash with brightness. It told me Aunt Thelma was awake and waiting, and I dreaded both the lecture sure to come for being out so late and having to confess the careless driving that put my car in the ditch. Just as I reached for the screen door, Aunt Thelma unlatched the wooden door and threw it open.

When I stepped through the door, instead of launching into a hissy fit, she grabbed me up and hugged me, squeezing me like a little girl engulfs a life sized stuffed animal from Santa. "Oh, thank God you are alright!!" she exclaimed. "How would I ever have explained things to your mom and dad? How would I have ever forgiven myself? Oh, you're bleeding, and you've torn your pants!! What on earth have you been doing, boy? Tell me you ain't been drinking."

"No, I wasn't. It's just some scrapes. No real damage. I tripped as I was hurrying home on foot."

"Oh, God! You wrecked the car and had to walk home!! Are you sure nothing's broken? Are you concussed? Let me get some alcohol and bandages. Let me....."

"Really, Aunt Thelma. I'm ok. And the car is, too. She's just stuck in the ditch a little over a mile from here in that really tight curve near the old rundown shack. She's in pretty deep, so I'm going to need help pulling her out."

"Well, I'll call Mr. Elmer up the road to help us right after I clean up those scrapes. People call him all the time asking to use his tractor to pull them out of that bog. I'll give him a ring. He'll be up at breakfast already any way. He's a really early riser." As she turned to go off down the hall to the telephone, she called back over her shoulder, "You're just mighty lucky that old Negro ghost didn't get you!"

"Ghost?"

"Yes, Mr. Jim's ghost! You never heard that story? Old Mister Jim who used to drive a tractor on Egypt Plantation got strung up one night about twenty years ago by some hateful old men for not saying 'yes sir' to one of them. He lived up the road there in that old shack. The story is they hanged him from that big oak right out in front of the house with his wife and kids watching. Folks say you can still hear him out plowing sometimes after midnight until just before daybreak, but you only hear him. You never see him."

So there it was, my brush with brutal history, my justified fear in what I couldn't explain! I admit that every time I passed that section of gravel road at night after that, I slowed down, almost to a crawl, to ensure no loss of control but also to listen for Mister Jim's tractor. Occasionally, I was brave enough to stop the car, step out, and call out to him, but not too loudly. Thinking ghosts hear you whether you yell out or whisper, I'd say, "You don't scare me, Old Man! But I sure as hell hope you're haunting the dreams of the living men who killed you! Hold her straight now, and plow on!"

5 Fighting Tigers

Jackson, MS   1969-70

The plan to stay in the Delta for my senior year fell through. My parents insisted I rejoin the family in Jackson since I would be leaving home for college in just one short year. It would be our final year living full time together as a family, and they just could not quite yet let me go. Knowing there was no use in protesting their decision, I said my goodbyes to Aunt Thelma and John Sylvester.

When I last saw John Sylvester, he refused to discuss my leaving. He told me, "You go on now. Doan be goin' all sappy on me wid no goodbye speech. You'll be seein' me again. You just git in 'ol Thelma and c'mon back to see me sometime." Somehow I never found an opportunity to do that, and little did either of us know it would be a number of years before we would share some stories together again.

I enrolled at Central High School in downtown Jackson, a school slightly integrated with about a 10% black student population. Through a "choice of school" policy, my parents decided to enroll me there because it offered programs other Jackson high schools did not. So I became a Central High School Tiger.

Though I usually sat in the front of all my classes, I was not what anyone would call studious since good grades came easily to me. Rarely would I have to study for tests, unlike my older sister Connie when she was in high school and had to study constantly to make her A's, but the counselors were concerned with my transcript from Greenwood because I had no foreign language credit. They insisted to my parents that anyone planning to go to college should have SOME background in a foreign language. So to complete my seven period schedule, I was enrolled in first year French, fifth period right after lunch with Mrs. Mahaffey.

That first day of French class, just before the tardy bell rang, Claire McAlister scurried into the room and sat down in the front row desk between me and a guy named Ralph who wore an Army ROTC uniform. In those first few moments of class, it was obvious from the way she looked at him and by his reactions to her glances that she and Ralph were a steady couple. Most of my teachers rearranged seating assignments that first day, putting us all in alpha order; but Mrs. Mahaffey left us to our own designs, which put the M girl beside this G boy.

Claire McAlister was not what anyone would call a particularly pretty girl, or even cute, but she had an aura about her that drew people to her, especially guys. It was almost like she threw off sparks, and many of us were hoping to catch fire from her. At barely five feet tall with dirty blonde hair, green eyes, and a slightly turned up nose, she was, in fact, quite plain in appearance but like lightning in spirit.

As the first few weeks of school dragged on, it became noticeable there was trouble in Ralph's world with Claire. They seemed to be arguing quite a bit over anything and everything. They came into French class giving dirty looks at one another. They constantly yelled at one another in the hall outside class during our split lunch. Looking from the outside in, it appeared he was quite domineering and controlling and she was in a state of rebellion against that. Every day she seemed to be reminding him, "You don't own me, Ralph, and you ain't my daddy! So just stop it; stop telling me what I can and can't do!" A showdown was brewing; all of us classmates knew it, and it happened in such a way I could not avoid getting involved.

Mrs. Mahaffey was late returning from her lunch and was not in the classroom. Just as I crossed the threshold into the room, I saw him slap her, hard, right there in front of everyone--- and no one moved! Except me. On pure instinct I shoved him against the wall and took a stance between them. I levelled my gaze and intended to put a stop to whatever was going on between them at that moment.

"That's enough, Ralph!" I said. "Sit your ass down and leave her alone." Claire was crying and a couple of other girls were petting on her to soothe the hurt and embarrassment. About that time Mrs. Mahaffey stepped into the class with no clue what had just happened; but Ralph sat down, and Claire and I took our seats. I saw Ralph pass a note to Claire and nodded his head toward me, telling her to give me the note. It simply said, "You're dead."

Now I could be as cocky a bastard as the next guy, so I merely looked at him and smiled, a big toothy smile. He turned so red-faced with rage I could almost see steam coming out of his tight collared, starched shirt cinched up with his ROTC tie. He looked like he might pass out from apoplexy at any second.

A cooler head evidently prevailed though, and we all three lived another day without a clash. Class let out and he just left. I guess he couldn't afford the demerits or possibly the rank demotion he would surely have gotten as an ROTC officer had he stayed to fight or started something on any other day. The next day in class, Claire passed me a note that simply said, "Thank you for yesterday. We broke up." I was not so cool that I did not blush with embarrassment like some wimp getting a first kiss. That feeling pissed me off, so I ignored her and made no acknowledgement of her note.

Within a week though she had convinced me I should ask her out on a date. "You have a car, don't you?" she cooed. "I see you wear nice clothes, too. I know you can afford at least a cheap date for a hamburger or something. I won't bite cha," she teased, "unless you want me to." When I picked her up and she saw Thelma, she knew I was the one for her, the one she wanted, and Claire McAlister usually—always—got what she wanted.

I didn't kiss her that first night though, and I didn't try any funny stuff on the next couple of dates either. Something about her told me to move very carefully because the electricity that sparked in me when she held my hand was enough for me to know I was in a danger zone. I saw her at school after the third date, and she passed me another note in French class. It simply said, "Do you want to kiss first or just fuck?" After class I told her, "Follow me." I took her into the back part of the auditorium balcony where I kissed her and pulled up her skirt, and she willingly climbed up on me as I pushed her against the wall. Before I finished, she took charge, taking me into her mouth just before my moment of explosion. And THAT was the end of me!! I became a dying star sucked into the vortex of a black hole. I lived only in her presence. Any other time and place, my mind and heart were lost in that space that only she occupied. I no longer belonged to my parents. I no longer belonged to Central High School. I no longer belonged to my church or to God. I belonged only to her. I was like a drunk with her, drunk on her touch, inebriated with her kisses, intoxicated by her sexual eagerness. Every time I was with her, I lost all sense of time, the world, sanity, and reason.

Try as we might, we could not talk her mother into letting me pick her up and take her to school or bring her home. She had to ride the damn bus!! Good ol' mom also had a hard and fast rule that Claire could go out only one night a week. So we had no choice but to meet in the balcony every day right after school before she caught the bus home. She was utterly delicious, and she knew she was. It made her even more stimulating. I could hardly bear releasing her to leave, knowing hours would be long and slow before we would have a chance again to slip away into our own universe of We. The tiger she was had opened the door to my cage, and now the two of us were running the jungle together with no other thought than racing toward our "next time" as fast as we could run.

We were both undeservedly trusted students who could easily get a hall pass for some made up excuses to get out of homeroom. We met up daily in different vacated parts of the school, even occasionally in a vacant restroom, for some steamy make out sessions and heavy petting. She was incredible with her love making. She was good at it, and even better, she **liked** being good at it. She knew things about a man's body no seventeen year old girl should know, but Cosmopolitan magazine had taught her a great deal, and she could drive me into oblivion with pleasure. It was exhilarating to know I could have her anytime, that she would always say yes, and she would say it with joy.

We fell into an abyss of love too deep for words and dated steadily the rest of the year. Anytime we were together we could not get enough of life, could not breathe enough, could not think enough of anything or anyone but us and what we wanted from each other. Being no different from any other steady high school couple, we talked about our futures and what we wanted in life. We even talked about getting married and having kids together. Being together all day and all night, every day and every night, was our idea of pure happiness and joy beyond description. We wanted the seeming bliss of married couples, never giving thought to the worries of paying bills and going to work. We just wanted to be us, to be together, totally absorbed in each other's every breath. She wanted every molecule of me, every atom of me, every single cell of me, and she made it clear she wanted the naked me with her more than anything else in the entire universe. And I wanted her equally with the most sincerity of devotions.

But everything else around us in school was coming apart at the seams. About the time Christmas break came around, the school was pretty much in chaos because of a recent ruling on desegregation by the 5th Circuit Court of Appeals in New Orleans. As if the Viet Nam War did not have us split up enough into different camps as students, the ruling opened up wounds that had all of us in turmoil. When we returned to school after the two week holiday, the desegregation order was all anyone could talk about.

The morning intercom crackled and screeched as the principal, aptly named Mr. Pleasants, came on to say, "Good morning, Tigers. I'm sure by now you have all heard about our order to immediately desegregate all Jackson schools by February 1st. We will be having class meetings today during homeroom to discuss the impact of desegregation on our campus. Be thinking of some positive ways we can make this work for us and not against us. Have a great day."

We heard this announcement several times because one homeroom meeting was not enough to say everything everybody wanted to say on the matter, and the first meeting was so volatile, teachers had to shut down the forum until some guidelines could be developed for the future meetings. The administration and faculty had their hands full trying to quell the anger but still allow free speech to voice opinions and concerns. An assembly was completely out of the question. The atmosphere was definitely too explosive to gather us all together in a single room auditorium! The school newspaper conducted several surveys so the student body could voice their perspectives, but many of the comments were so vile they could not be printed in the paper. Mostly, the majority of the student body considered the court order a communist takeover of Central High School and the state of Mississippi.

"We already have some niggers here at Central. How come that isn't enough?"

"Those judges are just a bunch of communist turds spreading their shit on the halls of our school." (Morris Sistrunk got a three-day suspension for that comment.)

"They are destroying America! This is just going to bring everybody down."

"I hate this ruling. They don't care about our education. They just want to boss us around like we're a bunch of slaves."

"We need to just walk out and protest."

"We ought to refuse to come to school." (Yea, that'll show 'em we mean business.)

"Blacks don't like this any better than we do. They're being forced into something they don't like either."

What most of us students did not realize though was the back story behind the ruling. The school districts had been dragging their feet on the matter for decades, littering the courts with piles and piles of appeals and revisions of a desegregation plan, and the lawyers for the predominately white schools had always found a way to skirt the inevitable. The court was done with unequal compromises and refused to allow any further delays. The inevitable was at hand. The hammer was coming down on Mississippi, and come hell or high water, things were going to change with utmost speed.

"They're messing up our senior year all to hell. Having to switch schools and teachers in February! That's just pure crazy. Those judges don't care crap about education for blacks or whites. They only care about mixing us up together. It ain't right."

"I know!! My sister has been assigned to go across town now to that black high school. She can't even stay here at Central with me. It ain't fair and it ain't right bustin' up families like that."

"Well, I'd never let my little sister go to some nigger school without me there to protect her. No way in hell!"

"I swear I ain't going to another class meeting. Nobody has anything good to say. They just want to talk about why they hate the niggers or why the niggers hate us whites."

"It's like we don't have any rights anymore. We are being pushed around more and more by the courts and the government. I say we protest and do it loud enough for the world to hear us!"

"The newspapers and TV sure ain't telling the whole story. I guarantee you people in other states have no idea what is happening right here right now in the MIDDLE of a school year!"

Among all this talk, various legal and administrative teams were meeting around the clock to redraw district lines to ensure at least a 60/40 ratio of black/white student bodies, which was difficult at best since the school district lost over 5,000 white students between Christmas and February 1. Districts also had to figure out a way to provide an equal ratio of black and white teachers for each faculty, so many were to be reassigned to new campuses starting in February. New bus routes had to be mapped out, and new student schedules had to be built. Everything was being turned upside down, and the same conversations were taking place among the parents.

"How do they expect these kids to learn in this fucked up situation? You know they don't want our kids in their schools any more than we want them in ours."

"What are black students supposed to do, being thrown into all-white schools mid-year with no support system to help them make such a strange transition?"

"The blacks? What about the safety of our white students, especially the girls? You know the black boys will attack and rape them if they get a chance."

So there it was. Every fear and prejudice imaginable brought to the surface. The desegregation plan was just about moving people around with no thought given on how to make it safe or manageable, only more undesirable. There were no student support plans even on the table. It was every Tiger for himself, on his own to make the best of it as he could. Protest as we might about the unfairness of it all, there was no going back.

The gavel of justice was coming with swift assuredness. More appeals would surely be filed, but the desegregation order was to be enforced immediately in the interim as those cases made it into the courtrooms. Based on my parents' involvement with desegregation efforts, I was one of a handful of students who seemed to know that no matter what ideas would be concocted to derail the desegregation train, Mississippi was moving forward and would never be able to undo what was happening right then. Little did I know though there is always more than one way to skin a cat, as they say.

Rumors ran amok every other day. There was to be a student walk out on this date or that date, and then it would be cancelled by threats of violence if students walked out.

"Have you heard the Jackson Police are going to shoot any student who walks out?"

"Have you heard the Black Panthers have secretly selected three white seniors from each high school to be assassinated on the spot if there was a walk out?"

"Have you heard there's a judge who says he will send every student to Parchman Penitentiary who participates in a walk out by charging them with rioting?"

No one felt brave enough to risk any of it. Everyone stayed in school, but the vitriol among students got so bad at one point that police in full riot gear were sent to occupy our hallways, one cop about every fifty feet, just to keep things civil. The stress was tremendous during that January for the teachers and for us. After February 1st, even though we were integrated inside the walls, many students, both black and white, still segregated themselves inside, during lunch, in our classrooms, in our locker rooms, on the buses. Everywhere you looked you could see pockets of white students here, groups of black students there, but no groups with both races interacting together. I guess you could say the inside situation was an unexpected anomaly --mixed and segregated at the same time.

We lost Mrs. Mahaffey as our French teacher, who resigned rather than be reassigned. My senior English teacher was replaced by a black English teacher from Brinkley, one of the formerly all black high schools.   Many of my friends were sent elsewhere, but Claire and I were left at Central for me to finish out my senior year and she her junior year because we were both taking courses not offered at any other high school. Thank God that counselor talked me into signing up for Office Machines. It would have been devastating to leave Claire in such a disjointed situation. Ralph and many others got to stay at Central, too, because of the ROTC Program and some Vo-Tech classes.

That whole spring was like living in a fish bowl with the whole world watching Mississippi.   I am ashamed to say we did not represent ourselves well. Everyone was scared of the changes, crazy with fear, and people do insane things when they are scared. Most just could not believe integration would be a good thing for everyone in the end. Not one good solution came out of all those class meetings in homeroom.

I was not afraid of the integration, but I did grow scared of Claire; scared of how much she meant to me and what all I wanted from life with her. Even though we had walked arm in arm up and down Capitol Street, window shopping jewelry stores for wedding rings one long ago cold, wet January day, it became obvious I wanted things she didn't. She didn't want to go to college. She didn't want "those niggers" sitting by her in the cafeteria; it was enough they sat beside her in class. I wanted the U.S. out of Viet Nam; she just wanted out of school. I was facing the draft while she was facing another year in a school under the thumb of a bunch of communists. I protested Viet Nam; she protested integration. We had many arguments about both of those subjects.

The Central High School Tigers managed to survive the chaos and turmoil though and finished the year without any major violence in school; Claire and I did not survive. She found herself another guy even before we finally had our last argument and broke up. I loved her, loved her too much for my own good, but we were just too different to make it work any longer. The last time we slept together she told me, "Bern, I just can't move that fast with all these changes." She rolled over with her back to me, her bare hips against my pelvis, lit a cigarette and said, "This Tiger just can't stay in this jungle anymore. There's too many apes here now. I'm quitting school as soon as the year ends."

Graduation was a strange and strained affair with so many of our friends there to see us cross the stage, a stage they too would have been walking had they not chosen to drop out in February. We seniors were now off the hook and getting away from the bedlam and mayhem of forced integration. Like Claire, though, many white students simply left school all together with an incomplete education. Many went off and enrolled in the dozens of "seg academies" that sprang up virtually overnight all across the state, but many just gave up on themselves and their futures and threw away their educations rather than share a coke machine or restroom with a black person. Within the next three years white flight was in a foot race to the suburbs, and more than 70,000 white students had abandoned the state's public school system. Most schools were over 85-90% black by then, and again, the great state of Mississippi had found a way to segregate itself once more.

6 **Darkness on the Delta**

Cleveland, MS   1970-1974

That final semester of my senior year in high school left me drained and cynical after seeing so much sulfuric bitterness and venom spewed among us students as lines were drawn and sides were chosen when the topic was integration. Some of my classmates seemed to turn almost animalistic in the face of desegregation, wanting to tear to shreds anyone who defended integration. There was a viciousness in tone of voice and expression in the eyes when conversations ended, even when they had begun in civility and with hope for understanding. The groups always seemed to degenerate into a meanness of spirit I had never witnessed before on a personal level. I had seen such in news reports, but I never expected to be face to face with such darkness of the soul.

As we guys faced the Viet Nam draft, there, too, were chasms of character and conscience. I could often be found on the corner of Capitol Street and N. West Street handing out underground newspapers that espoused full withdrawal from Viet Nam. It is hard to say how or when the "hippie" culture invaded my thinking and became my lifestyle other than that my parents were pacifists and railed nightly about the carnage during the evening news. Seeing war up close and personal on our TV sets for the first time in history surely brought home the ugliness of war, where we understood its veracity and ferociousness more deeply than ever before.

A couple of like-minded friends and I got involved in that anti-war movement more as a matter of integrity and not out of fear we might be drafted or even necessarily wanting to dodge the draft. We sincerely believed lives were being wasted to no avail, and that nothing good would ever be built or sustained from so much blood-letting. Such advocacy on my part did not impress my school counselors or administrators. As a matter of fact, it was my activism that got me blackballed from the National Honor Society for lack of character. My parents were highly disappointed in that turn of events, but I found it quite ironic that I was deemed lacking in character for wanting the killing to stop.

I, too, was disappointed to be judged as unfit in character, but I truly believed our war objective was both unethical and unachievable based on what we failed to learn from the French involvement before we entered the country and what we failed to understand about the culture of the Vietnamese. It appeared obvious to me the war was accomplishing nothing but thousands of deaths because it is difficult to defeat an enemy that has such a persistent patience with war, a philosophy that they would wear away the U.S. forces like water wears away a stone, the same way they had done to those who died there before the Americans.

Take those two events of desegregation and the Viet Nam War at its height, then couple them with college demonstrations that left unarmed dead students caught in the crosshairs of National Guard shootings at Kent State and Jackson State, and you've got a world gone crazy with killing and going to hell in a handbasket.

"I just feel like the world is so out of sync with what you guys have taught me," I told my parents one night. "I don't know how to reconcile all of this peace and love with war and hate."

My father took me aside and told me, "Son, the world is always with us, driving us often down roads we do not want to travel, but sometimes you simply must take your stand and be confident that you are on the side of justice and right, even when all others around you disagree."

"But Dad, how does one person make any difference?"

"Simply by trying to make a difference. Simply by trying," he said. Then he said something that completely surprised me because it was such an antithesis to everything he and Mom had taught us and what he had just proclaimed.

He said, "You just have to be smart enough to be cautious and know when to quit the fight."

"Wait! What?"

"It's like this, Bern. If a person is drowning and you try to save them, that is a noble and grand gesture. But then maybe you realize you don't have the strength or the skill to save them, so rather than drown with them, you might have to let them go. Let them drown without you."

I was stunned beyond words; I could not believe what my father was saying. At that moment I was so disappointed in him, heart-broken over his words and this seeming reversal of all I thought I knew of him. I had never heard of or known him to back down from a fight just because it was difficult. All I could say to him was simply, "I don't believe you, Daddy. I just don't believe that." Then I went to my room and cried in secret.

I think that conversation was the catalyst that created a complete change of heart about my career path. The family and I had always assumed I would attend Ole Miss like Connie had and that I would study law as my parents had done. It was a "given" I would be part of the family legacy to "continue the fight for equality and justice." Something had turned in me though from living in the midst of bitter hatred and deep disapproval of life among and with people "not like us." Living through the earliest parts of the Civil Rights Movement, seeing leaders and change makers assassinated in displays of public carnage never before seen and seeing once civil men, both black and white, prompted to violence and fighting in the streets, my world turned in a different direction.

I had a lengthy talk with my high school counselor about a teaching career, and Mr. Weems advised me to look into a small college in the Delta known for its strong teacher education program. That evening after supper, I told my parents I did not want to go to Ole Miss. "Even more so," I said, "I know I don't want to study law."

"What in the HELL are you talking about, son?" my unusually mild mannered father bellowed. I expected him to oppose my decision, but I never anticipated such an emotional explosion as what erupted in the Gresham living room that evening.

"We've given you every opportunity and advantage a boy could have for a college career at Ole Miss and a career in law. It's damn idiocy for you to turn your back on that!"

"Calm down a bit now, Franklin," my mother interjected, trying to intervene but cut short swiftly.

"You sit down and shut up, Nan," my father said. "This is between Bern and me, and we're going to straighten this shit out one way or another."

At that moment we all knew how serious this argument was because my father rarely ever cussed, and he would never have even dreamed of being even slightly rude to my mother, even when they had their biggest, though rare, arguments. Mother was stunned beyond belief, and Connie began crying. My upbringing was founded in civility and good manners, especially toward women, and my father's conduct set off an anger in me worse than my usual temper.

"No, Dad! YOU shut up for now! We're NOT doing this this way!" I grabbed my keys and stormed out. I honestly believe if I hadn't, the two of us would have ended up in a fist fight with our relationship forever damaged. I'm not sure what my mother said to him after I left, and Connie didn't know either because Mother sent her to her room. Whatever was said though brought reconciliation and resignation that I had to make my own decisions about my future and my career.

I applied and was accepted into Delta State University in Cleveland with plans to study English and become a teacher. Yes, I was going back to the Delta, and despite my parents' disapproval, I was determined to become an educator, believing education more than law was the best way to impact cultural divides and change generational attitudes. I had heard one too many Mississippians say, "They can make all the laws they want. They can't change our hearts and minds."

We were learning a similar lesson in Viet Nam, a place by the grace of God I never had to go. It turns out doctors found I had a couple of bad discs in my back. I guess I could thank Claire for that! That medical problem, coupled with my acceptance into Delta State, gave me a deferment from the draft and sent me on my way to let other young men go to war instead if they had no means of changing their fate.

During those college years I dated one girl exclusively. Shelley played French horn in the band, and I spent a great deal of free time accompanying her to marching practice. I got to know several of Shelley's band member friends, and all of them, in one way or another, expanded my knowledge of both classical and marching band music. I might as well have minored in music education for all the hours I spent at the band hall during marching season, practice hours, and recitals.

The most influential piece of music from that time that has stayed as an integral part of my life is the intro piece played when Shelley and all the band members took the field at half time each week of football season. Week after week, year after year, I eagerly anticipated seeing that Delta band step off to the tune of "Darkness on the Delta." I grew to love that tune, and pretty much each evening at sunset, I paused my studies to play that music in my head and even learned the words. I also grew to love that small college town and that small teacher college that helped me create both a dream and a career.

Initially, I did not do well in college though. I skipped classes to hang out in the band hall; I drank and partied too much, didn't do my research papers, and slept in late quite often to overcome a number of hangovers. I was put on Academic Probation for a year, and my parents threatened to make me come home. They could not understand how a strong student, such as I had been, could fail so miserably in college. Part of it was that now, for the first time in my academic life, I actually needed to study to pass, and I didn't really know how to study; good grades had always come so easily for me.

So I just tried to wing my way through classes but lost all focus. In order to graduate within the normal timeframe of four years, I ended up having to take courses year around for the next three years, and summer school sessions in lit classes were brutal. In my Shakespeare class, we had to read on average 80 pages a night, which doesn't sound too awful until you remember Shakespeare was in love with iambic pentameter. In my Southern Lit class, we read a novel every two days, including several Faulkner novels. Talk about a Herculean task! A class on Milton devoured hours of what could have been some great social time, and Transformational Grammar was as useless as a hat on a jackass.

Summers at Delta State weren't all work though. Each year there was a big watermelon bash on the Quadrangle, a beautiful shady grove stretching from the main entrance of the campus down to the student union. It was variegated green and pastoral, my favorite place to hang out late in the evenings for a good walk when reading grew tiresome and I needed a refresher.

All in all, my time at Delta State taught me so much more than just great literature and good writing technique. I learned a wealth of musical knowledge from my time with my French horn playing girlfriend. I learned I had a gift for poetry and an appetite for Hemingway and Sandburg. More than anything else though, I learned that my true passion in life, even more of a passion than writing, was teaching. While most education majors spent only six weeks doing their student teaching, I spent a full semester doing my required student teaching assignment at Ruleville Jr. High under a lady named Mrs. Burkhalter who was both the eighth grade English teacher and the assistant principal. She left me alone on my own with her classes after only my second day of observation in her room. When I reported to work that third day, we walked down to the room for her first period class and she announced out of the blue, "Students, this is your teacher now Mr. Gresham. He will be here for the rest of this spring semester. I will be in the office attending to duties there, and I do not expect to see any of you coming in for a visit." She then turned on her heel and walked out on us all. The only instruction she gave me was to start the unit on "Rime of the Ancient Mariner."

That "baptism by fire" in the classroom though was the best thing she could have done to truly teach me what the job was all about in a real setting. The classes had all the usual troublemakers—the spit ball throwers, the hair pullers, the plagiarizers, the bullies, the challengers to authority. But I also saw glimpses of genius during our discussions and in their writing, and I saw a few tough nuts improve their oral reading skills and conclude that literature wasn't half bad. I spent uncountable hours writing out lesson plans and grading essays. I hated the paperwork, but I loved the daily interaction with the kids.

They were finishing up their first full year as an integrated school, and I like to think I played a positive role in helping them with their transition into lives of full partnership. While many upcoming graduates abandoned the idea of a teaching career after their student teaching experiences, saying they would never teach another day in their lives, when I left Delta State that May in '74, I knew I had made the very best choice for my future. I would be one of the lucky ones who would work at a job I loved. All I needed was for Student Services to help get me in the market and find that job. I could never have anticipated the dedication and resilience needed to survive those first few years, but "Darkness on the Delta" still played in the background of my dreams.

It is a nostalgic song, with a sweetness to it; but looking back on it now, I'm certain some lines convey a naiveté that blots out the ugly violence and divisions. I guess the Delta finally won me over, where I didn't see just the negative things that seemed to be its total composite in my earlier years. I could now see a promise, and that one song convinced me life in the Delta could be good if we just listened to her music.

Darkness on the Delta

Lyrics by Marty Symes and Al J. Neiburg

When it's darkness on the delta
That's the time my heart is light
When it's darkness on the delta
Let me linger in the shelter of the night

Fields of cotton all around me
Voices ringin' sweet and low
Lord, I'm lucky that you found me
Where the muddy Mississippi waters flow

Lounging on the levee
Listenin' to the nightingales way up above
Laughter on the levee
No one's heart is heavy
All God's children got someone to love

When it's darkness on the delta
Only heaven is in sight
When it's darkness on the delta
Let me linger in the shelter of the night

7 Till Town

Money, MS   1974-75

I packed all my worldly belongings and left Delta State with my resume in the file at Student Services with a job preference to teach somewhere in the Delta area. Their job was to match me up with Delta school districts looking for an English teacher. No one called during June or July, and I was getting concerned I might not find a teaching job for the fall. Then August came, hotter than a pepper pudding as they say, and the Leflore County School District was hot in the hunt to find an English teacher. So they called me to come up for an interview.

I drove up to Greenwood to meet Aaron Meredith, principal of the Wilkes School. Although I had lived in Itta Bena and Greenwood for several years, I had never heard of him or of his school. He was desperate for an English teacher, and I was desperate for a job, though neither of us knew that secret about each other. Getting straight down to business though, the interview took less than five minutes.

Now I am no "small feller," but when I stood up to shake hands with Mr. Meredith, I literally hit him just above his waistline! When he shook my hand, half my arm was engulfed in his grip. He was massive and good looking, a black man of about 40 years of age who wore his hair in a short que of a ponytail. He did not look like any principal I had ever known, heard of, or met.

He told me I would be the only English teacher for grades 5-9 and asked me if I wanted the job. That was the only question he asked me. Without asking any questions of my own or assessing the extreme challenge of having five different classroom preps for each week, I said yes. Without any further discussion he told me I was hired and that he would be in touch within the week. Just like that. Nothing more, nothing less.

A week later he sent me a contract to sign along with a letter that said I was to report to work in eight days. That is when he lowered the boom to tell me the Wilkes School was located in Money, Mississippi, and had an all-black student body and faculty! He said he was delighted to welcome me as the first white teacher on his staff, and that is when the weight of the situation and the reality of it hit me.

Money, Mississippi is no ordinary Delta town. It is known throughout the South and the entire nation as the place where one of the most despicable, barbaric crimes of segregation took place. A fourteen year old boy named Emmett Till was kidnapped from his uncle's home in the middle of the night by two men who claimed the boy had whistled at the wife of one of them at the local country store. They took him out and beat him beyond all recognition, stripped him naked and shot him in the head. Such arrogance by a nigger could not go unaddressed, but just killing the boy was too good for his offense. Nope, killing him was not enough; there had to be more punishment. The two brothers, Roy Bryant and J. W. Milan, tied a 75-pound cotton gin fan to Till's neck using barbed wire, and then they threw the teenager into the nearby Tallahatchie River. Accounts say the next morning the two killers were in church as usual.

When the river gave up the dead, the body was found in such a horrible condition, Emmett's mother insisted on an open casket so the world could see the destruction of her son. Pictures of the devastated body circulated through magazines and newspapers all across the country. That happened in 1955, a little less than 20 years ago, and both the murder and miscarriage of justice when the two were brought to trial gave the entire country a wakeup call about the dangers of stepping out of line in Mississippi. Money, Mississippi would never outlive that horror and would forever be named as a place only one step above hell, where murderous insanity was the norm. I had to ask myself if I was really going to show up there to teach black children who just might still be angry enough to attack me. If I was committed to helping create change in the Delta though, I HAD to go.

Upon my arrival, I learned the school housed grades Pre-K through 9th grade and had a total enrollment of about 150, all on the free lunch program. The all black faculty was receptive enough to having a white teacher among them, but none offered any assistance or encouragement to this rookie, and no one offered to share their materials either. I had no ancillary teaching materials, no bulletin board materials, and not even a fan for my classroom. The school was not air conditioned, and classrooms often reached upwards of 100 degrees by 8:30 in the morning each day. I was told if I wanted a fan, I would need to buy it myself. I asked how children were expected to learn with that kind of heat beating on them all day long. I was told they were "used to it." No one else had any concern about their learning environment.

I did have some textbooks although they were outdated and falling apart. On the first day of school I was to issue a grammar book and a "story" book (aka literature book) to each child. I was not given a roster of students for each grade level I would teach. I was told to write their names down in a gradebook on the first day and that would serve as my roster. There being no compulsory school attendance laws, a class roster was made up of whoever might show up. So on the first day as each class filed into my room, all of them looking at me like I was from Mars and had four eyes and nine tails, I set about creating a roster.

Knowing how important our names are to us, I asked each student to come to my desk one at a time, write their name on a page in a spiral notebook, and then pronounce their name for me so I could learn to recognize each by name. It also gave me an idea about their handwriting skill, spelling aptitude, and diction. As they did so, I wrote their names in the two textbooks I was to distribute to them, and said, "It's nice to meet you, So-and-so. Here are your textbooks. Please have a seat."

The process went very smoothly; no one was disruptive or uncooperative. Then the eighth grade class showed up. Same drill. Until the fifth student came to my desk, wrote his name in the spiral and announced, "An' I betchoo cain't even pronounce it." Admittedly I had never seen this particular name before, but given the challenge, I ventured a good educated guess.

"Is your name Thee-offa-lus?"

"Damn, man! How you know dat?" he exclaimed, but he was smiling as he asked.

"Greek literature helped," I responded. I could tell he was impressed that I could pronounce the name Theophilus and would not be stumbling over it day after day as many of his other teachers had done in previous years. He was a bright and congenial kid, but I told him I was going to have to teach him some better vocabulary, that cussing would not be allowed in my classroom.

"Fine," he said. "Just doan be callin' me Theo."

And so went the first day. By the end of it, I had discovered I had a 19 year old in my ninth grade class who would be signing his own report cards. I had a boy in seventh grade who could read "and"

and "the" and write his name, but that was IT!! Nothing else!! I also learned that most students had a very difficult time pronouncing my last name.

On the second day, I had to really take charge of that same eighth grade class. As soon as they were seated, one girl raised her hand and asked, "Missa Gersch, what you goan do if we all decides to gang up on you and beechoo up?"

"Oh, shit!" I thought. "Here it is." I had no idea if she was serious or not, but one thing I knew for sure --- I had better not show any fear or let them think they could intimidate me. I certainly had better not escalate the situation. So I just gave her a level gaze and calmly bluffed, "I wouldn't do that if I were you. For one thing, you won't get away with it. And two, an awful lot of you are going to get hurt in the process."

"Why?" she asked. "You know karate or sumpin'?"

"You might be surprised what all I do know. Why? Is that your plan for today?"

She fell out laughing and said, "Aw, naw. I's just axin."

"Well, alright then," I said in relief at a crisis averted. "Let's then take another look at some common and proper nouns like we did yesterday."

In addition to my five academic preps, I also had one PE class for which I was responsible so I could have a full schedule. There was no gym, no playground, no sports equipment.

"How am I supposed to teach PE with no equipment?" I asked Mr. Meredith that first week. "What team games can we possibly play, air basketball or pretend baseball?"

"You just go outside and supervise, and make sure no one gets in a fight. They will make up their own rules and games. It'll be fine."

"You know good and well that is not right! Life does not let you just make up your own rules," I argued.

"Look, Mr. Gresham," he said. "You're new at this. I've been dealing with state budgets for many years. They will not give us a fair amount of money to really provide everything that is needed in these schools. You're not dumb. You know why we don't have money for things like that. We do well to have pencils for them."

I knew he was right. I could just imagine polite legislators, too genteel to really say anything nefarious out loud, but sitting in committees insinuating in code that money should not be "wasted" in such places as the Wilkes School.

So PE consisted of jumping rope and playing jacks. Two girls had 2 long jump ropes with which they jumped "double dutch." One boy brought a small ball every day so a group of his friends could play "jack rocks," which is the game of jacks played with the ball and several small rocks instead of jacks. The rest of the class just stood around in the shade of the classroom eaves. Since Mr. Meredith had flatly denied my request for money to buy some equipment, I knew the answer was the same old story. "If you want to buy something for the chirren....." So as soon I got my first paycheck I bought myself a portable electric typewriter, two box fans for my classroom, and a ball and bat so we could all play softball if jump rope and jack rocks weren't worthy of our time. We made bases out of cardboard boxes from the cafeteria.

Sometimes though things happen and get out of hand before you even have time to think. My little fellow Dorsey, who could only write his name and read two words, turns out didn't like my umpiring skills. When I called him out on strikes, he turned on me with the bat in his hands, threatening to "buss" my head open. I was most thankful he was a very tiny guy for his age, so when he swung at me, I was easily able to take the bat away from him. I told him he could only play jack rocks for the next week and banned him from softball. He never tried to assault me again, and by year's end he could identify the words ball, bat, base, strike, out, and softball in various sentences. I called it a win with a triple digit percentage increase in his reading ability.

Overall though, I failed repeatedly to bring the students up to grade level in reading, spelling, speaking, or writing. All of my students were significantly behind in every content area, so I was told not to worry about it. The educational philosophy in Leflore County was, "It's dat way in errybodies' class. They ain't jest behind in English. They just slow 'bout things."

And they were right. The students were slow, but not because they were dumb. They just had so little exposure to anything beyond their own front yards and the school. One sunny day as we played softball, a student asked if my sunglasses were "medicated." It took me a few minutes to figure out he was wanting to know if the glasses were prescription glasses. Another time I had a conversation on the ballfield that went like this:

"Missa Gersh, what you call white folk wid hair yo color?"

"Well, brown haired women are called brunettes, but brown haired men like me are called sexy." The joke went unacknowledged. I wasn't sure whether he believed that was the real answer or whether he just didn't think it was funny.

"What you call white folk wid dat yellow lookin' hair?"

"Blonde."

"What you call folks wid dat oinch color hair?"

"Excuse me? What color?"

"Oinch. You know like the fruit."

"Oh, orange. We call those people red heads."

"And what you call peoples with blue hair like Miz Melton in dat pre-K class?"

"OLD!!!" And we laughed like we were old friends.

But that conversation told me just how closed off they were in learning about the world around them. So I decided part of my curriculum should be teaching them basic knowledge about all kinds of things that most of us take for granted.

I also realized part of the problem was the way I communicated with them. I did not always ask the right question or give the best directions. One teacher asked me to work with Lorraine, a 7th grader, on her money counting skills during homeroom. So I explained money values, and after a couple of weeks of drill and kill, she finally got it. A quarter is 25 cents. A dime is 10 cents. And she could do a little addition as in three dimes would equal 30 cents. But when we got to money exchanges, things just did not compute.

"Ok, Lorraine. You have a quarter. How many nickels would you have?"

"I ain't got nay'un, Missa Gersh. I gots a quawta."

You get the idea of how we both struggled.

Then there was the day I taught a lesson on adjectives and their function in describing nouns. I gave plenty of examples and then called on each student to give me an example of an adjective-noun combo. They gave me great answers like black horse, blue sky, tall trees, short girl, fat pigs, hot food. Everybody got it!! I was so proud of myself for that lesson.....until it came to individualized practice. I had written 10 sentences on the chalkboard for them to copy. Each sentence had a blank in which they were to supply an adjective. On their papers they were to copy the directions and complete the assignment. The directions said, "Copy each sentence and fill in the blank with an adjective." Simple enough. But when I took up the papers and looked over them, over half the class had written "an adjective" in the blank of each sentence!

1. I live in <u>an adjective</u> house.

2. I drive <u>an adjective</u> car.

3. I like to read <u>an adjective</u> books.

Jesus, Mary, and Joseph!!!! But they HAD followed my directions. Literally. I told them to fill in the blank with "an adjective," and that is exactly what they did!! So I learned I was not the genius I imagined myself to be in the classroom.

Meanwhile, back in the state capital, committees were meeting and money was being discussed.

"Look here now, Senator Thomas. We can't pump hundreds of thousands of dollars into public education. It's a failing system. We all know that."

"Senator Burnbaum, those schools are failing because they have no money to improve! We hold the purse strings, so if they are failing, it is because we are not helping them do anything but fail."

"Senator! How dare you blame this committee for those failures! You know those people don't care nothing about their own education. They just care about those government checks. We can't make 'em wanna learn by just giving them money."

"Money is the only thing holding back those schools, you jackass! You can't teach without books and lab equipment and band instruments and on and on with dozens of things that cost money. Do you expect them to teach with just air?"

"Sir, you are out of order. I'll have the Sergeant-at-Arms remove you if you continue calling names and being ungentlemanly."

"What is ungentlemanly, sir, is your refusal to hear the truth. You don't want to fund the schools because they are predominately black. That is the truth of the matter."

"That is not true, and I resent what you say! As chairman of this committee, it is my duty to use education dollars where it will do the most good. And that simply means we don't pour money down a rat hole!"

"A rat hole? Did you say rat hole? My point exactly! Hold those purse strings tight enough and you might as well still have them all enslaved. It's just a covert way of still keeping them down, keeping them behind, keeping them less than whites, keeping them unequal. THAT is your motivation!"

"Sergeant, remove this man! Remove him now!"

And so it goes year after year. No money. No money. No money. Given just enough to pay the light bill of the school and the bare essentials, the public schools limp along, crippled with insult and injury. As George Wallace said in 1963, "Segregation today! Segregation tomorrow! Segregation forever!" He may have been from Alabama, but his words were adopted as the mantra of Mississippi when it came to budgets for public education, which as we all know in polite company, simply means "Bless their hearts. They can't learn anyway."

8 Nightmares and Mothers

Money, MS   October 1975

Jackson, MS   April 1976   April 1977   and July 1977

Delta State was a great training institution when it came to preparing the next generation of teachers for content knowledge, but just as with all teacher prep programs, they can never really teach you "the job." You simply cannot learn to teach by studying a textbook. As with any job, you never really know how much life it will suck out of you until you actually WORK the job. Every job has its emotional attachments, favorite parts of the job that thrill you to the core; and there are those parts that are as despised as a viper. Then there are those moments that hit you like a right uppercut that lays you out flat. That is how unprepared I was to deal with the death of one of my students during my second year of teaching.

Though I was well acquainted with all the murderous death that peppered Southern history, I had led a blessed life that had never been forced to deal with the death of a relative or close friend or classmate. I had never been plunged into flood waters so deep with tears too numerous to count.

I had never felt the ache of losing someone so dear that I wanted my own breathing to stop. I certainly had never known a young person to die. But it happens, and when it does, we are all left wondering how life can be so cruel with such a loving God.

Woodrow was my first of several in my career who left this world unexpectedly and tragically and incomprehensibly. He is the one I remember most vividly though because he took his exit long before any others, so I've had more years remembering him. He was an eighth grader, the same age as Emmett Till, when he met his doom.

One thing whites do not understand about blacks is that so few of them really know how to swim. It is assumed that growing up in the country with so many creeks and lakes and rivers that black children automatically learn to swim in those areas. They don't; and Woodrow didn't learn either. He died in a drowning accident, swept off into the Yalobusha River not far from where it empties into the Tallahatchie, the same river that gave up Emmett Till's body for the world to witness.

I had never attended a funeral for a black person, and I was not sure how well-received I would be there at Woodrow's in a time of such anguish and heartbreak. His funeral was held at the Wilkes

School in the cafeteria that was packed wall to wall with relatives and friends from all over Leflore County. I was given a stink eye by a couple of different people when I walked in to take my seat, strangers I assumed who did not know my connection to Woodrow or to the school. I did not let that deter me though from paying my respects.

There was an open casket, and poor Woodrow was so bloated from the river that I hardly recognized him. I stood beside the casket and read a quiet prayer for him from my Prayer Book as a few tears slipped down my face. "O, God, whose mercies cannot be numbered: Accept our prayers on behalf of your servant Woodrow, and grant him an entrance into the land of light....." The prayer was interrupted when his mother came and stood beside me. She took my hand in hers, a most unusual thing for a black woman to do with a white man, but we just stood there staring at Woodrow, alone in our own thoughts, but together in our acknowledgment of his being "gone" and lost to us forever. It seemed such a waste to lose one so young and fresh, so inquisitive and personable. I had had great expectations and hope for him, and now he was gone.

The funeral lasted about three hours; despite the fury of an early October afternoon sun and humidity, despite clothes soaked through to the outside with perspiration, despite pungent body odor cloistered inside the big room, no one seemed eager to end the singing and preaching. If people tired and grew weary, someone would suddenly wail out loud, and ladies in white dresses would rush to them and fan them to revive them and bring them back to their senses. Truth told though, no one wanted it to come to an end because it would mean the End of Woodrow for us all. Like all things earthly though, the time came to close the casket and wheel him away to the hearse waiting outside the school.

I remember standing in the blazing sun with several of his classmates gathered around me. Nearby stood three large bushes of knockout roses. His classmates, being too poor to buy flowers, picked roses from those bushes and threw them into the hearse, crying the kind of tears that were slobber-snotty as they called aloud, "Goodbye, Woodrow. Goodbye, Woodrow." It broke my heart that there was nothing I could do to help them make sense of the loss or to give them any comfort in their sorrow of losing a friend.

As the funeral home directors prepared to close the back door of the hearse, a lady I did not recognize unexpectedly jumped into the rear, threw herself across the top of the casket and caterwauled quite loudly, "Oh, my son! My son, Woodrow. My boy, my boy!" She looked to be about twenty-five, and not being Woodrow's mother, it was quite a spectacle to me though everyone else seemed to take it as normal. I asked a student who she was. "Oh, she da funeral home crier. Dat be her job, to do what da mudder cannot spress in public." What an ingenious and generous gesture, I thought. Whites tend to be so stoic at funerals, we would never have thought to do such a gracious thing for a grieving parent.

As I walked away toward my car and the hearse was driving away, the last thing said to me was, "Missa Gersh, I knowed you dint haf to come her today, but I preciates yo comin.' Woodrow liked you a lot, sayed you uz always respectful to 'im. Thank you for bein' kind to our boy." It was one of the three preachers from the funeral, and as he turned to go, he said, "Doan you worry nayun 'bout our Woodrow. He be wid God now and alive betterin us." Little did I know that just a few months later I would be attending another funeral, one even harder, and one far more devastating than my first loss of a student.

It was my father on the phone telling me, "Bern, you must come home right now. Drop everything and get down here. Something really bad has happened, and I can't tell you on the phone, son. Just come home. Come right now." So I drove like a bat out of hell, my mind racing as fast as I drove.

When I got to my parents' house, Connie was already there, and I could tell she was highly distraught. She came running down the driveway, grabbed me around the neck and squeezed me so tight I almost couldn't breathe. Crying uncontrollably, she blubbered in my ear something barely audible, as if she could hardly find enough air to say the words, but it sounded like "He's gone, Bern. Will is gone."

"Connie, what do you mean he's gone? Run away? Missing? What?"

"No, Bern, he's dead. Will is dead. Someone shot him, shot him twice in the head and left him in a ditch out on the...."

"Shot him!! What, why would someone shoot Will? He's just a kid. Who goes around shooting sixteen year old kids?" As these words poured from my mouth, my tears flooded my face and a fog suddenly clouded my brain.

"We don't know, Bern. Police have no idea who did it or why. Dad is holding it together for right now, but Mom has come totally undone. She's barely one step above catatonic. You and I are going to have to handle everything for them with the funeral home once the coroner releases his body later this afternoon."

"How could this happen? Where was he found?"

"They left him in a ditch beside the road going out to Camp Kickapoo off Highway 49. An old man found him just after daybreak as he was out for his morning walk for his heart. Seeing Will like that almost gave him another heart attack. Police say he could barely talk to them when they got out to scene."

"Are they sure it's Will? How do they know it's him if they shot him in the head?"

"Mercifully, police say, they used a small caliber handgun, and the bullets did not exit, so everything looks...... Jesus, Bern, what are we going to do?" Again the dam of tears broke with sobs such as I had never heard before from my sister, even when her fiancé absented himself from the church during the wedding rehearsal. I slipped my arm around her waist and all but had to carry her back inside the house.

Dad had not even realized I had arrived until Connie and I walked in. He stood up from where he was sitting on the sofa, walked up to me, and just hugged me. He didn't say a single word, just hugged me and then walked toward the back bedrooms.

"Mom's asleep right now," Connie said. "Dr. Pharr gave her some tranquilizers. She has just been out of control in grief since the police showed up at the door. I don't know if she will ever be the same again."

"None of us will ever be the same again," I muttered just above a whisper. Getting words out audibly took too much effort. We were defeated in mind and spirit. We were cast into a living hell brought on by murder too close and answers too distant. We had no idea what motive anyone would have for killing sweet, even-tempered Will. We had no idea who would do such a horrific thing. It took months for us to get any answers to the myriad of prickling questions.

At the family viewing of the body, upon first seeing Will lying there so pale, I almost fell to my knees, barely able to remain standing. My mother wept uncontrollably, as did Connie, but my father was stoic after having downed a couple of glasses of scotch beforehand.

During the funeral, I inwardly questioned every person, especially his friends, who came into the parlor suite where Will lay during the visitation.

"Were you the one who did this?"

"Was he involved with drugs and owed you money?"

"What was the last thing he said to you when you were with him that night?'

Did you have an argument with him that got out of control?"

"Are you the killer?"

"Are you my brother's killer?"

"Are you?"

"Are you?"

My dad bought four cemetery plots for the family. Will would be the first to occupy that land. The other three were intended for my parents themselves and whoever might need the fourth, in case Connie or I died unmarried. I found it quite odd that my parents thought several years into the future at a time I couldn't even think toward the next hour.

Finally, after eight months of haunting, torturous questions without answers, December news reports identified the shooter as Sandival "Taboo" Robertson, a twenty-three year old security guard. His accomplice was a two-time offender named Morris Greenlee. They had kidnapped Will at gunpoint with the idea to rob him and get some drug money. Since Will had so little money on him, they decided to kill him. During what would be about a twenty-minute ride, with Will crying and begging for his life the entire time as they drove him outside of the Jackson city limits, they were undeterred in their murderous plan. On a lone gravel road, Robertson forced him into a ditch at gunpoint, knelt over Will with his knee in his back, and fired three times. The gun misfired the first time, a split second reprieve from death for Will and possibly a glimmer of hope, and then life was ended.

Police were able to solve the murder because after killing Will, the two criminals drove back into Jackson and robbed two convenience stores at gunpoint. Police had arrested them for those armed robberies, and while awaiting arraignment, Greenlee offered to solve a murder for them if they would cut him a deal. Having been incarcerated twice before in the state prison system, and Mississippi having a "three strike" law, Greenlee knew with those two priors plus two armed robbery charges, he could face a death penalty. He gave up Robertson as the shooter in exchange for a life sentence.

Robertson, it turns out, was a preacher's son. As we sat in court in late July of 1977 to hear pre-trial motions and prior to jury selection, the preacher had a talk with his son and convinced him to own his sin and plead guilty so avoid a death penalty. There was no doubt a jury would find him guilty of capital murder given the information provided by

Greenlee and Robertson's own confession to police, which he had since recanted.

The preacher father cried and pleaded, "You break yo mama heart doin' dis kinda thing. She cain't take you dyin' too. Day'll puts a needle in yo arm sure as Jesus is King. Betta fo us all to have you in Parchman than in da ground. You know you did it. We all know you did it. It cain't be undone, but you can live through it. So tell 'em da troof!"

Crying not for Will but for having been caught, Robertson admitted the crime to the judge so Judge Caldwell would sentence him rather than a jury. By law the judge cannot order a death penalty, no matter how much he might wish he could in some cases. Will's case was one of them.

Judge Caldwell, while apologizing to us as a family for having to hear what was about to happen, insisted Robertson inform the court as to the details that led to the murder; he would not accept just a simple statement of guilt. It was not the judge's intent to be cruel to us, but by requiring Robertson to divulge the specifics, he ensured Robertson would have no grounds for an appeal. In replaying the events of the evening, Robertson finally admitted they decided to murder Will because he had only two dollars, and it pissed them off. They wanted drug money!

So with two convictions for armed robbery and one for capital murder, Taboo Robertson was sent to the Mississippi State Penitentiary in Parchman for what was intended to be the rest of his life without parole. Unfortunately, our lives would be forever entwined with his for what remained of our years on earth, because in truth, in Mississippi there is no such thing as life without parole.

We were left to carry on with our lives, each with our own guilt for not having protected Will better, each to sort out our anger that he was killed for so little reason, for just two fucking dollars. Every time I pulled a couple of dollar bills from my billfold to pay for something, I thought of that moment when those two cold blooded killers discovered it was all the money Will had on him, that moment when they must have said, "Then let's kill him."

Mom was completely crushed under the weight of loss. No parent expects to outlive a child. She lost all sense of time, all sense of joy, all sense of responsibility and duty. She quit her job. She stopped going to church. She stopped cooking, and Dad had to hire a maid to clean house. Mom was so lost in her grief that she could hardly breathe on her own without prompting. If Dad didn't tell her to bathe or get dressed or wash her hair, she just sat on the couch and stared at the television, not really seeing, hearing, or comprehending anything going on around her. She became a wasted woman, withering away in loss and confusion.

I thought of Woodrow's mother. I wondered how she was doing and if she was still in the grip of grief, choked off with just enough oxygen to stay alive. It was almost time for school to start up again, and I needed to get back to the Delta, to my job. The only thing my mother said to me when I left was, "I don't know how you can go back there and work with 'those people' after what they did to Will." I knew then the mother we had known as strong and committed to justice was now in a well too deep for the hand of equality to reach. This one act of violence, after seeing so many other unjustified deaths, had turned her heart toward that Delta disease of an "us vs. them" mentality. Will's death had taken from her every sense of justice she ever had and cultivated, along with any belief in the goodness in others.

In as kind a voice as I could, I told her, "Mom, THEY didn't do this to Will. One man did it. Not all black people are to blame. My students and teacher friends had nothing to do with Will's death. You know that," I gently reminded her. But she just turned her face away from me as if to say she did not believe it. I tried to tell Dad she needed some professional help, but his own denial kept him from discussing it with her or taking any action. I could only assume he had decided to let her drown without him because he didn't have the strength himself to save them both. They each got through day by day as best they could, separately, silently, secretly harboring the anger and nursing their pain with pills and alcohol. Our family was in shambles, and I wasn't sure it would or could ever recover.

As I drove through the early heat of spring to return to my Delta home, I thought about my mother and her talk of "sensible shoes." I needed to hear her talk to me like that again. I discovered that no matter how hard our Founding Fathers tried to set up a patriarchal society of male dominance, it is our mothers we look to most when crisis and heartache come into our own lives. When we most need guidance, comfort, or strength of will, it is our mothers we seek out and long for, whether through phone calls, letters, or earnest prayers. It is the reason dying soldiers cry out in delirium for their mothers.

It is the mother's way that points us in the right direction when we come to confusing crossroads. It is the mother's whiskey-strong will that pushes us to do the right thing when the color of the necessary course is gray instead of black and white. It is the mother's waltz that gives us the courage to join the dance even after our knees have been cut from under us, and she teaches us to invite others to the party. It is the mother's wave goodbye that makes us pause in our busy lives to remember the silly things, like three-inch red high heels to walk a gravel road, so we can laugh in the loss and brokenness of our universe when she leaves. And it is the mother's warm hand on our winter dreams that brings us comfort from her ever burning fire of love.

My mother never recovered from Will's death. The loving, insightful and delightful woman I had known as a driving force in my younger years faded away into fathomless nothingness, a hollow and hateful woman too hurt to ever love anyone again, another victim of Robertson as surely dead as Will. The destruction of such an indomitable spirit was a thing I could never quite believe actually happened, but a year after Will's death, before Robertson ever came to trial in July of '77, she took all of her pills and quietly lay down and went to sleep with Will.

9 World Without Will

Money, MS   April   1976

On a spiritual level I knew he still lived with me, but on a physical level he is nowhere to be found. Emotionally, he was only tears, wretched guilt, and haunting dreams. With Will having been six years younger, we had never attended the same school together; we were never together in youth groups at church; there was never a club or hobby we participated in together. Since his death, I realized there had always been a separation that kept us just beyond each other's reach, something more than just the veil of daily living and running our own lives in our own circles. He was really too good to live in my world.

At thirteen, though, he had fallen in with the "wrong crowd" and had gotten into some minor trouble with the police. It was serious enough the judge thought he needed some form of intervention. The judge ruled that Will was to be removed from home for a short while, although not to a juvenile detention center. So for a year and a half, Will had gone to a group home for troubled youth down in Hattiesburg. All were troubled enough as to be headed toward prison, but still deemed salvageable and redeemable, caught in time before their crimes became really serious. There, in that setting, Will really came into his own. He developed confidence and became a leader, and even older kids looked up to him.

Will lived on a different plain. He had no temper at all, so unlike me in that way. I couldn't recall a single instance when he needed to borrow Mom's high heels to hike off down a gravel road to inhibit a fit of anger. Upon his release from the group home, his house monitor had filed an evaluation of Will for the court's consideration on releasing him. It read in part, "Will Gresham is a negotiator, a fixer, a compromiser with viable solutions that give benefit to all with little loss on either side. His heart is in the right place to see the needs in others and take whatever action necessary to relieve the impasse, the anger, the distress, the sorrow. He has a high level of empathy and a smooth temperament, soothing to all those troubled around him. He has had a remarkable transformation while here, and he has made a positive impact on us all, adults, older teens, and younger youth."

When I had returned to work following Will's funeral in April, I had been out for almost two weeks. I was still unfit to be teaching in my current emotional state, but I needed to get back to work for many reasons. One really important one was an eighth grade graduation ceremony to plan and practice, speeches to write, prayers to design, parts to assign. It was an all-student production, and it was a really big deal because it was assumed across the board that a black child's eighth grade graduation would be his only graduation. I wanted to change that mindset. But there was this new world now, a world without Will, a world where I had little to no will to move, to breathe, to teach. Like my father whose numbing drug of choice was scotch, I had little desire to live outside a vodka bottle. How was I supposed to work my way through this kind of loss?

"Missa Gersch, Missa Gersh, Missa Gersch, whur you been? You been gone most two week. Dat sub wuz turrble. We thought you done leff us." I knew from their questions that they had been told nothing about Will's murder. The faculty had collected money and sent a funeral wreath with condolences, but no one had told my students a single thing about my prolonged absence. I took it as a teachable moment with my eighth graders.

"Look, kids. I need to tell you something that's really hard to talk about. I can't explain it all at one time; I'll probably have to break it up into parts, but you need to know. I've been gone because my little brother was murdered two weeks ago." As those words hung in the air, my own breath seemed to be sucked out the windows, and "my chirren" all drew a collective breath inward.

"How old he was? What whur his name? Where'd he stay? Who kilt him? Why day kill him?" These were the questions whirling through their minds at the time, questions that came out later but which they held inside that first day I was back. They just sat there staring at me like I was lying, playing a joke. In their world, white folks don't get murdered, only the black ones. Telling them that Will was killed by a black man would take time. That first day back was not the time, being as it was we did not know then who had killed him.

Softly a voice rose from the back of the room; Ernest Westerfield stood up and said, "Errybody pray for Missa Gersch!" Though the sound was compassionate, it was like a demand, so all eighteen heads bowed. I bowed my head, too, and closed my eyes to refuse tears, but I heard footsteps coming toward me. Ernest and five of his buddies came to stand around me and put their hands on my shoulders. "Keep prayin', Missa Gersch," Ernest said. "Don't look up. You jest keep prayin."

I told them we could talk about the murder if they wanted to know, but that I insisted they use the time to learn something valuable from all of it, to honor Will that way, and not ask questions of pure curiosity. I also had to set limits—just one or two questions a day. I felt it was all I could handle. So each day before class ended, Ernest appointed the next inquisitor for tomorrow. They had deep, probing questions, not just about Will's murder, but about death in general.

"Do you think he see you teachin' each day you come her?"

"Do you think when we be raised up, we be in dis body, or could we maybe be white?"

"Do you cry 'bout it since mens ain't spost ta cry?"

"Was he doin' drugs?"

"What gone happen to dem killers if day finds 'em?"

"Do dis make you wanna go out and kills somebody?"

"Can wees tell udda students or would dat be disrespecting to you?"

"How yo momma doin'?"

One day, I walked into that class and a girl named Carolyn Edleman stood up and approached my desk. She was a very studious girl and destined to be named the Valedictorian of the class. Her English speaking skills had improved tremendously since the beginning of the year, and sometimes the other kids made fun of her, saying she was just trying to be white or be the teacher's pet. She paid them no heed and fearlessly pursued her studies and her mastery of speech. "Mister Gerscham, we wanted to get something for you, but we didn't have a lot of money. So all we could get you was this here card." Then she added, "We didn't all help pay for it, but we all signed it." The class and I laughed together for the first time since I had gotten back.

It was a sympathy card, neatly signed by every one of my eighth grade students in their best handwriting. T.W. Jones, a less studious charge in my room, told me later Carolyn had told them if they couldn't write neatly, she would write their names for them, but she didn't want no scribbling on it. She wanted to ensure it looked nice and clean, "not like some of the homework papers y'all turn in looking like you slept with it in your underwear," she had said. It was a beautifully thoughtful gift. Even if meager, it was a true treasure to my heart.

I knew though that sympathy for grief can last only so long for those on the periphery of it. Life has that way of recycling and getting back on track with routines and patterns. I knew my students had reached that point when there was no "Question of the Day" and when two days later there was a disruptive incident in my class.

It happened during silent reading time. To set a good example, when they read silently, I also sat at my desk and read a book. We did not have a large number of books to read since the school had no library. We did, however, have a full set of old encyclopedias, so each student would just choose one and read that for their twenty minute assignment.

About ten minutes into the reading time, a boy named Melvin came charging up to my desk, encyclopedia in hand. He slammed the book down on my desk with all the force of a muscular male teen, pointing to a picture of a Coca-Cola machine. He raised his voice to me, yelling, "Do you see that? Do YOU see that?" In the picture, you could clearly see the words FOR WHITES ONLY written on the machine. Again Melvin demanded, "Do you SEE that?" It had obviously angered him, and he was indignant and looking for an argument. "Look at that!! Do you SEE IT?"

I lowered my voice, just audible above a whisper and as calmly as I could I said, "Yes, Melvin. I see it. But I didn't write it on there." It was the only answer that came to mind and the best answer I could offer.

He half jumped backwards, like one does when lightning and thunder come together at the same time and shake all the windows in a house. He hadn't thought of it that way. "Oh! Dat's right," he said. "I sometimes forgets when I reads that it ain't really happnin'. It jest bees in my head dat way. Sorry, Missa Gersch." He went and sat back down.

So the days wiled away into graduation practice and speech rehearsals. Our speeches centered on the concept "This is One of Three!" They emphasized to all class members and their parents that this graduation was just the beginning, that each one of them had intention of also having both a high school graduation and a college graduation down the road. Each day that we practiced a speech or the selected poem, I thought of Will who would never graduate....from high school or college.

As week after week passed, I slowly came out of the numbness that had protected me, when the pain exploded to the surface. The pain of the grief was so deep —deep and dark as the place where sea vipers sting, a place too deep for words to breathe.

My father's wisdom came to me. "Our words have life of their own. They may be children sometimes, happy to play in our own front yards, but eventually they grow up and demand to find their purpose. They will want to go off around the corner, for a hike in the woods, to hitchhike across America, to live a full and boisterous life. Never lose your voice for justice, Bern. Never let anger overtake you to the point where fists or guns replace the words of peace and love. Let your words have a good life."

In the depth of grief though, I could not find the words to assuage the feelings of loss and despair that were boiling under the surface, coming to a head. I could not speak his name without coming undone. I couldn't say it aloud. I couldn't whisper it in the dark. I couldn't even write his name on paper.

I could not think of him that I did not recall the words of his evaluation from the group home—"Will Gresham is a negotiator, a fixer, a compromiser..." But in that night of murder, there had been no breakthrough in negotiating. Beg as he did, his murderers were unfazed. Cry as he did, the killers were undeterred. I so desperately wished I didn't know what I knew about the details of the murder, of how desperate Will was, enough to revert to his juvenile crime of breaking and entering, telling the two he would break into some place for them and steal the money they wanted. It broke me, seeing in my mind a boy so young and at the same time so desperate, facing death alone among two ruthless strangers intent on the most evil, with no help in sight.

I cried for his useless tears. I cried for his hopelessness. I cried for that next-to-the-last moment of his life when the gun misfired and all he heard was a click, a click that still sounds like a cannon in my dreams. I cried for the prayers I hoped he had the presence of mind to pray. I cried for the girls he would never kiss, and for the woman he would never marry and sleep with. I cried in anger over the black hearts that stole him. I cried for my own brokenness that prevented me from fully living with any joy because even a small smile seemed like a betrayal. During those days, all I did was work, eat, cry, and sleep in a world without Will that hardly seemed worth the effort of reclaiming or redeeming.

Like my mother, I too was floundering in the grief that nightly took me to the grave of a boy gone. I did not question why God let it happen. I only questioned why I wasn't given the opportunity to save him or to trade places. I longed for some peace with it, but there was none to be found. I was bitter and angry and full of rage. I was wrecked out in an emotional collision, in a ditch as bloodied as the one where Will was executed, all tires flat, all windows blown out, roof caved in, doors smashed shut, and I was trapped under the steering wheel of a grief I was too powerless and hopeless to chase away . I was a broken, haunted man when Coleman found me.

10 High Heels and Halston

Money, MS   1976-77

Starting my third school year just a few short months after Will's murder had me all out of sync with days and classes. I truly felt like an old man who had no life left to enjoy, no more idealistic dreams of improving the society and culture around me, no more desire to do much of anything but be alone in my thoughts. I lived almost entirely in my own head, thinking and rehashing what all had happened that awful night, and how things could have turned out differently....if only.

When Robertson and Greenlee drove up in their car and pulled the gun on Will, he might could have gotten away if only he had thought to run in the opposite direction of their car. Even if they had been brazen enough to shoot at him, they likely would have missed since most people can't hit a moving target. If only he had run, knowing the gun misfired on the first shot, I'm sure he could've gotten away to safety in the nearby convenience store. They would not have come in after him. If only they had had a single moment of compassion for a crying kid begging for his life. If only they had stopped to truly hear the desperation in his offering to burglarize a closed store and steal money for them. If only there had been a single moment of clarity of what a heinous thing they were about to do. If only... if only... if only.

My life was bleak and scourged with self-loathing for things I did not do with my little brother, for things I did not say to him. Thanks be to God that I was somewhat functioning in my depression, enough to do an acceptable job at teaching, but certainly not excelling at it. My only goal was simply "just don't get fired!" Each day I clawed my way through normal living as much as I could make it normal. Then at the start of second semester, God in His infinite mercy sent me a lifeline, a beautiful diversion on which to refocus my life. And yes, despite the anguish and desolate living, I still had to believe in a merciful God.

She appeared at my classroom door unannounced, with no precursor in January. "Oh, hi. Good morning," she smiled, a very engaging smile, I thought. "I'm the new Migrant Program teacher, and I need to steal a couple of your students for supplemental study this hour." She called them by name and off they went, down the hall to the first room on the left. I watched her as she led them away, wearing three inch high heels, with a walk like she owned a fashion runway.

Essie Coleman entered my world when I was still dazed and numb with grief. She appeared like a visiting angel comes in a dream, and she got my attention instantly. She was petite and pretty, friendly and fashionable, classy, sophisticated, and tempting. New on the campus mid-year, she acted as if she had been among us from the very start. There was nothing shy or withdrawn about her, mingling among various teacher groups and making friends so easily she might as well have been her own Welcome Wagon in the Neighborhood. She laughed easily and was flirtatiously playful around me and other men, but just in a fun loving friendly way, not with duplicity. She was single.

I can't say I fell in love with her instantly, but within three days I was definitely interested in getting to know her better and most assuredly was somewhat charmed. I never saw her in the same outfit twice, and she must have owned 200 pairs of shoes, shoes that always matched her outfit in color. She stood out in a room like a rose in a weed patch; after all, who teaches in three inch heels and wears Halston in the Delta? Answer: no one except Essie Coleman.

She must have known early something was going on with me. Maybe I smiled too easily when she was around, or perhaps she saw me constantly looking at her across the cafeteria every day. Perhaps it was my eagerness to engage her in conversation during our mutual conference period. I looked forward to going to work and grew to hate weekends when I would not see her. She came to my classroom several times a day to pull out students for reading support, and each visit was a boost to my sunshine quota. She did not like for anyone to call her by her first name, so I, along with everyone else, just called her Coleman as her preference, and even when we became more than just colleagues, she rarely called me anything but Gresham.

It turns out she had family living in Jackson as well as I, so if one of us had plans to make a family visit over a weekend, we made plans to carpool together. I liked having her sitting beside me as we rolled away the miles. I liked the ease of our conversations, our query of one another as we searched for mutual interests, of getting to know one another on a very personal level outside of school confines.

My mother at this time was still in a slow decent to purgatory, not really dead but not living either. I tried to see her at least every other week, so if I wasn't initiating a trip to Jackson, Coleman was planning to go visit her family there. So it seemed we were on the road together almost every weekend.

After one such weekend foray into Jackson, on the way back to the Delta I told her, "I want to ask you out, but if I do and you say no, what does that do to our little carpool here?" I wanted badly to date her, but I didn't want to damage the friendship we had built during our time in conference together and carpooling. I truly enjoyed her company aside from just the physical attraction I felt toward her.

"You know you can't take me out, Gresham. Quit thinking silly. Where would we go where we could just relax and enjoy ourselves? No place! Even if we took off to Memphis," she answered, without addressing the carpool issue.

"Oh, I don't know, Coleman. Memphis is a big city with lots of places people go to have a good time just hanging out and feeling free. I bet we could find someplace if we both really want to give it a go. Do you?"

"Are you seriously asking me out? I mean don't be playing around. You're not just pulling a prank on me for fun, are you?"

"No, Coleman. Not kidding around. Yes, I'm asking you to go on a date with me sometime......"

"Well, I'll have to think about it long and hard. After all, we live and work in the Delta, and I doubt your kisses are worth getting killed over."

She was right to immediately acknowledge the inherent danger we could face going down that road. The fact that she said she would think about it though was enough encouragement for me. At least she didn't say no. So I called it a win and told her to let me know as soon as she had made up her mind.

A month passed and she had not said another word about our conversation on dating. I grew impatient and decided to approach the subject again, so I just asked her straight out, "Coleman, are you going out with me or not?"

"I really don't think it's a good idea."

"Why not?"

"Because you are who you are, and I am who I am, and this IS the Mississippi Delta; reasons all good enough to avoid the kind of trouble we would be flirting with."

"It's just a date, Coleman. We might find out we can't even dance well together. It's not like we are going to marry or anything."

"I just don't think it would be worth all the trouble."

"Oh, trust me, Coleman. I'm worth the trouble," I joked. "And you know you like me." I flashed a Cheshire cat grin at her and looked at her sideways. "C'mon," I pleaded, "give it a shot."

"Sometimes you can be such an ass, Gresham; granted a sweet jackass most of the time, but I just can't date you here. We just can't do this."

"So let's go to Memphis together. We could have a good time in Memphis, and we're not as likely to even raise an eyebrow there."

And just like that, she was in full load black-woman mad, hands on her hips, wobbling her head, and bugging her eyes. "Go to Memphis!!!! You are one crazy ass white man if you think I'm going to Memphis and spend a weekend with you in some hotel. I'm saying I'm not sure it's even a good idea to date you, and you think I'm going to sleep with you the first time we go somewhere together? You must be crazy ass, for sure!"

"Oh, good God, no, Coleman! That's not what I meant. I would not presume to think you would ..." I half chuckled through the words to make light of it.

"Good!!" she interrupted. "Because I'm not nearly ready for THAT with you."

"Well, I'm not ready for THAT with you either, Miss Hot Pants!" She laughed. "No, seriously, we can get a room with two beds, or I'll get a room to myself. I promise I won't pressure you or harass you. I'll be a total gentleman."

"Gresham, if you were any more of a gentleman you'd have to be a Mormon with some secret underwear."

"So date this Mormon Episcopalian. Say yes. I promise you'll have a great weekend. We will have so much fun together. I know we will."

"I'll think about it," she said.

"Last time you said that we didn't discuss a date for over a month. Am I going to have to wait that long again? Because I hope not. I may be a gentleman, but I'm not a patient gentleman. I'll be totally honest with you, Coleman. I'm about half crazy over you."

"And I'm about half scared of you, Mr. Fast Eddie, but no, I won't leave you guessing. Give me a couple of days, and I promise I'll give you an answer."

"Fair enough, as long as the answer is yes. You know you want to," I teased. She just turned and sauntered away with her runway walk in those three inch heels, and she looked as good going away as she did coming into a room!

Two days later she was doing early hall duty near the main office when I arrived at work. As I came through the front door, she walked past me as I was signing in and pretended to be getting mail from her mailbox. On her way out, she passed even closer by and whispered, "Yes," and kept walking. I knew she did not want our colleagues knowing her business, especially when it came to me, but I lit up like a fine Cuban cigar next to a glass of Scotch. I could hardly wait for our conference period so we could talk and make plans. It was going to be an outstanding weekend; I just knew it.

We were coming up on Spring Break, and that Friday after school she went home to gather her weekend things, and I picked her up from her duplex on Henry Street to head to Memphis. On the drive north, we were both a little nervous, much more reserved with each other than we had ever been on any previous trips.

"Gresham, why are you driving like a granny?" she asked.

"I just didn't want to attract any attention from some Mississippi Highway Patrol. I feel sure if we got stopped, he'd find some reason to detain us, search the car, and harass us just a bit. I don't want anything messing up our plans."

So on down the highway we rolled, doing just two miles over the speed limit. Just outside Memphis, I reached over and took her hand for the first time. She closed her fingers around my hand in reciprocity.

Just inside the city limits of Memphis, we pulled into a motel parking lot.

"A La Quinta? I was expecting the Peabody" she announced, trying to act as if she were serious.

"On a school teacher's salary?" I shot back. "Lady, you must be delusional, or else Leflore County is paying you a lot more than they're paying me!"

"As a matter of fact, the federal government helps pay my salary, so I probably do make more money than you. But I'm still not paying for my dinner or anything else on this date," she advised.

"Take it or leave it," I joked about the motel, "but if you leave now, you'll have to get yourself a bus ticket back to Greenwood because I'm staying in Memphis this weekend. In case you haven't heard, I have a hot date!"

We often teased each other like that; it was that easy banter that seemed to cement our compatibility as both friends and colleagues. I went into the motel office and got two rooms, one with a double bed for me, and one with two double beds for her, just in case she asks me later to stay in the same room with her for company. I parked and took her to her room and handed her the key.

"I'll bring your suitcase in just a minute and then meet you back here at the car in an hour for dinner," I said, and handed her the key to her room. "I'll be next door if you need me."

"Living up to your promise to be a gentleman, huh?" she asked.

"Yes, ma'am. All weekend long—unless you tell me you want something different," I said, half joking, but half hoping for something beyond holding hands and smiling. She gave me that easy smile of hers I loved so much, and I could tell at that moment she really trusted me; so I leaned in and kissed her cheek, and she did not back away. In fact, she stepped closer and kissed me full on the lips right out in broad daylight in Memphis, Tennessee. I'll always love Memphis if for no other reason than that one kiss.

11 Dancing by the River

Memphis, TN   March 1977

As she bathed and perfumed and primped for a night out in Memphis on her first date with a white man, Essie Coleman couldn't help but recall a contentious conversation she had had with a neighbor one Sunday night after Gresham had dropped her off at her place following another carpooling to Jackson. Just a few minutes after he had driven off, there was a knock on her door. She assumed it was Gresham returning, thinking perhaps she had left something in the car. But it wasn't Gresham.

"Oh, hey, Miss Tiny. How are you doing? Come on in."

"I thinks I needs to! Sumbody needs to talk to you 'bout what's goin' on," the neighbor said with deep concern in her voice and anger scattered all over her face.

"Ok. Tell me what's going on then. Sit down. I'll get you a glass of lemonade, and we can talk."

"I ain't gone be her long nuff for no lemonade," she said. Coleman had never known her neighbor to be so curt and abrasive. Miss Tiny was always sweet and generous with her smiles and laughter, a good neighbor who shared cookies when she baked, and one who would give you her last dollar or last cigarette if she thought you needed either one.

Looking at Miss Tiny with a sideways glance, Coleman had said, "What's going on, Miss Tiny? Tell me straight up."

"It's dat cracka man you been goings off wit 'most erry weekend. I doan know whur you bees goin' but I knows you leaves her togedda and you comes back her togedda after bein' gone two whole nights. I thinks you's done loss yo mind, girl."

"First of all, Miss Tiny, that 'cracker man' is a teacher I work with, and he is a friend."

"No such thang assa cracka man friend," she said. "You might thinks he be yo friend, but he's still a cracka. Ain't no changin' dat, and all crackas be trouble and all crackas be the same."

"Gresham is not like that..." She had tried to defend him but got interrupted.

"He DO be like dat!! And her you be ruttin' up wid him, and errybody be talkin' 'bout hows you betray yo kine."

"I am NOT sleeping with him!!! We just carpool to Jackson together, as if it is anyone's business here in the neighborhood. And even if I was, I am a free woman and can do as I please. You've no right to judge me this way when you don't know the facts."

"I knows enough to know you spends a mighty lot of time wid him. Sooner or lader, it gone come to trouble if you ain't keerful. I'm tellin' you, girl. Don't be bringin' yo cracka man friend to our part of town no mo."

"I don't want to be rude, but please leave now, Miss Tiny."

"I be leavin'-- but we's all still be watchin.' You bedda lissen."

Coleman looked at herself in the motel room mirror and wondered how she had ever agreed to be there in this moment, in Memphis, going out with a white man. She was getting cold feet and debated calling off the whole thing. Gresham had said he wouldn't pressure her about anything, and she believed him. But she had kissed him, kissed him on the mouth... first. He would think she was just a big tease, the kind of tease that makes men crazy angry. But no, she decided there was no going back, at least not right now anyway. They were here for some fun and good times; she would not let Miss Tiny and the others ruin that.

****

At 7:30 sharp I knocked on Coleman's door. I was dressed in my best suit and wore a blue pin striped shirt with a fashionable tie and pocket handkerchief. I held a bouquet of daisies in my hand. When she opened the door, she looked like a real knockout, and I almost lost my breath. She looked even more stunning than usual.

"Oh, my! You even brought flowers? You didn't have to do that," she said.

"Well, I thought it wouldn't hurt, and a gentleman brings flowers "just because." You know that is the

Southern thing to do for a big date, right? Are you ready?"

"Do I look ready?" she said with a coy look.

"Oh, yes, ma'am. You look ...smashing! But then you always look great, Coleman, and tonight is no exception."

"Well, come in for a minute and let me find something so I can get these into some water."

As she took the flowers and turned away and I followed her into the room, she made the comment over her shoulder, "And you look especially handsome this evening as well." Ok then, I thought. First impressions are SO important.

"So what is on the agenda for this big date this evening?" she asked as she filled the ice bucket with water for the flowers.

"Oh, I thought we'd go to McDonald's and really blow my entire paycheck on a couple of Happy

Meals," I quipped. She gave me "the Coleman look" that said, "Oh, no, you don't, buddy. You are not getting away with that."

We both laughed and headed across the parking lot to the car. Thelma was as clean and shiny as an uncirculated Morgan silver dollar. "We have a reservation at the Pyrenees. It's one of those revolving restaurants on top of a big skyscraper so we will have a beautiful view of the city while we eat."

"Ooo! Good choice. I like a lot of ambiance with a good meal."

We arrived a bit early and decided to have a seat in the lounge area of the bar for a drink. She ordered a Chivas on the rocks, and I ordered a dirty martini. We sat in a pair of comfortable lounge chairs facing each other. That was when I really took note of her, seriously examining her so I could keep this picture of her tonight in my mind forever.

She wore a beige skirt, cut straight with a slit up the side that revealed a portion of her thigh. She leaned back in the chair and crossed her legs, revealing even a little more thigh. She wore a teal green blouse with an Oriental brocade design, sleeveless with a Mandarin collar but cut low at the neck, quite sexy but also very fashionable. Her high heels matched the color of her blouse. It was typical Coleman, always well dressed and always very appealing. I loved looking at her, the way she held her glass, the way she crossed her legs, the way she looked at me over the top of her glass as she took each sip. I realized she was looking at me as intently as I was gazing at her.

"So, Mr. Gresham. Tell me about yourself. Why should I want to date you more than just this one night?" she asked.

"Because you like the way I dress, and I didn't take you to McDonald's." We laughed. "Besides, who said I was going to ask for a second date?"

"No one had to say it. I could tell by the way you looked at me just now. You're thinking this might really turn into something."

"And what do you think, Miss Coleman?"

"I think it's too soon to be thinking anything beyond just this drink we have right now."

"That's part of what I like about you, Coleman. Living fully in the moment.   Never in the past. Never in the future. Just here and now."

They called us for our table and seated us side by side looking out the windows over the city and the river. We ordered medium rare steaks and another round of drinks. As we waited for the meal, I presented Coleman with an unexpected surprise. I handed her a sheet of paper and said, "This is strictly for you. No one else." She opened it, saw it was a poem of some kind, and asked, "What's this? I mean, I can tell it's a poem, but it has no title. Who wrote it?"

"Just read it for now. I think you'll understand," I said. She turned the page a little more toward the candle on the table for better light and read silently....

Dance in my life

Black dancer in black dresses.

Castanets clicking

With all my life ticking

Away to your time.

Dance a little closer

To my table, Sable Dancer,

Dance my time.

Red fingernails clinging

To red wine glasses clinking

While I'm drinking

While I'm sinking

But not singing

My life away.

Dance a little closer to my table

While I am now still able

To see you so clearly

Through eyes already red---

Yes, already read

For you know what I'm

thinking.

Dance in my life

Black dancer with black dresses.

Come remove the presses

That are pressing on my head.

"What is this?" she asked. "Did you write this?"

"Yes, I sometimes write a little poetry, and I thought this occasion warranted a poem just for you. Anyone ever write a poem for you before?"

"No. No, they haven't. It's lovely, Gresham. I really like it. I didn't know you wrote poetry."

"See? Now there's another reason we MIGHT should have more than one date. There's a good deal about each other we don't know."

"So do you dance as well as you write about dancing?"

"Absolutely!" I joked. "My club foot and I enjoy a good spin around a dance floor every now and then."

"You don't have a club foot, you silly man," she said as she laughed and leaned into my shoulder and touched my forearm. She always liked to touch the people with whom she laughed. I had seen her do it a hundred times with different colleagues and with children. The times she had done so, with me and everyone else, made the laughter sweeter for us all. Coleman had a special touch that way.

The steaks arrived perfectly cooked. We were both starving, and the liquor was beginning to make us a little too unreserved for such an elegant eatery. We talked with food in our mouths and laughed too often too loudly. Our waiter smiled congenially though obviously embarrassed for us. As soon as we finished the meal, we declined both coffee and dessert and headed out on the town.

Once when Coleman had excused herself to refresh her makeup, I had asked the maître de about a good night spot in the area. He had recommended Fernando's, which he said had good drinks and a great DJ who played the best Top 40 music. I made sure to ask if we'd be turned away at the door as a mixed race couple. I didn't want any kind of issue like that to ruin the evening, and I was assured it wouldn't be a problem. Turns out the dance club was just three blocks away, so we were there within minutes.

As I rushed around to open her car door, she advised me I didn't have to come around and open every door. "You've been hopping around like a jackrabbit to get to the doors first all evening. I mean, I like that, but you don't have to do that to impress me."

"It's something I was raised to do, opening all doors for all ladies. I got knocked on the head by my dad if I didn't, so get used to it."

Inside the place was just one step above a dive. The chairs were all mismatched. The floor was concrete. The tables were all sizes, shapes, and colors. Lighting was white, dripping candles stuck into the neck of long neck beer bottles. But it was packed wall to wall! And everyone looked to be having a great time.

"I'm sorry," I said. "I thought this was a nicer place. We'll find somewhere else. I guess the maître de just played me by recommending this place since we were a little rowdy in his place."

"It's fine. I know you're trying to make this evening perfect, but seriously. Get a grip. I'm not some princess, you know, although some people do refer to me as Queenie."

"Seriously? That's your nickname?"

"Hell, no, boy. I'm just playing with you," and she leaned in against me and touched my arm again, smiling that beautiful Coleman smile that always seemed say, "Life is easy." So we stayed.

We sat against the far wall, several tables away from the dance floor and DJ but close to the bar. No one paid us any special attention most of the evening, which relieved my anxiety enough that I could stop looking around expecting trouble from every angle. Our waitress, named Cindy, was friendly and kept the drinks coming. The bartender wasn't scrimping on the liquor either, and the lights, undulating with the music, were as intoxicating as the drinks.

We tried talking to each other, but we ended up just watching the people rather than sit and yell in each other's ears. Looking at all the couples, it was almost like being deaf or in a dream. Everyone was smiling and talking, but no sounds or words could be heard coming from their mouths as they moved.

About the time Cindy brought our third drink, the DJ switched into full blown disco mode. Coleman looked at me with a raised eyebrow that had a question mark in its expression. I shook my head in the negative, but she took my hand and insisted we go to the dance floor. That's when she got her second surprise for the evening.

Thelma Houston started blaring through the speakers singing "Don't Leave Me This Way." I took her hand and whirled her every which way around that dance floor in the usual disco patterns, and what a great dance we had! She loved it and was able to keep up step for step, turn for turn, even in high heels. It was like we were made to be dance partners.

Out of breath, laughing and stumbling back to our table, a loner who had been sitting at the bar approached us as we sat down.

"Hi, I'm Roger. Mind if I join you?"

"Well, Roger, we're kind of having our own little party here, if you don't mind," I said.

"Oh, yeah. Sure. I get it. I'm a reporter though, and I'd be interested to talk to you about your interracial relationship for a story I am working on." He slurred a few words that made it obvious he was three sheets in the wind, and his ruse was easy to detect.

"We're really not interested in anything like that. We're just out trying to have a good time. That's all."

Suddenly things turned ugly. "Why the hell not? Your uppity nigger girlfriend wouldn't like it, pussy?"

I took a deep breath and let out a heavy sigh that said, "Ok. I'm so tired of crap like this, and I've had enough of this joker," but Coleman reached over under the table and gently patted my knee. I took her hand off my leg and put her hand back in her lap. I stood up.

"Man, someone should put you in a sink and cut your guts out for messing with that black whore." About the time the word whore came out of his mouth, a haymaker aligned his left molars with his nose, and down he went. Out cold and good riddance, but the next thing I knew I was being jerked around by the collar of my suit coat and my belt, being shoved toward the door by a bouncer that looked twice the size of Mr. Meredith, my principal. Coleman was trailing behind and saw me hit the pavement as I was bodily thrown from the threshold.

"Dammit! I'm sorry you had to see that, Coleman."

"Are you ok? You didn't break your hand, did you?"

"No, but I've torn a hole in the knee of my best suit!" It brought to mind that night on the gravel road when I stumbled in the moonlight and tore a hole in my favorite pants, the night I put Thelma in the ditch. It also brought to mind my mother's words about how to handle anger, and it crossed my mind I should have pulled out some red high heels to walk off my anger as she had so often told me to do.

Out of the blue I just started crying; thinking of her in her present condition of despair and anger, I couldn't hold back the flood that had been building since Will's death.

"Gresham???"

"I'm ok, Coleman," I assured her. "I'm just drunk.
Just give me a minute."

"No, you can't tell me there's not something bad
wrong here. You better share with me whatever it
is. Just being drunk doesn't make a man cry like
that."

I just sat in the parking lot and poured out the story
of Will's death just under a year ago and my
mother's withering decline into oblivion, the agony
of seeing her deteriorate into such a mess of
unkempt hair, unbathed body odor, untrimmed
nails, unbrushed teeth, and my helplessness to
reverse the situation, to help her find herself and
some happiness again.

Coleman didn't make fun of me or pity me. She
just kicked off her heels and sat down on the
pavement beside me. She laid her head on my
shoulder. The only question she asked was, "What
made you think of her at a time like this?"

I told her, "She would be so disappointed that I let my anger take over in that situation rather than handling it with logic and reason and some compassion. At least the mom I used to know...."

"C'mon," she said. "You may have ripped your pants, but the night is not ruined. Let's just go for a drive out along the levee and look at the river. No one will bother us there. We can talk without having to yell at each other. Let's stop and get us some coffee and sober up some more. I'm not giving up on the evening just yet, and I have my heart set on some Jack Pirtle fried chicken before going to bed."

I couldn't help but laugh. "You're always full of ideas, aren't you, Coleman?"

"Well, someone has to keep you on the straight and narrow. Looks like it's me tonight."

We ended up near a public parking lot that also had a dirt path where you could drive along the levee. We took the dirt path and got out to watch the river slowly slip past. The big Mississippi rolled by as fog began to stream up from the middle of the river and swirl around the barges moving through Memphis. We got out, leaving the car doors open and radio playing. We held hands and walked a short distance along the levee. I took off my jacket for her to sit on, and we sat in the wet grass and just didn't care. The moon was not quite as full as I would have wanted for the evening, but it was beautiful anyway. We both found it odd that in all our time together, neither of us had talked about our families. I told her all about the things that lead me into teaching and how my parents' work had influenced me to believe so strongly in compassionate living and truthful work that could make lives better.

I found out her father was an electrician, and her mom was a cook in an elementary school. Despite their meager income, they had insisted she go to the best school possible, that there would be no Jackson State or Alcorn or Mississippi Valley State for her.

"So your mom and dad are lawyers, yet you went to little ol' bitty Delta State?" she asked.

"Yep! They weren't happy about it, but they paid for it anyway. They couldn't complain too much since tuition was so much cheaper than Ole Miss. What about you, Coleman?"

"I graduated from Vassar."

"Holy shit, I'm dating a Vassar girl!! That is incredible!! How'd I get so lucky?"

About that time Dorothy Moore came over the radio singing "Misty Blue."

"I love that song," Coleman said. "I love to slow dance, and that song is so lonesome, like I feel sometimes."

"Dance with me, Coleman." I took her hand and helped her up. She took off her heels so she could dance in the grass. There by the headlights with the radio playing in the background, I took her in my arms and pulled her extra close to me. We embraced the dance and each other, we slow danced in the champagne moonlight, by the river in all its dark mystery, and we left the rest of the world to its own darkness.

12 An Anniversary to Remember

Jackson, MS   April, 1977

I deeply dreaded the approaching one year anniversary of Will's death, and I was concerned about its impact on my mother. Since she spent her days staring into space, though, I wasn't sure she was even aware of the approaching date or if she knew one day from the next. For the sake of her sanity, what little she seemed to have, and as unrealistic as it was to think, I secretly hoped she would not remember anything as specific as the date or the terror I imagined Will felt in his final minutes and seconds. Perhaps God in His mercy would spare her that much.

Coleman finally told me about the warning she had had from Miss Tiny several weeks prior to our first date in Memphis. There was another visit after she returned from that date.

One day during conference, she drew me aside in a secretive way, saying she had to tell me something really important. "You can't come by my house anymore," she just blurted out.

"What are you saying, Coleman? You don't want to see me anymore?"

"No, Gresham. I do. I really do, but we will have to find another way to make that happen other than your coming to my place to pick me up."

"Why? What's the problem with that?"

She told me about Miss Tiny's first visit, and then relayed the warning words of the second one.

Miss Tiny said, "I ain't comin' ova her to try and save yo ass no mo. I dun toad you not to be bringin' yo cracka man back to our side o' town. I bees tryin' to hep you, girl, but you ain't lisnin'. If the mens 'round her ketch him, days goan hurt 'im. If day ketches you bof togedda, days sure goan hurt you, too." She admitted this last conversation had scared her, scared her badly. She was scared for her own safety, but she was worried about mine as well.

So we decided it was best if I just stayed out of the black part of town and that we would choose various convenient meeting places whenever we were carpooling or going out together. Since our date in Memphis, we had escaped the Delta two more weekends to share dinner dates and drinks and to dance the night away. We truly enjoyed each other's company out of town, being so free to just be. I remained a gentleman, even when she asked me on the first date to stay in her room with her even though it was just for company and safety. I slept in the other bed and made no attempt to violate the promise I had made to her. We held each other intimately close when we danced. We kissed intimately, and we stood for long periods just holding one another each time we were about to get in the car and return to Greenwood. Admittedly, I was as unsure as she was about moving toward a sexual relationship, so there was no rush for either of us.

"Coleman," I said, "I don't know where all this is headed for us, but I know what I feel for you is something deep and inescapable. There's a part of me that wants so much more, but I know if we cross that bridge, the level of danger increases with that, and the last thing I want to do is put you in any kind of harm's way."

"It would put you in just as much danger, Gresham. And I don't want you getting hurt on account of me. We just really have to take this walk together very carefully and not let our emotions make us do something that can't be undone."

"I just don't know how not to want all of you. Are you struggling with that part, too?"

"I am. You know I am. Why else would I kiss you the way I do? I'm just scared and that makes me hold back. I'm just not ready to do what my heart is telling me to do."

I was still a very broken man in many ways; so I held back as much as Coleman did, and we took what pleasure we could in each other's presence. I grew to depend on her embraces and kisses to carry me through dark times when Will would come into my dreams asking me to help him. She was of great comfort to me when I would wake from dreaming about Will, alive again and well and happy, only to realize upon waking that he was none of those things. He was gone, gone forever, except for what I could remember of us at family gatherings. That is why Coleman was the first person I called when Connie notified me that Mom had killed herself.

"Coleman, my mom has killed herself. I won't be at work tomorrow. I have to go to Jackson right now."

"Oh, baby! I am so sorry. What can I do to help?" That was the first time she had ever called me anything but Gresham.

"Just check in on my classes for me to be sure the sub is ok and that the kids are actually working to learn something. I'm not sure exactly how long I will be gone, but for now at least through the weekend. I'm lining up a sub for Thursday and Friday. I doubt I'll be back by Monday, but I'll just have to see what funeral plans we can make and such."

"You want me to come down to Jackson this weekend? I will, you know. I know you need me, and I want to be there with you."

"Oh, God, Coleman, you can't imagine how comforting that would be for me at this time. My family is going to be a wreck dealing with the anniversary Friday of Will's death and planning a funeral for mom. Can you come down after school Friday evening?"

"Sure, baby. When I get to my folks' place, I'll call you. What phone number can I use to reach you?"

With plans made for Friday, we ended our conversation, and I began packing. Since I had torn up my pants leg on that first date in Memphis, I had not bothered yet to get a new suit. I had a couple, but I needed a really nice one. Mom was always extremely particular about having me dress like a real gentleman, so a suit from J C Penney or Sears would not be acceptable. I would just have to shop for a suit once I got to Jackson. I packed what I could, loaded the car, and set out for the two hour drive.

During that drive I steeled myself for the moment I would have to look my father in the face and not be callous toward him. It would be important to be loving and kind, to see him as a man who has lost his wife, his world fulcrum, instead of seeing him as the man who stood by as she spiraled into darkness, a man who drowned himself in work during the day and drowned himself with glass after glass of stiff Scotch each night. The fact that in the past year he had done nothing to get my mother the mental help she had so desperately needed, despite my repeated prompts to him to do something, seared an anger in me that was both vicious and mean, one that would be toxic to both my father and me if I gave rise to it. I literally wanted to beat the ever loving hell out of him once I laid eyes on him, but I prayed he would not see any accusation in my eyes or hear any in the tone of my voice. But I wasn't sure I could pull it off. I prayed earnestly for understanding and compassion toward him during the entire two hour drive.

Upon arrival Connie had taken charge, keeping a list of people who had called, people who had already started bringing over food, a list of to-do things for the funeral, a list of possible people to contact to serve at the altar and for special music, and a dozen other things that would demand our attention. Dad was seated on the couch holding a letter of some sort.

"So good to see you, son," he said as I came in. He got up and walked toward me, threw his arms around me, and sobbed like a lost child in a huge department store. I let him cry. I cried with him. We stood with our arms around each other that way for probably ten minutes before he told me, "She left a suicide note."

He handed me the letter he had had in his hand when I first walked in. I didn't want to read it, but I had to know her final thoughts. So I opened the letter, sat in the rocking chair, and read by lamplight words too hard to understand and words so much more lucid that we had ever dreamed she was for this past year.

My Dear Living Loves,

I know you think this is about Will, and it is. But it's not just Will. It's also the betrayal that has been killing me. For years I devoted my life to those people. I stood up for them, worked my fingers to bone for them, fought tooth and nail for justice for them. I scratched and clawed at the eyes and ears of the courts for years, struggling and wrestling against the best lawyers in the state like a raped girl scratches the forearms and chest of her attacker. I demanded dignity for them, and I took no prisoners! I was relentless; you all know that. But they killed my boy, my baby boy—ruthlessly, brutally, and selfishly. I might could have eventually learned to live without Will, but I cannot live with their betrayal, too. So yes, it's Will, but not just Will. The grief is deep enough to kill me, but the betrayal cut a second wound just as deep, and I could not carry both pains any longer. The two together I could not overcome. I just need to rest—a rest the world cannot give me. Please know I love you all still. Please forgive me. I'm sorry.

Nan

Mom

What was there left to say after that, I wondered. Connie came in and found me too dazed to even cry at that moment. I felt so numb I could barely even feel any part of my physical self. Every heartbeat, every breath, every word spoken, everything about living was sickeningly difficult and exhausting. It was done, and there was no undoing it. There was only going forward to wherever God and the future would lead us.

13 Scraping Rock Bottom

Jackson, MS   April 1977

Thursday morning bright and early Connie had us all up for a big full breakfast. "We might not have a chance to eat any other time today or a chance to eat together. So sit and eat. We have a busy day ahead of us." For the first time I could ever remember in my life, my father said he just couldn't do it and asked me to say the blessing over our meal.

I was ordered to go get two suits as soon as the stores opened, one for the visitation and one for the funeral. Connie and Dad were going to the florist first to select the blanket that would sit atop the casket during visitation and then on over to Wright and Ferguson Funeral Home where all our family funerals had always been held dating back to my great-grandparents, including Will's just one year ago. I was to meet up with them once I had the suits in hand.

Millie Sullivan, a neighbor two doors down, came early to stay at the house, answer the phone, and take in food from those who would drop by. She was also a church member whom Mom and Dad had known for several years, so Dad agreed when Millie asked if it was ok if she organized the church reception following the funeral. It was standard practice in the Episcopal church to hold a reception afterwards to celebrate the life of one who had left us. We weren't sure if a reception would be in order given that Mom had committed suicide, so we just told Millie to check with Father at the church and go with whatever he said.

Millie was a really good neighbor, and I know she was a big help to Connie in taking over all those duties. Women always get the hard parts in the Theater of Death. We men don't seem to know how to deal with the flood of emotions, so we just sit around and stand around and do little more than shake hands and greet people.

By noon all decisions had been made and everything was in place. The body would be ready for family viewing by 7:00 that evening, the visitation would be Friday from 10:00 a.m. to 8:00 p.m. Episcopalians do not normally have such a long visitation, but it was nothing unusual in Jackson, Mississippi, regardless of the denomination, and it was just what my family had always done. The funeral would be Saturday at

10:00 at St. Andrew's Cathedral on Capital Street where both my parents were members.

Once all arrangements were made, we were left with time on our hands as to what we would do until that evening when we were to come back to the funeral home for the family viewing of the body. Connie and Dad went home to nap. I drove back to Greenwood to see Coleman. I so much needed to lay eyes on her, to touch her, to see her smile at me in my emptiness and to reanimate me, to fill me up again with some measure of joy. I drove out to the school and left a note on her car, telling her to call me at my apartment as soon as she got home after school.

We arranged to park her car at the bowling alley since it was always crowded and wouldn't be noticed by anyone keeping an eye on us, and that's where I picked her up and took her to my apartment. We had coffee and kisses. I told her I had only a short time before I needed to leave, and she understood I couldn't stay long. I told her I was just totally beat down, scalded to the bone with both anger and grief, and why there was equal measure of each. That is when she reached over into my lap and touched me. She then crawled into my lap facing me, and she kissed me with hard kisses and began rocking herself against me. I held her in a grip like a dead drunk in rigor mortis holds a whiskey bottle. She held my head against her breasts and just rocked me.

I wanted the world to instantly disintegrate and leave us alone. I wanted Will back. I wanted my mother well. I wanted things I could never have again. So I chose just to stay in those few moments and give them my fullest breath. I cherished the intimacy she was giving, but again we both backed away from a full commitment to the flesh. We were just two people lost in each other's lives and the one we wanted with each other, but just too unsure if we could cross that line and never look back. Too many things interfered, so we slowly separated and I prepared to leave.

"So, I'll see you tomorrow afternoon in Jackson, I guess," I said as she stepped out of my car to return to her own at the bowling alley.

"Sure thing, baby. I'll be there." And she blew me a kiss goodbye as she drove away.

When I arrived back in Jackson, there was a house full of people and a table loaded to capacity with food of every kind: fried chicken, three hams, chicken and dumplings, vegetable soup, chicken soup, sandwich meats, fruit and vegetable trays, cakes and pies. You name it, it was in our kitchen or refrigerator somewhere. There is no limit to the generosity of friends and neighbors when there is a death in the family.

I grabbed a piece of fried chicken and ate it hastily, took a quick shower, and dressed for the funeral home visit. We left the house, still packed with people, and drove to Wright and Ferguson. Mom had always been a striking looking woman, even as she aged. She was tall and lean, almost as tall as my father who was over six feet. She carried herself with assurance and grace and was always ladylike even in her most ferocious court fights. She knew how to work a room at a party. She knew how to sway juries in a court. She had a commanding presence of both grace and courage that I had surely missed in the last year.

So, since she was no drab, mousy sycophant, but a genuine force of nature in all its beauty, we had had her dressed in a rose colored outfit that she wore during her last court appearance. We had hired her own hairdresser to fix her hair and do her makeup. We put her favorite necklace on her, the 14K gold one with the legal scales that had a diamond on each side inside the scales. God love her, she hadn't looked that good in a long time.

In her designated parlor she lay already arrayed with funeral sprays wall to wall. As she lay there among all the flowers, I somehow found a way to be happy for her, there in her full bloom of beauty and peace. "She was always such a beauty, wasn't she?" my father asked. I think he had forgotten over the past year and in all the Scotch just what she really looked like when she was fixed up.

"Yes, Dad, she was," I said, and he turned to cry on my shoulder again with Connie who was already crying on my other shoulder. I stood between them, like the rock they needed me to be, solid and smooth like a river rock with no jagged, hurtful edges even though I was not feeling particularly loving toward either of them at the moment. I blamed them both—for seeing her every day and doing nothing. I blamed myself for not insisting more that my father do something. I felt blistered by their inaction, withered by my own meanness of heart, parched by tears too many to count that had already fallen but were now too dry to fall, hot with anger and in need of cooling words to soothe me. But I stood as their rock, a monolithic fortress in which they could seek shelter and their own comfort because I knew one day I would love them again. One day.

The next day, visitation day, was truly exhausting. People from law firms all across the state had come by to pay respects. Hundreds from the church had come. Relatives and friends who had known Mom and Dad for decades showed up and helped us wring our hands at the pity of it all. When Coleman showed up, the funeral home directors would not let her come upstairs to the parlor suite where we were all gathered. They came to tell me there was a "Nigra Lady" downstairs insisting on seeing me.

I immediately went to bring her upstairs to meet my family, but the directors vehemently protested and simply would not allow it. I was furious. Coleman was embarrassed and angry, but rather than cause a big scene, we both decided to leave. I told Coleman to wait for me in the parking lot as I went back upstairs to tell Connie I was leaving.

"Connie, I'm leaving now. My girlfriend is here downstairs, and they won't let her come upstairs here because she is black."

"Black??? Really, a black woman??? You're dating a black woman?" Connie acted astounded over the idea and shook her head like she was shaking off a hangover or some such. "How could you even think of bringing a black woman here to visitation knowing how Mom felt about the blacks after Will?"

I exploded. "Because, dammit, Connie, Mom doesn't care about shit anymore. She's GONE, in case you haven't noticed! She's been gone from us for months now, and this is the end of her anger and pain. And I can't believe you let her misdirected racism infect you like this. It goes against everything we were ever taught."

"Well, the white girls in the Delta must not be what they used to be if you have to scrape the bottom of the barrel and date a black woman!"

"Just get the fuck away me right now," I said through gritted teeth.

Her words stung me to the core. I could not believe what I was hearing from my own sister, the sister who grew up in the same house with the same values as I had been taught—that God loves all people, that all people deserve dignity and respect, that blacks especially needed champions to help fight for their rights, and on and on, but now all that had somehow been lost among the willows. How had that happened?

I just turned to walk away, but as I pivoted, I almost walked right over the top of Claire McAlister.

14 Burial and Resurrection

Jackson, MS   April 1977

"Hello, Bern," she said. "I hope you're not leaving!" Claire reached out and wrapped her arms around my waist and stepped in close against me, laying her head on my chest. Seeing her again after all this time took me by storm. Her touch, still feral and intimate, created a firestorm and had the same stiffening effect on me as she always had years earlier.

"I see you remember me fondly," she quipped. "So I'll just stand here close until you calm down so neither of us has to be embarrassed."

"Much appreciated," I said. "I'm sorry about that. How did you hear about this?"

"I like reading the obits in the paper each morning just to be sure my name isn't there," she joked. "When I saw your mom's name, I knew I had to come. I knew you needed me here."

"Look, Claire, I'm sorry but I've gotta go. Someone is waiting for me right now."

"That's ok. I knew you weren't expecting me, and I'll be back tomorrow for the funeral anyway. You won't have to face this without me, I promise, and afterwards we can maybe have lunch and catch up."

"Sure. Sure thing, Claire." And I left. By the time I finally reached the parking lot, after conversations with both Connie and Claire that took way too long, Coleman was gone. I couldn't blame her. It was such a bad situation, and now, after what Connie had said, I knew having Coleman with me at the funeral would cause huge discord, not to mention Claire's intent to attend as my comforter. I really didn't know what to do about any of it. I didn't have a Jackson phone number for Coleman; I would just have to wait for her to call me. I just went home to my old room and went to bed. As had been my bedtime pattern for months, sleep did not come easily; and when it finally took over, again I dreamed about Will asking me to help save him.

The morning of the funeral, I dallied around showering and shaving, taking far longer to get dressed than usual. Coleman had not called me by the time I had left the house, so I had no idea if she would come to the funeral or not. Secretly I was hoping she had decided against it after the incident last night of being turned away. I didn't want her having to face that indignity again of being treated as even less than a second class citizen, but I was concerned that she had not called.

I didn't know where she went when she left last night, and I didn't even know if she got back to her parents' house safely. I was worried beyond reason that something bad could have happened to her. After what had happened with Will, I had grown quite paranoid about all my loved ones whenever I was in Jackson; so shortly after Will's funeral, I bought myself a gun and had taken to carrying it with me. I didn't tell Dad, or Connie because of the disagreement, and debate was sure to take place. To me though, carrying a gun was my only means of comfort from further danger. I remembered far too distinctly standing over Will as he lay at rest in his coffin and thinking to myself, "One day somebody might kill me, too, but it won't ever, ever be that damned easy." I said a quick prayer for Coleman's safety and left for the church.

Episcopal funerals are a bit dry for those who have never attended one since there are no open caskets and florals sprays are not allowed inside the sanctuary. The idea is to keep things simple and let nothing take the focus away from the cross and the resurrection message. I had always liked our funeral traditions and liturgy though because they were all about hope and our life as Easter people.

St. Andrew's was packed by the time those of us in the family were escorted to our reserved pews. Claire had found me as she promised, and asked about sitting beside me. Claire had never been much of church-goer, but she had come to church with me a few times back in high school, so she had an idea what to expect.

From the back of the church, Fr. Ellison began the liturgy for the Burial of the Dead by announcing, "Please rise." We all stood, and Claire instantly reached around and put her hand around my waist just under my suit coat and put her thumb inside my belt. Resisting the fire in that touch took every ounce of strength I had.

Fr. Ellison began, "I am the Resurrection, and I am Life, says the Lord..." She laid her head against the shoulder of my arm.

"As for me I know that my Redeemer lives...After my awaking, he will raise me up, and in my body, I shall see God."

"Claire, please stop," I whispered. She gave me a pouty look but released her contact with me.

"I myself shall see, and my eyes behold him who is my friend and not a stranger."

"Is it ok if I hold your hand?" she asked, and she reached for it anyway without waiting for an answer. I resolved not to look at her but just detach myself as much as possible and listen to the words of comfort being offered.

"So, then whether we live or die, we are the Lord's possession."

"I'm yours," she whispered. I just closed my eyes, pretended not to hear her as the first prayer was offered. "O God, whose mercies cannot be numbered: Accept our prayers on behalf of your servant Nan, and grant her an entrance into the land of light and joy..."

My mind wandered to question if my beautiful, once courageous mother would be given what was asked, under the circumstances of her death. The second prayer began, "O God of grace and glory, we remember before you this day our sister Nan. We thank you for giving her to us, her family and friends, to know and to love as a companion on our earthly pilgrimage..."

And so on it went with scripture readings, a recitation of the Apostles' Creed, and special music that had been especially selected for Mom by Dad and Connie. Fr. Ellison had met with us early on the morning of the visitation to discuss joyful remembrances we wanted included in the eulogy and to advise which scripture he had selected for his homily. He did an exceptional job with both, blending them seamlessly. As is common in our church, we stood; we sat; we knelt; we bowed as the cross passed by; we did what we lovingly but laughingly called our "pew aerobics." And we got through it, burial and all.

"Lord Jesus Christ, we commend to you our sister Nan who was reborn by water and the Spirit in Holy Baptism.....Father of all we pray to you for Nan, and for all those whom we love but see no longer..."

That was the point where I broke, with Will coming to mind so young. When the tears began, Claire reached up and pulled a handkerchief from my suit coat pocket and handed it to me, endearing and tender, not sexual and predatory.

"Grant to them eternal rest...."

"... a rest the world cannot give me," my mother had written.

"Let light perpetual shine upon them. May her soul and the souls of all the departed, through the mercy of God, rest in peace."

I bowed my head and squeezed my eyes shut as hard as I could to stave off more tears, but all to no avail hearing the words "Acknowledge, we humbly beseech you, a sheep of your own fold, a lamb of your own flock, a sinner of your own redeeming..."

Well, she was God's lamb now, no longer a lioness of the courts, no longer the mother who had taught me so much about what a good woman looks and acts like. Just like Will, she was gone never to be seen again by me except in dreams. It was an incredibly hard loss, immeasurable because she had been the hub of our universes, collectively and independently. With her absence, our worlds were spinning out of control, flying through a blackness searching for brighter light to see again.

With the funeral and burial concluded, it had been decided to have no reception in the parish hall afterwards. We had so much food at the house that we just invited everyone to come help clear out the kitchen. Claire rode with me to the house, and our conversation along the way was quite enlightening.

"That really is a great looking suit, Bern. You wear it well."

"Thanks. So what have you been up to in these seven or eight years since high school? I've lost track of time."

"Well, I've been married twice and divorced twice...."

"Whoa! Twice divorced? What happened?"

"Well, the first was just a little crazy and killed himself when I was five months pregnant." Then suddenly realizing the similarity of her first marriage and the reason we were now riding together in the same car, she began trying to apologize.

"No, really, Claire. It's ok. Don't give it a thought."

"Well, the second wasn't much better. We were married only six months before I had to send him packing because I had had enough of his shit. He started slapping me around, and I didn't want my one year old son seeing that."

"So you have a son now. That's great, Claire."

"Yes, he is eighteen months old now and truly the biggest love of my life. I want you to know I named him after you." She said it as such a matter of fact, I almost didn't understand the depth of what she had just said.

"You named him after me?" I asked in surprise.

"Of course, I did. You were the love of my life, and now he is. So yes, he has your name. Halford Bern Mayfield. I call him Bern, too, even though that's his middle name."

"Wow! What can I say? I never expected you to do anything like that."

"Yeah, well, I knew shortly after we split up and you went off to college that it was unlikely I would ever have that kind of love again."

"I'm sorry you feel that way, Claire. You deserve to be happy."

"But what about you? You haven't even married once! Was I so good I ruined you on all other women?" We laughed but I knew she has half way serious in asking.

"Maybe so," I joked. "I've had a couple of serious relationships. Matter of fact, I am currently dating someone I'm pretty serious about."

"Yeah, me too, but he's married, and he's my boss."

"Aww, shit, Claire! You can do so much better than that!"

As we drove into the driveway at the house, I told her, "Get ready. It'll be a madhouse. We probably won't get another chance to talk again today until you get ready to leave."

She opened her purse and took out a little notepad. "Here's my home phone number. You call me. I'd love for you to come over and meet my son, and I'd love for him to meet the man he is named after."

15 Fighting Words

Jackson, MS   April 1977

Greenwood, MS   April 1977

With the house full of people, I took the opportunity to slip off into my bedroom to try and contact Coleman. I didn't know if she drove back to Greenwood when she left or if she stayed in Jackson at her parents' house. I pulled the hall phone into my room and closed the door. I first called her home number in Greenwood but got no answer, so I just started calling each Coleman listed in the Jackson phone book that had an address located in the black sections of town. I must have called at least twenty houses before I finally reached her.

"Hello."

"May I please speak to Essie?"

"Essie?"

"Yes, sir. Is this Essie Coleman's house?"

"Just a minute," the man said rather gruffly. In the background I could hear him calling Coleman to the phone, and he did not sound happy.

"Hello?"

"Coleman! It's Gresham." I could hear the man in the background asking rather angrily, "WHY is a WHITE man calling you at MY house?"

"Oh, hey. Look I can't talk right now. We'll talk soon."

"I'm sorry," I said. "I didn't mean to cause you a problem. I just wanted to know you were ok. I haven't heard from you. And I'm sorry about the other night...."

She interrupted me saying, "Gresham, I really can't talk right now. Please. We will talk soon." And she hung up. About that time there was a knock on my bedroom door.

"Come in." It was Claire.

"I followed the phone cord down the hall and figured I'd find you here." Looking around the room, she said, "Not much has changed in here. Do you remember the two times we were together in that very bed?"

"Yes, Claire, I remember. But that was long ago."

"Not so long ago. Just a few years. We were young then, sure, but we've both learned a lot since then." She came and sat on the bed beside me. "I hope I'm not interrupting too much, but whenever you are ready, I need you to take me back to the funeral home to get my car."

"Oh, sure. I'll be just a minute. I need to make a quick stop by the bathroom to throw some water on my face." As we both stood, she put her arms around me and kissed me with the same hungry energy as she had always done back in high school. As much as I wanted to, I couldn't break away. I was the man being electrocuted who can't turn loose of the wire!

Finally I was able to get a full breath. "Look, Claire, I can't do this. I told you I was seriously seeing someone. I don't want to mess that up."

"I understand.   But I still love you, Bern," she confessed.   "I still think about you so often, and I would do just about anything, short of setting my hair on fire, for a second chance."

She tried for a second kiss, and I just walked out, telling her, "Just go get in the car, Claire."

On the ride back to the funeral home, she apologized for being so forward. "I can remember a time when you would have taken me right there even with a house full of people, a time you weren't such a gentleman," she said.

"Yeah, well, you keep this up, and I might have to do the ungentlemanly thing of putting you out at the next gas station and calling you a cab."

"You really are upset with me, aren't you?" she asked.

"Yes. Very.   I mean you waltz up in here in the middle of a family crisis, you come on to me even though you are dating a married man, you come on to me even though you know I am serious about someone else, you create all this chaos in me by kissing me like that, telling me you still love me, you've named your son after me, knowing I am not thinking straight right now; you're just taking advantage of the situation. You gotta stop, Claire. Just stop it."

"Ok, Bern. I'm sorry. I really am. I just wanted to see you again, to tell you how I felt, and to tell you about my Bern. I wanted to see if maybe we might work this time. But I at least want us to see each other occasionally, even as old friends. I really want you to meet my son sometime."

"We'll see. I'm not sure. That's the best answer I can give you today."

"I'll take it," she said as she squeezed my hand and stepped out of the car. I waited to be sure she got into her car safely. Once she drove away, I drove to the liquor store and bought a fifth of vodka with intentions of drinking myself into a stupor so maybe I would have a good night's sleep without dreaming about Will.

I was still quite angry with Connie over the comments she had made about Coleman, in addition to her complicity over Mom's death. As soon as I woke up Sunday morning, I packed to return to my home in the Delta. This would likely never be my home again. I was pretty sure Connie knew why I wasn't staying longer, but she was unapologetic, which made things even more strained. I left her and Dad standing side by side in the driveway waving at me as I pulled away.

Once back home in Greenwood, I was hoping Coleman would call me whenever she got back from Jackson. I knew she had to go to work in the morning, so there was no reason to think she wouldn't be returning to Greenwood sometime that Sunday. I waited up past midnight, waiting for her to call, but she never did.

When I got back to school for work on Monday morning, Coleman was again on duty in the cafeteria for breakfast. It took several people to monitor because every kid was on free breakfast and lunch, so the majority of kids were there. Bus routes were arranged to get them there in time for a breakfast if they wanted it or needed it. When Coleman saw me walk in, headed in her direction, she gave me a head shake indicating, "No, not right now." I turned and went down to my classroom.

Given the wrecking ball that had lately smashed almost every important relationship I had had, I was itching for a fight with someone. As I stood looking out my classroom window, I noticed that the grass on our "ballfield" was almost knee high. Our janitor, Malinda, was a middle aged black woman, and she was usually assigned the job of mowing the field with a push mower. I went to talk to Malinda to see why it wasn't mowed and if I could help somehow. I knew my fight would not likely be with her, but with the man who holds the purse strings, but I needed to know what was going on first. I was really going to blow sky high if it was something as simple as needing a can of gasoline.

"Missa Gersham, I toad Missa Murdith 'bout that mower breakin' down three week ago. But he ain't did nuttin' 'bout gettin' it fixed. I did all I knowed to do about it, check the gas, the sparks, the oil. I even putted a new spark in it. It still wouldn't do nuttin."

"Well, Miss Malinda, I guess I need to talk to Mr. Meredith about that damn mower. I got a PE class to teach, and we can't learn in knee high grass."

Like a firecracker half a fuse from blasting, I walked into the principal's office and immediately launched into a fit of indignation. I hadn't even bothered to knock.

"WHY has that mower not been fixed? My ballfield is knee deep in weeds. How do you expect us to play softball if we have nowhere to play?"

"I'll get around to the mower soon enough. I really didn't expect to see you today, Mr. Gresham. I was really sorry to hear about the loss of your mother." He made me even angrier for him to first, act like the mower was a non-problem, and second, for him to mention my mother.

"Yeah, well, that still didn't get the mower fixed or the grass mowed." I was being quite surly and truly borderline insubordinate, but Mr. Meredith, for all his foot dragging on spending money, saw through the frustration and knew my anger was about more than just a broken lawnmower.

"Sit down, Mr. Gresham," he said. "Take a breath. You've had a lot of stress lately."

"I don't want to sit down. I want that damn ballfield mowed."

"I understand. But as I have told you many times. We do well to have pencils. The chirren need classroom supplies, and the mower will have to wait."

"This shouldn't be an either-or situation. The 'chirren' need both!! I tell you what. Get me a sub, please, for today, sir. I'm not staying. I'm taking another grief day, but I'll be back tomorrow though. Count on it." I turned and walked out, got in my car, and left.

If Coleman didn't have time to speak to me, and if Meredith wasn't going to solve such an easy problem, then I decided I would. I went home, changed into some work clothes and went straight to the Western Auto. There I used my credit card and purchased a riding lawnmower for $329.89. I rented a trailer to haul it out to Money, and I mowed that field while my kids and their substitute in class watched. Once I finished, I was stinking worse than wet dirt that had been soured with too much moisture. Stinking or not though, I went into my class, introduced myself to the sub, and told her the kids would be going to PE that afternoon at 2:00. The field was ready. The kids clapped and cheered. I just walked out.

I walked down to Coleman's classroom to see if she had any kids in class right then. She did not, so I asked if I could come in.

"Sure, Gresham. I can't believe you are here. I really am so sorry about your mom."

"I know. And I'm sorry about any trouble I caused at your parents' house when I called for you."

"Yes, well, if I had called you, it could have been avoided. But when you didn't come back outside at the funeral home pretty quick, I just didn't know what to think. So I left. And then I didn't call because I didn't know what to say."

"Can we meet this afternoon after school? I promise I'll clean up and won't smell so bad."

"What is that all about anyway?"

I told her about the problem with the old mower and my conversation with Mr. Meredith, about buying the riding mower and bringing it out and mowing the field myself.

"Let that temper get you again, huh? Forgot your momma's high heels, huh? Done spent a bunch of money you won't be reimbursed for, huh?"

"Yep, yes, and yes ma'am."

"You're a special man, you know that, Gresham? I believe there is nothing you won't do for your students, is there?"

"Not much. They desperately need someone to take their side and stand up for them. Looks like today it's me."

"Go on home then, and clean up. Meet me at the bowling alley at 4:45. We need to talk about a lot of stuff anyway."

"I wish you could have been there with me."

"Me, too. Me, too. Sometimes things just get crazy. But I'll see you later."

"I so much want to kiss you goodbye right now, but I know it would jeopardize both our jobs. Besides, I have a lawnmower to pay for, so I need this job. Kiss you later." As she laughed, she leaned close and touched my arm.

Before leaving the school, I went by to see Malinda again. I took her out back and showed her the mowed field, the new mower, and showed her how to drive it. I hated the idea of a middle aged woman "mowering" with a push mower in that kind of Delta heat. I gave her the keys, and I told her my next plan was to have Mr. Lucas and his woodshop kids build a little shed to keep it in.

"Thank ya so merch, Missa Gersham. You's a good man. Dees chirren be lucky to have you her." She hugged my neck and went off dabbing her eyes.

When I returned to my apartment, there was a note on my door from some anonymous "neighbor."

"Don't bring that black bitch to these apartments again! You will pay for it if you do."

"Well, ain't that a fine hidey-do," I thought. "Chicken shit!" I looked around to see if anyone was watching me from their apartment windows. I didn't see anyone, but just in case anyone was looking, I tore that note into a million pieces, threw them as high in the air as I could to let them sail all over the parking lot, and then I went inside. Even the garbage heap is too good for some pieces of trash.

16 End of An Era

Greenwood, MS   May 1977

We are never prepared when love and violence cross paths. We want to literally vomit when we hear of a woman severely beaten by her husband, or we read about a child starved to death by a parent. We always empathize with the victim, but we go about our lives the same, thankful for the peace we have and assuming violence would never come to us.

With Will's death, I learned how close violence can come and how quickly love can turn to hate, as it did with my mother. The biggest mistake though is thinking once we've had our turn at a close encounter with violence and mayhem, the odds favor us that violence will never again be part of our lives; we are safe from a second assault.

Since my mother's funeral, Coleman and I had spent almost every evening together. Since dating in Greenwood had its troubles for us, we usually just drove out into the country down a gravel road to a calm place under a bridge crossing the Tallahatchie River just to be alone together, to talk, to dance, to share some wine, to touch. One such night about a week before school was to end for the year, one hot and humid May burst of coming summer, Coleman kissed me and whispered in my ear, saying she wanted to stay the night with me. We drove back to Greenwood and went upstairs to my second floor apartment. It was really too early to go to bed, but we did anyway, like old married people often do.

"Give me one of your old shirts to sleep in," she said. "I like that one you wore the day you bought the mower for the school."

I pulled it from the drawer. As I turned to hand it to her, she was stepping out of her slip, revealing matching panties and bra but still in her high heels. Typical Coleman, I should have guessed.

"So, your wardrobe is entirely coordinated? Nice!"

"Remember who you are dating, Gresham. Vassar girls are always put together head to toe."

She came toward me and wrapped her arms around my neck, pressing herself ever tighter against me. "I'll let you remove the rest," she said, as she turned her back to me to unsnap her bra. She then turned toward me to give me a full look at her, unashamed in any way. She took my hand and led me to the bed where she sat down and reached to unbuckle my belt. I thought to myself, "She's really here with me now. She is fully here and ready to commit to me. Give thanks and be tender."

I unbuttoned and removed my shirt. Then she did something Claire used to do! She ran her hand, flat palmed up my stomach to the middle of my chest and held it there. "I just want to feel your heart a moment," she said.

Dismissing all thoughts of Claire, I said, "Oh, it's beating alright, Lady! It's about to jump out of my chest!" and we laughed and fell across the bed side by side. There were no candles, no music, no flowers, no wine, just us in shadow from the street light, naked and forgetful of the world, blissfully ignorant of what waited for us outside.

We both had to go to work when morning came, but we stayed up most of the night, in peace and the loving arms of the other, wishing the morning would never come. Daybreak did come though, and when we stepped outside into the glare of the morning sun, there sat Thelma trashed out almost beyond recognition! "Go back inside, Coleman!" I said, but it was too late. She had already seen what I was seeing.

In all these years I had had Thelma, I had kept her in pristine condition. I had kept her oil and transmission fluids changed on schedule, the belts replaced on schedule, the radiator flushed on schedule, the brakes replaced. I kept a beautiful wax job on her. You name it! Whatever Thelma needed, I made sure she got the only the best treatment.

As she sat there so desolate in the sun, I cursed like a deranged sailor. Her tires were all four slashed. Most of her windows were broken out, and the interior front seats were slashed to ribbons. The hood was open and every belt and hose had been cut. Black spray paint was used to write DIE NIGGAR LOVER on one side, with the same message on the other side written in holes where they had evidently used a drill bit on poor Thelma.

"Goddamned motherfucking ignorant sons-a-bitches couldn't even spell nigger correctly!" I spewed. I yelled at the top of my lungs, "You jackass shit hook bastards, when I find you....." I ranted and raved like a schizoid off medication. Coleman came out and got me to come back inside.

"Look, you need to settle down a bit and call the police. I need to call a cab so I can go home and get dressed for school. You also need to call Mr. Meredith about getting a sub for you since you can't drive that car in that condition." Coleman just had that way of making logical plans when they were needed, the calm voice heard in the middle of a ravenous storm, whereas I was almost hyperventilating, enraged as much for what they had done as WHY they had done it.

"Coleman, I'm so sorry. I'm so sorry." After such a memorable night, one with such tenderness, now a devil in me was rising, and I was ready to set fire to the whole damn town! It seemed the world was about to bury me if I didn't fight back. Between Mother's suicide and now Thelma's demise, with Will's murder and Woodrow's death, the broken mower, the asshole in Memphis who almost ruined our first date, and all that shit with Claire, I was like dynamite itching for the match. I had come so far recovering from grief and brokenness with Coleman, but this latest incident had me slamming head first down a steep path toward explosive decimation if I didn't get some perspective that would extinguish the fuse now flying along that destructive wick.

I sent Coleman home in a cab and made the call to police. Given the reason for the vandalism, they did not seem too interested in solving the crime, just assigning the blame to me and giving me fair warning. They took pictures and made the obligatory notes, but it was obvious that would be the extent of any investigation.

"So why do you think they wrote that on your car?" they asked.

'So, you are dating a black woman, huh?"

"Well, you knew that could cause problems with your neighbors, right?"

"For your own good, you better find some other place to do your diddlin' with your Nigra woman. Several Citizens Council members live around here."

"Well, fuck you and thank you very much for nothing!"

I went inside and called a wrecker to haul off Thelma to a car dealership. No reason to expect much of a trade in, given her condition, but a new car was a necessity, and I needed it by the end of the day so I could get back to work tomorrow.

I bought a swanky black Ford Thunderbird, and also gave notice to the apartment manager that I would be moving. I took a cab to a realtor's office while the dealership prepped my new car and told them I was looking for a place to rent out in the country anywhere in Leflore County.

I was lucky. There was a farmhouse for rent that had been on the market for several months. The owners were eager to find a decent, reliable renter, so a meeting was quickly arranged. By the end of the day I had a move-in date for the following weekend to a small two bedroom house near Sunnyside just up Highway 49. I didn't see Coleman that evening, but we talked on the phone and I told her about the new car and the new place where I would be moving.

When I drove up to work in the new Thunderbird the next morning, Malinda, our custodian, and several of the cafeteria ladies were outside smoking. They started hooting and whistling at me as I got out, laughing and teasing me.

"Ooowee,, Missa Gersham, you goan be catching you some ladies now! Might eben be married by next week!"

"Yes, sir! Dem womens goan be switchin' day skirts to get yo tention fur shure!"

"Why you traded off Miss Thelma for dat dare black lady? She wuz sho a pretty thang you had."

"Long story, ladies," I said as I entered the building. Down in Coleman's room we had a quick conversation to arrange a date for that evening, or at least what I thought would be just another date.

That evening we drove over to Greenville to sit out on the levee. Coleman was subdued and pensive during the drive over, making very little conversation except for commentary on the impressive features of the Thunderbird, such as a great speaker system, the electric windows, cruise control, the receding antenna that disappeared when the radio was turned off. Once on the levee, I knew something bad was about to happen when she did not immediately move over closer across the seat.

With her eyes averted, in a softly distant voice she said, "Look, Gresham, we can't keep doing this. Dating me puts you in a lot of danger; this morning proved that. Frankly, it scared the hell out of me, and I know you would never want to do anything to endanger me..."

"Don't do this, Coleman. Please don't do this. We'll figure out something, we'll...."

"No, Gresham, we can't. There is no way to fix it. It is too big, too wide, and too deeply engrained. We are both stuck in this Delta because, for all its faults, we don't want to leave it. We love this place. We love our jobs and the kids we work with..."

"Coleman, listen to me. I love you, and I do believe after the other night you feel just as much for me..."

"That doesn't matter now. It can't matter now. I don't want to see you get hurt any more than what's already been done. Don't you understand that what they did to Thelma is just an example of what they have planned for you, except much worse? If you truly love me, you need to protect me..."

"I WILL protect you, Coleman...."

"...by letting me go back to my side of town and staying there, and working my way back into my group of friends and neighbors who have cut me off. Since Miss Tiny's last visit, hardly anyone will even speak to me. I am alone there, Gresham. Do you understand that? Do you know what that kind of isolation feels like? If I needed help, there is not one single neighbor I know who would come help me right now. And from the looks of what was done to Thelma, there's not a neighbor to help you either!"

I swallowed hard, knowing full well the truth of what she was saying but still unable to agree. "Don't. Don't do this."

"We have to end this before one or both of us end up dead. I know death threats have been part of your family's life for years because of your parents' work, and you don't pay much attention to that, but I take them seriously. After all you have been through with deaths in your family, I know you couldn't live with yourself if you were the cause of something happening to me—the least of which would be rape and the worst would be who knows what, but probably something really sick before being killed. We are in a dangerous place, Gresham. You have to accept that fact, dreamer and poet that you are. It's time to get real about the two of us."

"Tell me you love me, Coleman."

"No. I won't do that to you."

I decided if the serious side of me couldn't sway her, perhaps I could charm her with some humor. This conversation had gotten way too morbid and serious, so I started singing to her the disco song we first danced to in Memphis.

"Remember these words, Coleman?" I began to sing, "Don't leave me this way...I can't survive, can't stay alive, don't leave me this way..."

"Stop, Gresham. You don't sing that well anyway," she joked. At least for a brief moment there was that easy smile that comes between us when we shared inside jokes.

"Come on satisfy the need in me, 'cuz only your good loving can set me free....don't leave me this way."

"Seriously, baby. We have to stop before something really bad happens to us. After the other night, I am scared, REALLY scared, and forgive me but I'm TOO scared to keep seeing you, much as I know I will miss you and regret doing this."

There was no way to turn things around. She was right about all of it. There was no fix. I lowered my head. "I know, Coleman. I know you took a big chance on me. I know you trusted me, and it has cost you a lot, time and again. You've been called things no lady should ever be called, and I know the threats that came through Miss Tiny unnerved you; but you gave me a chance anyway, and I can't tell you how thankful I am for that trust you put in me. I know you're right, and I'm sorry I can't change it to make it work out for us."

"Well, as you so often like to quote Hemingway...it WAS pretty to think so."

"Yes, achingly pretty. But I will tell you this ugly fact. I WILL kill anyone who hurts you, and I won't think twice about it. You just be sure I am the one you call first if you are ever in serious trouble and need help."

"Well, at least school will be out in another week and summer break will make separating a little easier for us both since we won't see each other every day."

"Yes, there's always summer," I said with resignation. I recalled from my teen years how brutal summer could be, full of killings in the past, full of putrid hate, and now it was costing me yet another loving relationship.

"I don't know how to get through a day without seeing you, Coleman. It will take a lot of getting used to without that smile, and those damned matching high heels. I've grown very fond of your shoe fashion. There's so much I'm going to miss about you, Miss Essie Coleman."

"I know, Mr. Gresham. I've grown pretty fond of your shoes, too, and I am glad, I truly am glad, that you walked into my life." She leaned over and kissed me.

"So, was that my kiss goodbye?" I asked.

"No," she said. "I'm not going to just kiss you goodbye. You're going to take me to a motel nearby, and I'm going to love you goodbye. Then we're going back to Greenwood and pretend WE never happened." And that was what we did.

I kissed her hand as she stepped out of the Thunderbird at midnight back in Greenwood, leaving me bitter to the bone and angry at myself for letting her go, but what else could I have done to keep her safe?

I could not change the culture of separation that grows as rampantly in the Delta as kudzu grows in the hills around Yazoo City. We knew we were playing with fire when we started our dance, and we pretended it would work out in the end. But the Delta is what the Delta is.

For all the ugliness and distrust to be seen among the races in the Delta, the land itself is a beautiful lady, especially when she is clothed in the green and white garments of new, sprouting cotton. When you look at her in the early morning light, she fills you with an unexplained joy, like when you see a beautiful woman naked for the first time at sunrise.

And she is so much more than a high-yielding lover putting out her crops. She is a fertile paramour that grows inside your soul and demands your love. You can never resist her; and once she has invaded your bloodstream, you can never really leave her behind. No matter how much heartache you find living within the social confines, the peace of darkness on the delta soothes those wounds enough to stop the tears and the bleeding.

Neither Coleman nor I would ever abandon the Delta. As much as we loved each other, loved each other enough to let go to be safe, we never left the Delta for any bright lights in a city, preferring the dark peace of each Delta evening where we could let our hearts mend and dream about the freedom to love "maybe one day."

17 The Mean Season

Jackson, MS   Summer 1977

As soon as school let out for the summer, Coleman headed to New York to visit old Vassar friends for a couple of weeks. I moved to the old farmhouse in Sunnyside with no plans and no focus except to eliminate the rat infestation under the house. I adopted two cats, named them Mildred and Maxine, and turned them loose to solve my problem for me. I just wished my emptiness could have been solved as easily.

Summer is that time of year when people get to be what they can't be any other time of year. We can be kids again. We can be swimmers and divers. We can be sun worshippers and go around half naked. We can be relaxed and let time become less of a master. We can be whatever we want to be. Me? I just became an ass.

I was negative about everything, picked fights with practically everybody, friend or stranger. I argued with cashiers and bank tellers over trivial things. I criticized food served in restaurants when there was really no reason to complain. I almost got into a fist fight once with the owner of a Chinese place because I didn't like the fortune in the cookie I received with my bill. I made no effort to smile at anyone or to speak to them with any form of courtesy or respect. All my encounters were singed with sardonic words and tone. As far as I was concerned, everyone was culpable in Coleman's leaving, and I hated them for it, including myself.

With Coleman absent in my life, I built a massive wall around my heart and decided there would be no more Mr. Nice Guy. The world is too damned mean to let you be good hearted, and if you can't lick 'em, you better join 'em! I turned to stone, cold and unfeeling. When I ventured beyond my wall of protection, I went out in full fighting mode, cagey and defensive. I just flat out didn't give a shit about anything!

I spent more time at the liquor store than I did at the grocery store. I rarely went into town; I just stayed at the farmhouse and tried to make my mind forget what drove Coleman away. I tried to revive myself by reading the novels and poems that brought me the most pleasure. I read the books that made me think and evaluate, books like Thoreau's WALDEN, looking for the secrets to peace. I toyed at keeping my brain from going to mush during the day, but I killed off a number of brain cells each night with Stoli. Just as I had right after Will's death, I was drinking way too heavily, to wash down and drown all the monsters eating me alive.

Toward the middle of June as I stood in line to check out at the grocery store, a folded slip of paper fell out of my wallet. It had a purple and blue butterfly design on it, and I could not for the life of me imagine why I had such a note in my billfold. I opened it to see Claire's name and telephone number written on it. I had forgotten all about her giving me her phone number when we saw each other back in April. I started to throw it away but tucked it in my shirt pocket instead, to think on it. After all, I was alone and lonely, emptied of everything but anger, and Claire was easy. If anyone could soothe the seething, bitter rage in me, Claire would find a way, sort of like putting out one fire by starting another.

A week later Dad called, saying he would like for me to come down to Jackson for a Fourth of July BBQ he was planning. Connie had moved in with him to help around the house and with cooking, and he told me she had a new boyfriend. He was happy about that. Since she was left virtually standing at the altar, we all wondered if she would settle for an overtly bland life of old maid habits and attitudes, thinking she might never trust anyone enough to date again. Dad startled me though when he made the offhanded comment, "...and I just might start dating, too."

How does a son even respond to a statement like that just a couple of months after burying his mother? Many things can happen to a man, many tragic and horrifying things like buddies blown to bits in war, but he can push on and put those feelings in a locked box to keep them in check. A man is never the same though ...once... he... loses... his mother.

He is like a planet that has spun off its axis, and it is unlikely he will be able to right himself again. He just has to learn to spin differently in another orbit. Accepting that my father was spinning differently as well was a challenge I had not anticipated coming so quickly. Being still relatively young and fit, I figured he would have a choice of several widows and divorcees interested in him. I just didn't expect him to be interested in another woman this soon.

He might have been "fishing" to see how I would respond, but I told him I would think about the party and made no further commitment. It really was not my decision to make about his future. Plus, I was still holding a grudge against both him and Connie for not intervening enough to prevent Mom's suicide, so I was not anxious to spend any time with them.

One night just a couple of days after Dad's call, one very late night, after several drinks, I lost track of time as drunks so often do, and in poor judgment so typical of drunks, I called Claire. She should have been mad at me for calling so late at night, but she wasn't. She just asked if I was drunk, and I admitted that I was. "Well, if you remember making this call come morning, call me back tomorrow evening when you're sober. But call me after 9:00 tomorrow night because usually Billy is gone by that time."

"Billy?"

"Yes, remember my boss? The one I'm dating?"

"Ah, yes. The **married** boss." I emphasized the word "married" with a sneer.

"Don't judge me, Bern. I do what I have to do to keep a roof over my head and feed my boy—that baby boy I named after you. Remember?"

"Did I really mean that much to you, Claire? How do you have another man's baby and then name that baby after a former lover? Why'd you do that?"

"I told you why. You just don't remember right now. Call me tomorrow night and I'll remind you. Goodnight, Bern." I hung up and within minutes was sound asleep, all liquored and languishing. I wanted to dream about Coleman, but I dreamed about Will instead.

It was that same recurring haunt of a dream I had several times a week since Will's funeral. We were all at our grandmother's house on Bailey Avenue. He had been to the store up the street and was walking back when he was jumped by a pack of wolves. I saw them run out from behind some trees toward him and immediately knew they would tear him to pieces if they caught him.

I began running toward Will and the wolves as fast I could, but they got to him first. He began yelling for me to help him, screaming awful little girl type yelps of pain. "Help me, Bern! Get 'em off me! Help me! Help me!" I punch them, kick them, wrestle them away as best I could, but they are focused only on tearing Will apart. He starts to yell one more time, the word "help" coming only half out as the largest wolf rips open his throat. "Hel..." and I wake up.

Coleman was beside me many times when the dream woke me in a terror. I missed her so much all the time, but most of all when I awoke alone and crying in desperate grief for the brother I could not save in real life or in my dream.

I didn't call Claire the next night. Not because I didn't want to talk to her, but because I was drunk again. If I was going to try to reconstruct any kind of relationship with Claire, I needed a few more days to drink away both the abiding grief and the joys of Coleman and a little more time to sober up.

A week later I finally called again, after 9:00 p.m. as I did remember her to say. "Hi, Claire. It's Bern. Sorry I didn't call back last week. It's not that I didn't remember; there were just some things I needed to work out in my head."

"I figured as much. I know when guys start drinking a lot that there are usually some demons working them over."

"Yea, well, that's a discussion for another time. But look, my dad has decided to throw a big bash for the Fourth, so I was thinking about coming down to Jackson. I was wondering if we could maybe get together for dinner or something, or maybe even you could be my date for the BBQ."

She did not hesitate for even one second. "Sure thing, Bern. I know Billy will be tied up with his wife and kids for the holiday anyway, so getting together shouldn't be hard to do."

"Well, look, Claire, if seeing me will be a problem for you, just say so. I surely don't want to mess up 'some good thing' you got going," I said with a sarcastic tone in my voice.

"Dammit, Bern! Did you call to ask me out or to pick a fight with me?"

"Well, if I recall from our past, we do a pretty good job of combining the two. Plus, I have to admit this ten tons of gorilla shit that has landed on me over the past year has just kind of turned me into a mean, hateful sonofabitch."

"Well, I have a better plan this time around. So let's just get together and see what happens. The BBQ sounds like fun. What time should I be ready?"

"Given our wonderfully high humidity and ninety-plus degree heat, we're not starting until right at sundown, hoping for cooler temps by then. So I'll pick you up around 7:45. How's that?"

"Perfect. See you then. And Bern? When do you want to meet your namesake? Before or after the party?"

"Maybe both, if he's not asleep by the time I get you back home."

"I can't tell you how excited I am about you finally seeing him. He's a good looking kid, and crazy as it sounds, I think he even looks a little like you. Silly, huh?"

"Poor kid doesn't stand a chance then," I said, mocking myself. It made us both laugh, and it gave me a small catharsis.

When I picked up Claire, I found her living just outside of Jackson in a little place called Raymond. She lived in a house trailer on top of a hill about 300 yards from the metal building where she worked as secretary for the heating and air-conditioning company that Billy owned. Billy had set her up in that location, which made it quite convenient when he wanted to visit after hours. His truck could still be at the shop, giving the appearance he was working late, if his wife ever bothered to check on him. I decided not to bother thinking about any of that. It might just make me crazier than I already felt.

Once inside the trailer, I was introduced to the babysitter and Little Bern was placed in my arms. "Here's our boy," Claire said as she picked up the tottering brown haired boy and handed him to me. I admit that for a brief moment I felt a twinge of joy again. The smell of his hair, the smell of his breath, the way he looked at me so inquisitively, almost as if to say, "Uh huh, yep, I think I know you." Then with a mischievous grin he offered me his little truck but then instantly snatched it back, teasing me. He then dropped the toy, reached out and grabbed my nose with one hand and my ear with the other and giggled with delight. All those things consecrated him in my heart.

We stayed a few minutes more, long enough for him to release a contagious giggle with a farting crescendo that produced a pookie diaper stench that almost drove us all out of the house! I set him back down in his playpen as Claire gave final instructions to the babysitter, telling her we would be back around midnight. He waved bye-bye as we stepped out the door.

The BBQ and fireworks really lifted my spirits as well. The beer was ice cold, and the steaks were tasty, thick, and juicy. Seeing neighbors and friends from church, sitting in groups playing dominoes or spades, and telling old stories about our youth, I was enjoying life a little for the first time in over a month. I wasn't able to crawl completely out of that well of bitter water, but at least I was making an effort to climb the rope.

Claire and I talked about where our paths had taken us and where we hoped to go in the future. I did not tell her about Coleman, and she didn't ask about the girlfriend I had been so serious about just three months earlier. She held my hand and put her arm through mine when she sat beside me. She would lean in close and whisper in my ear. Once she kissed me on the neck. It was good to feel a soft touch again, even if it wasn't Coleman's.

Back at her house well after midnight, she invited me in for another beer. With the babysitter now gone and Little Bern asleep, we stood side by side watching him, like parents so often do with sleeping infants.

"He should have been your baby," Claire said. "I wish he had been."

"If he had been, we'd be tied together forever. I'm pretty sure that is not what you wanted at the time. Looking back, I'm not sure it would have been what I wanted either. I just wanted you."

"Come here," she said. She led me off down the hall into her bedroom. "I've waited a long time to do this again," she said.

In my mean heart I violated the first rule of Southern etiquette. I spoke aloud the brutal truth without a speck of politeness. "And just what is it you want to do exactly? Cheat on your married boyfriend who is cheating on his wife?"

"You ass," she said. Then just as she had said to me back in French class years ago, she giggled and asked, "So do you want to kiss me first or just fuck?" Since nothing in the world meant anything to me anyway and I had no care about consequences, I laid her down, hard and rough, without the least bit of tenderness or intimacy.

We had learned back in December who had murdered Will and why. We had been waiting since then for the trial to start, and it was a blessing in disguise that Mom was not alive to sit in court. A week after the BBQ we collected ourselves as the remaining family and went to court for the trial of Sandival "Taboo" Robertson, which made me even meaner in spirit. Hearing him recount the details of that black night, the devil took over my heart, and all I wanted to do was kill, to kill with no remorse as Robertson had done, to kill and see the blood and life run out of him. Only then, I thought, could I find my true self again.

Thank God He gave me a poet's heart instead of a killer's. I penned my pain to pages of poetry, hoping that by pouring it out like dirty bath water,

I could cleanse my way back to a more tender heart and escape the mind fixated on fantasizing on death. I needed an escape to a cooler climate.

Montana Mountains

Montana mountains speak to some of us.

They speak to me...calling my name across

thousands of miles

the way one lover calls to another

across the canyon or through the ages.

One day I will follow that voice

even though I know

Montana can break a spirit

like water that freezes

in the stone and breaks it apart.

I know, too, that when I answer that call,

my hibernating bear heart will awaken,

and for a time that grizzled heart will soften,

only to be broken again,

and eventually those jagged, broken rocks

will reclaim me.

Just as the bear rends its prey,

So will my bear heart—my bare, raw heart—

be ripped from my chest and

shredded like paper

by the claws of loss and love unwisely spent.

But the hope is that in Montana

My heart will rest

when it becomes the dust

holding the footprints of real bears.

18 The Siren of Summer

Jackson, MS   Summer 1977

Claire had a way of making things seem so much easier than they really are, a true gift that made her lovable; but she had a way of driving you insane as well with all the complications that came with loving her. Just a couple of hours after our late night secretive liaison, she threw me out way too early in the morning "because Billy sometimes comes in to work real early, and I don't want him seeing your car out front."

Not being fully invested in a renewed relationship with her at that point, I threw on my clothes and left. I told her to call me if she needed another perspective on romance, if Billy couldn't take care of her by himself. I was truly an ass about her dating her boss and letting him treat her like a prostitute. I was already mad with the world enough as it was. It made the fires of hell in me flare even higher to think of how she had lowered herself over the years.

Time and again I had to remind myself that she was not my problem to solve. Her life was what she had made it. I was just a visitor, there for the fun and games in the traveling show called Claire McAlister: twice divorced. Claire McAlister: who was dating a married man while screwing around with a high school sweetheart, and naming her baby after him when the father had no idea how she came up with such a name. Claire McAlister, a sweet poison, a caustic blend of exhilarating sex and deadly disappointment. As I walked down the steps of the trailer, she said, "Call me again whenever you come back down here to visit. I hope to see a lot of you this summer since school's out and you're not working."

And so it was. I was home at the farmhouse maybe two or three nights a week, and in Jackson the rest of the time, specifically to see Claire. As much as I resisted any emotional involvement, telling myself it was just sex, her tenderness turned me from a sharp edged, jagged rock with cutting angles into a smooth, round river stone. A man could not spend that much time around Claire and not fall in love with her. She nurtured that male ego and could make any man believe he was the strongest man alive and that she needed him in every way a woman needs a man.

In the times we spent together, however, we could never go outside the trailer for her fear of being seen by Billy. We stayed inside the trailer house, living a very docile life together playing with Little Bern and watching Johnny Carson on late night TV, and later in the night living a wildcat life in her bedroom. Night after night we would crash and burn together, and she was always willingly giving, never saying no. She always made sure "her man," whichever one she happened to be with, had a very satisfying and fulfilling sex life. That was her magic, and she could weave a spell with it better than any woman alive, I believe.

Afterwards, the pillow talk would turn to dreams shared aloud about becoming a family, the three of us. As much as I loved the idea of being an influential part of Little Bern's life and having a salacious sex life, I knew inside it was all illusion. I couldn't reconcile her situation with Billy, and we began to argue more than we kissed, much like we did when we broke up in high school.

"Don't you think it's some kind of kismet for us?" she would say. "I mean, neither of my marriages worked out, and you haven't even tried to marry someone else. It's kind of like a sign that we belong to each other, don't you think?"

"How can you tell me you want to marry me and for us to be a family when you're still putting out for your damned boss?"

"Look, Bern. If I ended it with Billy, he would surely fire me on the spot, and that job is the best paying job I've ever had."

"Oh, you can bet on that! He's paying for a lot more than just a secretary!"

"Ask me to marry you then and I'll stop seeing him."

"NO. You need to stop seeing him first before I ask. I'm not going to ask you to marry me when I know just an hour before I show up to see you that you just crawled out of bed with him! I may not be the brightest guy on the planet, but I'm not a half brain idiot!"

"I can't stop seeing him until I know I have someplace else to go and that I'll have some financial support for me and the baby. I'm tied up with Billy until I have some other options."

"So what do you suppose he's going to do when you walk in one day and say—oh, by the way, I'm getting married next week? He's going to know then you have played him for the fool. He's going to know you've been screwing around with someone besides him."

"He will probably throw me out of the shop and out of this trailer before nightfall. That's what. So I'm damned if I do, damned if I don't."

"Claire. Claire. Listen to yourself. You know this whole thing is crazy. You have to know he's not in love with you, that you are nothing more than a whore to him!"

"It's called getting by until your ship comes in and your dreams come true!" she vehemently protested.

"No, Claire, it's called settling-- and selling yourself like a slut. And do you really think I'm your dream who can take away all those problems out of your complicated life?"

"I told you I've known from way back I made a mistake when I left you and started dating ...hell, I can't even remember the guy's name!"

"Dusty." I spit out his name as if dirt really was in his name when said aloud.

"What?"

"His name...was Dusty. He was a drug store cowboy who wore blue jeans and boots."

"Well, I'm sorry, Bern. I messed up then, and I don't want to mess up now. I really want us three to make a life together, but I just can't drop Billy and all the financial help he gives me if I have nothing in the other hand."

"And I can't hold your left hand and put a ring on it while he is holding your right hand. I never was very good at sharing."

She couldn't argue with that statement, so rather than continue the argument, she offered her most placating gifts. "Let's not argue again right now.

For now, Bern, for right now, with us here together, let's just forget Billy. Let's get Little Bern bathed and patted down for the night, and let's just go to bed and do what we do best together—make the world disappear for each other."

It was easy to do with Claire—letting the world slip away under the waves of some dark sea. But each morning brought the same divisive problems, and we were at an impasse. As much as I wanted to stay around and try to work things out with Claire and maybe raise a son together, I knew she could not be trusted in the long run. During our catching up phase, she had admitted to several affairs during her two marriages. She was a cheater, and she'd always be a cheater, one who got bored easily and would be gone on a whim off into some fake paradise with the next guy. I just couldn't trust the idea that a life time with Claire could be a good life. It would always be a mess.

It couldn't be the dream she conjured up in her mind or the hope I still secretly held onto from that time we walked Capitol Street looking in jewelry store windows. On the deepest level I knew Claire did not really love me as a wife loves her husband. She loved the idea of me as her husband. My gut told me Claire would never be anything but a heartache to me, no matter how lovely the song she sang. Like those Sirens who lured ancient sailors to their death, she would lull me into the depths sure to drown me like Woodrow was, waters so powerful and deep, I would be crushed under the pressure and turned into a jellied death as I sank lower and lower under the waves of broken vows.

So two weeks before school was begin again, I went back home to Mildred and Maxine and hoped never to see Claire again. That was not to say I wasn't devastated. My heart broke that it also meant leaving Little Bern behind, leaving him out of my life, and never having a baby of my own with Claire.

19 Return of the Native

Money, MS   1977-78

With my fourth year of teaching on the horizon, I actually looked forward to school starting up again. I was beginning to think I had an inkling of an idea about what teaching really involved, though it would take several more years to actually master the art. There was that one worry though about how I would handle seeing Coleman every day and her seeing me. It seems that damned Miss Tiny took care of that though.

When teachers reported back to Wilkes three days before the students were to arrive, there was no Coleman anywhere in sight. When I came in that first morning, Mr. Meredith told me to come by his office right after our first workshop. I knew that could not be a good sign.

"Do you know Miss Tiny that live up in Greenwood?" he asked.

"I've heard of her, but I've never met her," I confessed.

"Well, she came by her the first of summah break, and she told me you and Miss Coleman were becomin' an item of talk around the black neighborhood. She threatened to go to the school board if I didn't do sumpin about it, so I axed to have Miss Coleman transferred to Amanda Elzy High School. She won't be her to make a problem worse or to distrack you from yo duties this year."

"Sir, you had no right to interfere that way! We had worked out a solution Miss Tiny knew nothing about, a solution at our own great expense I might add. You should have called us to come in and talk, and you should have sent me to Elzy High School, not Coleman."

"Mr. Gresham, I did it to save bof yo careers!" he boomed, taking me aback. "Talk like dat amongst the community would have bof races up in a big snit! They'd try to run you outta town on a rail, boy; and frankly, I need you here. You do the chirren a lotta good. I couldn't afford to let sumpin like a mixed affair, whether true or not, drive a wedge 'tween you and me and dat school board. So I did it to save yo ass! Miss Coleman will be fine wherever she land."

I didn't want to hear any more about how the school board might have felt about my dating a black woman. It called to mind Mark Twain's quote: "First God made idiots. That was for practice. Then He created school boards." I thought it highly applicable in this case. Likewise, I didn't want to hear Coleman's name flung around in the air anymore; it hurt to hear it. It was disconcerting that she had to take the ax at Wilkes instead of me. Once again the white gets the benefit and the black takes the consequence. The whole system was so disgusting it made me want to puke right there on his desk.

"May I go to my room now, sir? I see no need for further conversation or discussion on this matter."

"Alright, Mr. Gresham, you go on along now. I don't speck you'll be too innerstid in the new Migrant teacher. She ain't no looker like Miss Coleman, nat's fo sure."

"Just shut up and don't mention her name to me again," I said as I walked out. I retreated to the solace of my classroom and decided I would not speak to him again unless it was an emergency or some urgent matter. He was to blame, too, for Coleman leaving. Because of his action, now I did not even have the comfort of knowing she was close by, just up the hall, a few steps away. I had resigned myself to the pain of not being within a touch of her, but my respite was in knowing I could at least see her; I could look at her. Now I didn't even have that. Some other something would have to be my focus and comfort. My students and my classroom would have to be my place of ease and joy.

The great thing about working at the Wilkes School in Money was that each year I only lost about 15-18 students to the eighth grade graduation. I rarely had new students to train since all of my other students would return to me, a year older and a grade up, but they would be back sitting in my classes just like the year before. My first fifth grade class was now my eighth grade class, and for some inexplicable reason, I always was partial to my eighth graders. Maybe it was because of the challenges they presented to me my first year; maybe it was because that was the year they seemed to develop a more inquisitive nature about things beyond their own lives and experiences. They wanted to know about things beyond their own front yards and the school yard.

Whatever the reason, I was ready to pack their brains with as much knowledge as I could find they needed. I loved the fact that there was no established curriculum dictating what I was to teach. That freedom to teach opened up mounds of material we could cover whenever I discovered they lacked significant knowledge on a certain topic. I decided this would be the year I would bury myself in my work to expand their core knowledge. I would leave no stone unturned if it was revealed to be something foreign to them. I wanted their world to be as big and wide as it could be, bursting the tight belt that cinched them up in the confines of their Delta shacks. So I set my goals far beyond the typical language arts curriculum and opened myself up to guide them through canyons and up mountains, across rivers and among forests. The entire world would be our subject of study for the year. I did not expect to be their white savior who arrives to finally give them the "good" education they deserved but usually didn't get. But I did expect to be their travel guide who knew which trails to trek and where the rivers were too wide to cross.

That evening I called Coleman. It seemed only right that I should apologize about her being transferred on my account. I couldn't just leave it as is, as if it was just part of the way things got done.

"It's ok, Gresham, it really is," she said. "I found out several weeks ago, so I have been at the school a lot to meet people and look at the Migrant Program that has been in place there. It needs some work, and I'm just the one they need to make those changes. I'm ok with it."

"Well, I'm still sorry you took the brunt of it all, but I hope you will be happy there. You'll let me know if you need anything, right? I mean, for your classes or whatever?"

"Sure, Gresham, sure," she said, but I knew she wouldn't. I just said my prayers for her safety and happiness each night and resigned myself to my work and my need to get lost in it.

I looked at all our readings with different eyes, our short stories and poems. Rather than looking for symbolism and figures of speech and analyzing character development, I looked for "foreign" things and concepts. I tried to see things the way they see them, and I questioned, "Will they know what (fill in the blank) is? Do they have any idea where that place is or what it looks like?" I built my lesson plans on the unknowns I anticipated from their lack of exposure.

The fourth day of the first week opened an opportunity to go off track like that. We were reading a story set in an ice cream parlor, and the two main characters were sharing a banana split.

"What dat?"

"What?" I asked.

"Dat nanna split?"

"Well, it's an ice cream dish made with a banana that is cut down the middle, and in between the two pieces they put three different kinds of ice cream, three kinds of toppings, and on top they put whipped cream and a cherry, sometimes maybe even nuts."

Suddenly I was being peppered with questions.

"Whut udder kine of ice cream there be sides banella and chocolate? You said dere was three kines."

"What's dat whupped creem thang?'

"Why any buddy want to eats a banana wid day's ice cream?"

"How you eat sumpin like dat?"

I tried to draw them a picture of a banana split on the chalkboard, but I am no artist; and without some colored chalk, it just all looked vanilla. Then a student over by the window said, "It's so hot in her, I sho whist I had me some of dat ice cream!" And an Idea was born.

I went to the grocery store after work to buy bananas, three kinds of ice cream, whipped cream, and all the other extras needed to make a full blown banana split. My plan was to have the kids build three of them in class the next day and each person get a bite or two. I wanted that banana split to be real for them.

I rounded the corner from the ice cream freezer, headed to the checkout, and there was John Sylvester Hamilton! He noticed me about the same second I noticed him.

"Well, I'll be a sombitch!" he said, as he galloped toward me with his hand out to shake mine. "Look at you, Buddy Boy! I never expected to see you again!"

"It's good to see you, John Sylvester! I've been living around here for the past few years, but no one I asked knew where you were. Damn, it's good to see you! Where you been and whatchoo been doin'?"

"Yeah, well, I married Dimple Tate about six months after high school when she got pregnant. We moved off down to the coast so's I could work on the offshore rigs. It paid good money but damn near killed me. We got twin boys named James Ray and John Ross."

"Really? That's great, man!! How old are they?"

"They're seven and live with their mama. Dimple and I divorced after two years. I moved back up here to be closer to them so I can see more of them now that they're in school and playing T-ball."

"I'm sorry to hear that your marriage didn't work out, but at least something good came out of it. You gotta be pretty proud of those boys."

"Oh, you bet I am! They're good boys, too. Not little hell-yuns like you and I were!"

"Well, they ain't in high school yet either! So we'll see how that turns out later. But I see you have learned some better language skills since you left the Delta. You don't talk nearly as funny as you did back then."

"Well, yours has gotten worse from living here, you damn hick!" We had a good laugh over that change of skills. "So you lawyering up here or what?"

"No, I changed my mind about law school. I teach language arts up at a little school in Money, just started my fourth year there. I really like it, but damn, these Delta public schools are so shit poor. If I ask for anything other than a pencil, the answer is always no."

"Still trying to set right the world off kilter, huh?"

"I guess so. But look, let me put this ice cream back in the freezer, and I'll come back and pick it up later. You got time to go get a beer somewhere and let's catch up a little more?"

"Hey, that sounds great. Let's do it."

We met up at Lusco's, a hole in the wall kind of place, old and dusty, but they served some of the best food in the whole Delta. It's the kind of place where you never knew who is dining there with you because every table is set in a little room blocked off by a curtain. It reminded me of a place where maybe Mafia guys would hang out, but I liked it. The beer was really cold, and we could sit in a private room with a buzzer to ring whenever we wanted the waitress to bring more beer or something to eat.

John Sylvester told me about his parents moving off to Tupelo when he and Dimple moved to the coast. He liked his offshore job, but it was really back-breaking work. He had landed a job here in Greenwood out at the John Deer place as a mechanic with steady hours. Inevitably, talk turned to my family.

"So how's your mominem?" I smiled at the way he said "mom and them" but I knew immediately he knew nothing about Will's death or Mom's suicide. Telling him was difficult, and he took it hard, making me remember what made him such a good friend. It was a relief to talk to someone about all of it now that I didn't have Coleman to talk to, but I did not tell him about Coleman. I just didn't want to chance hearing something that would ruin the reunion.

"So how come you never married, Buddy Boy? You ain't gone queer or nothing, have you?"

"No, you jackass, I'm not queer. I just haven't found that right woman. I've come close, but no cigar. And how come you haven't remarried?"

"Dimple was hell, that's why!! And I just ain't ready for more hell. She made marriage a bad word in my dictionary."

"Shit, you don't even know how to use a dictionary, you dumbass bastard."

"Well, I know enough to know hell would be found under the D's for Dimple Tate! Sending her back to her momma and daddy was the best thing I ever did. They spoiled that girl rotten to the core, and she expected me to treat her like some damn debutante. Shit on that!"

"Well, looks like the two of us are right back where we left off that summer I moved back to Jackson. Single and drinking beer. God help us!"

I so much enjoyed that evening with John Sylvester at Lusco's. We laughed and cussed, reminiscing about fishing trips and girls on gravel roads. The only thing we didn't do was spit and scratch. I realized I had really missed him over the years and that I hadn't had a close friend like him in a long, long time. It felt good to be just a guy with no strings, hanging out with a friend, having a few laughs.

"So, are you dating anyone right now, John?"

"Nobody seriously. I got a girlfriend I been dating now about six months. We just like each other's company, but it's not like we're in love or anything like that."

"How do you date someone for six months and not be in love with her? She ugly or what?"

"Naw, man! She's alright. Not no Delta Debutante though, that's for damn sure! She's a real down-to-earth kind of girl, smart and funny, even college educated. Likes to fish, too."

"Well, I'll have to meet her sometime. She got any friends looking for a date? I need to get back in the game. I miss female company. It's sure a lot better than yours," I joked.

"Yeah, well, it's all you got tonight unless you meet someone at the store when you go back to pick up that ice cream. What the hell you have so much ice cream for anyway?"

"It's for the kids at school," I said, but I did not elaborate on my lesson plan for tomorrow. "Look, here's my phone number. Call me when you need another beer buddy night."

"Sure thing, Bern. Maybe we can set up a double date or something, just like the old days."

I thought of nights running the road with John Sylvester and Thelma, and pictures came to mind again of all the damage done to my sweet lady. Between those thoughts and the one-beer-too-many, I suddenly wanted to throw up. It was warm inside the closed off booth, and I needed some air.

"Sounds like a plan, John. I'll take care of the bill on my way out, and I'll see you soon. It really was good seeing you again. I'm glad you're back in Greenwood."

"Say, Bern?"

"Yeah, man?"

"Thanks. I enjoyed the evening."

"You bet. See you soon."

I got in the Thunderbird and drove out to my quiet place under the bridge where Coleman and I often went. I just sat and listened to the crickets and the river running. I thought about how life seems to have run full circle, and how talking about Will and my mother would always be part of my story from now on with each new person I meet. I didn't know it at the time, but meeting up with John Sylvester was about to change my life again in a significant way, just as he had changed my life when I first came to the Delta. God has a way of drawing intersecting lines like that. Thanks be to God. I then drove back to town to buy ice cream.

20 All the News Fit to Print

Sunnyside, MS   October, 1977

The school year was clicking along at a rapid pace, and each day brought new topics to explore. Close to Halloween time, I received a flyer in my school mail about a new program I thought would kill two birds with one stone. It was called "Newspapers in the Classroom," and with it I figured we could improve reading skills and bring current events into school discussions. The flyer offered a class set of newspapers once a week for a very reasonable price as long as they were paid for by a school and not by an individual teacher.

I thought it was a brilliant idea, one that could open all kinds of avenues to help students understand the world around them and how those things might impact their lives. They were tired of reading the same old encyclopedias anyway. The trick would be getting the money from the school budget, which meant another round with "Got-No-Money" Meredith. Surely he would see the value in bringing this program into the school. After all, once we had the weekly set of newspapers in hand, they could be used in several ways. I formulated my plan of attack, and my objective was not leaving his office until I had approval to order those newspapers!

I talked to Mrs. Lucas, his secretary, and asked her to set up a meeting for me with Mr. Meredith after school the next day. I also asked her about money available for supplies and supplementary materials. She was well versed in the "Meredith Budget Plan" and quickly told me, "We ain't got no extra money for whatever is on yo' mind."

"Well, maybe not, Mrs. Lucas, but I'm going to ask for some anyway."

"Wastin' yo breff, Mr. Gersch. Wastin' time, too." But she did put me on his schedule for the next day, so at least that was a start. She just didn't let him know I was the one coming for the meeting. On his appointment book, she just wrote "teacher conference." She was sly like that at times. I loved her for it.

As I walked in the next afternoon, you could see him start shaking his head "no" as soon as I crossed the threshold. Mrs. Lucas started giggling in the background. I showed him the flyer and just stood there quietly to give him time to look it over. He gave it what I considered a fair amount of perusal, and when he looked up, I launched into the vantage points of moving forward with the newspapers.

"Bringing a set of newspapers into the classroom is going to open up all kinds of experiences for these kids. They know nothing about the space program or computers coming onto the market. They know nothing about what other countries are doing that could impact their lives and even lives of their children, like all this nuclear bomb testing that's going on in France and Russia and even here in our country."

"Well, it ain't like they even know where those places are, and none of 'em damn sure ain't ever going to the moon in a space ship."

"You don't know that!! I can teach them the geography they need to understand those things. I can teach them to read maps as well as read the newspaper. Besides, they are sick to death of reading twenty-year old encyclopedias! They NEED this exposure!!"

"We ain't got no money for newspeppers. Even if we did, it would be a waste. Most of 'em can't read on that level; you know that. It'll just frushtrate them."

"Mr. Meredith, listen to me. These kids won't ever rise above where they are today if we don't push them. It's our job to challenge them. Then if it 'frushtrates' them, it's our job to teach them some coping skills so they learn how to push on, to persevere, and to hang tough."

"We ain't got no money. Why don't you just order the prescription yo'self. Teachers gets extra stuff like dat for the chirren all the time."

"But they shouldn't have to. Besides, it clearly says it must be paid for through a purchase order from a school, not from an individual teacher."

"Are you deaf, Mr. Gresham? Did you hear me? No money! None! Zeeee-row!"

"Look. I know we have a tight budget. We do every year. But think of this as an investment. Once we have them, they can be used in all the secondary reading classes, not just the eighth grade. There are parts of the paper even the fifth and sixth graders will want to read, like the sports page or the comics. If we can give them material they are interested in, they will WANT to learn to read better. And after we have cycled them around the upper grades, they can go to the little kids for their art classes, if you can really call them that. Everybody in the whole school could benefit from this one resource. Besides, I've been here four years now, and you have YET to approve one single request for me. Stop being such a tight-purse granny and give me the damn twelve dollars!"

He got the most surprised look on his face. "Is dat true? Four years and not one dime?"

"Yes, sir. Not once have you said yes to any of my requests for additional resources."

"Humph! Well, I guess I better approve dees damn newspeppers then. Tell Mrs. Lucas to do the pepperwork, and I'll sign it."

I was ecstatic!! "Wow!! I knew somewhere inside there I'd find a GREAT principal, sir!! This is fantastic!! You're going to see what a difference this makes! Thank you so much!!! "

As I left the office, Mrs. Lucas gave me a wink as if to say, "Good job! Can't believe you did it, but good job!"

And just like that, the "chirren" who were locked into the space of Money, Mississippi, had the world come to their doorstep. We kept track of what plays were being performed on Broadway, and they learned about nudity in "Hair" and about Don Quixote in "Man of La Mancha." They learned about the election of the first black mayor of New Orleans, and where that city was located in relation to their homes. They learned about the test flights of the space shuttle Enterprise and the unmanned exploration of Voyager I and II. We learned about the treaty being discussed to return the Panama Canal to Panama. We kept tabs on the upcoming Presidential Inauguration for a peanut farmer from Georgia. And on and on and on. It was an exciting time to be at the Wilkes School in Money, Mississippi, and teaching was more of a blessing than I ever imagined it would be.

That night after Mr. Meredith and I had our newspaper conference, though, Claire called. She wanted me to know she was getting married again. "Maybe three times will be the charm," she had cheerily quipped.

"Is Billy really divorcing his wife?"

"No, not Billy. I've been seeing a guy named Doug, and he has asked me to marry him."

"Does HE know about Billy?"

"No. Which is good, because I am pregnant, and it could be Doug's, but it could also be Billy's." After a long pause she added, "Or it could be yours, Bern. I haven't had a period since you left at the end of August. But it doesn't matter. Now that abortions are legal, I'm not going to have it anyway."

"Wait! What??? What if it is mine?"

"Most likely it isn't. And if it's not yours, what difference does it make?"

"Claire, don't do something you're likely going to really regret in the long run."

"Well, I may not have many scruples, but I do have some standards. I'm not going to marry one guy when I might be carrying another man's baby. That would just be too much. It'll be best for my new marriage if a baby is not part of the equation. I really just wanted you to know I was getting married again. I shouldn't have even told you about being pregnant."

"Are you sure this is what you want, Claire? I mean, this new guy? It's awful quick to be talking marriage. You can't have known him more than a couple of months."

"It is fast; I know that. But it's my chance to break things off with Billy, and Doug loves me. I know he does."

"But do you love him?"

"I will sooner or later. For now, he's an answer to a prayer, so I'm going to take my chances."

"Claire, seriously. Do you think there's really any chance that baby could be ours together?"

"I don't know, Bern. I just don't know. I don't even want to know now that it's clear we aren't getting married. I just want to start a new life for me and Little Bern that has some shred of normalcy and decency. I'm tired of secrets and sneaking around. I just want a regular life with a nice man, and Doug can give me that. He has even said he eventually wants to adopt Little Bern as his own if things work out that way."

I really didn't know what to say to her after that. All I could think of was a silent "Poor Doug." Admittedly, I felt a twinge of regret that I hadn't asked Claire to marry me back in early August when she wanted me to, but that was water under the bridge long gone down river. I reminded myself that marrying Claire would have been the biggest mistake I could make in life. People's hearts play such tricks, though, and Claire's heart could turn on a dime. For a brief moment I wondered if she had a heart at all.

Shortly after we hung up, John Sylvester called, wanting to meet up for a few drinks at the Ramada Inn lounge where a really good all-girl band was playing. He had wandered in there a few nights before and found the place packed with standing room only; the band was that good, and the bar was making money like mad. They had never had a band pack the house like this one. So I agreed to meet him.

I managed to get there just as one couple was leaving, and I immediately grabbed their table. The place was packed to the gills, and the band was really rocking it out. Greenwood had never seen an all-girl band who played their own instruments. A girl on drums? A girl playing bass guitar? A girl playing lead guitar? Nowhere in the Delta was there such a thing! In our part of the country girls in bands were usually just singers or keyboard players; but these girls could really tear it up, and their playlist included Top 40, some oldies, and some country! They had something for everybody in the crowd, and they were all four good looking enough that every guy wanted to go out with them. Their tip jar full of five dollar bills was proof of that.

When John Sylvester walked in, he had a lady with him whom I assumed was the college educated girlfriend who liked to fish. She stood about five feet tall, a brunette with glasses. She was not what one would call pretty, but she was attractive in a subdued way though she had rather angular features. I stood up and waved at them from the corner table I had snagged, and John Sylvester flashed a grin and steered the young lady toward my direction.

"Hey, Buddy Boy!" he yelled over the crowd. "This is Marin Walters, my girlfriend who is a better fishing buddy than you are," he joked.

As we shook hands, he turned to her and said, "This is my high school buddy, Bern Gresham, I told you about."

Marin and I immediately shared a laugh together when the words "It's nice to meet you" came out of our mouths simultaneously, as if they had been synchronized by a Swiss watchmaker. It was a great way to start off, having a laugh together.

The crowd around the bar was four deep, so we just had to be patient for the waitress to get to us at our table. John Sylvester and I both ordered a Tom Collins. Marin ordered two shots of tequila straight up with salt and lime. John Sylvester noticed my eyes go wide and said, "Yep, she can drink you under the table, too!" You could tell he was proud of her in a number of ways.

It turned out to be an incredibly fun night, and John Sylvester told no lie. Marin Louise Walters could hold her liquor better than any man I knew. She was fun, with a sharp sense of humor and quick wit, not easily offended and holding no expectation of special treatment as a lady. She was as easy to talk to and joke with as John Sylvester was. I really liked her and fully understood why John Sylvester enjoyed her company so much.

There were some things though John Sylvester just was not going to do, and dance in public was one of them. When he told Marin she'd have to find another dance partner, she turned to me and asked as easily as if we had been friends for years.

"Come dance with me, Bern," she had said with no duplicity or intent beyond a dance with a friend.

"Don't mind if I do," I said as I rose from my chair.

"Yeah, Twinkle Toes. Go ahead and dance with her."

"Well, just don't drink all our liquor while we're away, Peg Leg!"

As we got to the crowded dance floor, the band kicked into the techno beat of Donna Summer's "I Feel Love." Marin leaned in close to tell me, "I can't disco dance."

"That's ok," I said. "Most people on this floor can't disco either. We'll just do our usual dance moves, how 'bout that?"

Turns out not only could Marin not disco dance, she couldn't dance at all. She could find the beat well enough, but basically all she did was bounce a little and step side to side. I was amused but disappointed. It was so crowded and hot on the dance floor, though, we went back to our table before the song ended.

We sat down and Marin took a long swig of John Sylvester's drink. "It's so hot up there near the stage lights, you could die of dehydration from just one dance!"

"You call that dancin', do ya?" John Sylvester teased.

"Well, hell yeah, John; it's better than sitting your butt in a chair! I know I can't dance worth a doodlelum damn, but that's part of the fun. You just do it anyway!"

I found it very endearing that she had no illusions about herself or her sex appeal on a dance floor and that she could laugh at herself so easily. It showed a good deal of confidence, and I liked that about her. I had no doubt we would become good friends over time.

The band cranked up an oldie by Dusty Springfield called "You Don't Have to Say You Love Me." Marin leaned over to say, "I may not dance well on my own, but I'm really good at following in a slow dance. Shall we?"

"My pleasure."

She turned to John Sylvester and said, "Order us another round of drinks, will ya? We'll be right back. I'll take a Tom Collins this time, too."

To me there was always something special about slow dancing with a woman when she is willing to let you lead. It's a trust thing, letting you be close enough to smell her hair, her breath, the perfume behind her ears, to feel her breasts against you, her hand in yours. We danced closer than we probably should have, but not so close as to be overly intimate. She was right; she could follow well. She was smooth and relaxed, picking up every nuance to the next step or turn. It was an easy and enjoyable dance. Not once did we step on each other's toes.

It reminded me of the time I was in junior high when school dances would be coming up throughout the year, and Connie had taught me how to slow dance, telling me several times, "Watch the toes! Watch the toes!" Connie and I used to dance to records all the time together. I longed for that easier time of living when slow dancing with a girl was the most stressful thing in your whole life.

Again Claire's words rattled through my heart—"or it could be yours.....but I'm not having it anyway." I wanted that baby to be mine, but I felt pretty sure it wasn't, and there was no way I'd ever know for sure if she followed through with the abortion. Claire's comment was likely just one last ditch effort to torment me for leaving her. It was her revenge. It was her way of making sure she could haunt me for years, and she couldn't have chosen a better way.

It seemed poetic justice though that I spent that evening drinking with friends and dancing with Marin Louise Walters. That was my sweet revenge that refused to let her keep twisting the knife in my gut. Claire's scheme of torturing me for years ahead really exposed her hateful heart, and for the first time ever, despite how deeply she had hurt me in the past, I despised her for the meanness. Isn't it funny how you can love someone so much, how you can have such pretty dreams of building a life with them, and also hate them to their very core all in the span of a few spoken words? Just like Dad had said so often, "Words do have power." They were her sword with which to spear me, and my sword with which to cut myself loose from her web of deceit and mind games.

21 Hard Facts

Sunnyside, MS   November 1977

As much as I wanted to ignore Claire's declaration about a third impending marriage and aborting the baby, whosoever might be the father, I simply could not escape the stated implication that the baby could be mine. The idea crawled all over me like ants on a discarded scrap of bread. It needled me and would not stop. If it was indeed my child, I needed to dissuade her from an abortion; but with Doug's proposal and my refusal to propose, she seemed determined in her plan to abort rather than wait to see who the father might be through paternity testing.

Claire's words continuously flashed through my mind daily, sometimes hourly, like a scrolling neon marquee.... "Or it could be yours." Dozens of questions haunted me and plagued my mind day and night. Could that baby be mine? What if the baby really is mine? Am I prepared to be a father? Am I prepared to have my life forever twisted up in a tangle with Claire? Should I marry her if the baby is mine, knowing her propensity for divorce? Could I tolerate being a divorced father with shared custody? Or could I make it work with Claire even though it never had succeeded before despite two attempts? Questions, questions, questions!

I wanted to be free from Claire and her wily ways, her toying with me when I knew she didn't really love me as much as she wanted me to be believe she did. Nevertheless, as the air turned cooler and fall colors began to appear, I knew there was little time to waste if I was going to have any influence on Claire in changing her mind about the abortion, about delaying both the marriage and the abortion until we had answers. Her upcoming third marriage in December meant November would have to be the month of action and decisions.

Then late one night an epiphany came to me. How come none of the other girls or women ever came up pregnant? It certainly wasn't because I frequently used protection or took precautions. I thought about the gravel road girls I had that last summer with John Sylvester. I thought about the year Claire and I had together at Central. Hell, I had had a four year relationship with the same girl all through college and she never got pregnant. The idea was even more disturbing than the idea that Claire could be carrying my baby. Oh, God! Have I been shooting blanks all this time? What if I have? Could I really be...? I couldn't even bring myself to say the word.

All night I tossed and turned in bed thinking of the consequences. I immediately clutched at denial. No, there's no way I'm sterile. Hell No! After all, Capt. John Smith had always risen to the occasion when a girl offered her Pocahontas. He never failed to complete his task. I had never experienced any kind of sexual dysfunction. By the light of morning though I knew I needed a final answer from a professional, not just my own self-diagnosis, so the next morning I called my doctor and made an appointment. I had to know the odds of the baby's being mine (or not) before I could approach Claire about reconsidering the termination of her pregnancy and maybe even the third marriage.

Dr. Fleischman was thorough and professional, but curious why I would have doubts if I was not even considering marriage at the time. I told him about all the relationships that I'd had over the years that had never produced a "need to marry" situation, and then I admitted to him there was a paternity matter in question and that I needed answers as quickly as possible since the young woman was debating an abortion. He then understood my urgency in wanting an answer and promised to submit blood and semen samples to the lab with all expediency, even labeling them as Priority. I felt assured I would have my answer soon, and that answer would direct me as to what I should do next. So the waiting game began.

During the waiting period of three days, though, I grew anxious, and for some odd reason decided to call my dad and talk things over with him. He and I had not had a father-son talk in several years, certainly not since Will's death. I was still angry with him for such inaction with Mom's depression that led to her suicide, despite my repeated assertions that he needed to get her some serious professional help. Angry or not though, I needed to talk to someone I could trust to give me good solid advice. With John Sylvester being such a jokester, I had immediately ruled him out as my first choice despite the fact that I was meeting up with him and Marin almost every night at the lounge to hear "the girls" play, to drink and dance.

Marin seemed to notice I was preoccupied and asked what was going on, why I was quieter and more reserved than usual. I lied, of course, and said it was just school stuff, the usual work stress. I could tell she didn't believe me, but she did not press the issue. She just slow danced with me in a comforting kind of way, leaning into me in a tender way, different from other times, like she understood something she could not possibly have understood, but giving me space to just slide into the music and escape with her. Her efforts were endearing, and they made me realize something I had never thought about before. As much intimacy as I had shared with Claire, I had never danced with her. Never once.

The next morning after meeting with Dr. Fleishman I took a day off from work to drive to Jackson to meet Dad for lunch at the Mayflower Café on Capitol Street. He looked stronger than when I last saw him at the BBQ on the Fourth, almost younger in fact. I resented it the moment I saw him, and that was something I would have to deal with eventually, but not right now. Later. Right now I needed my father's help and advice and was desperate to talk about the Claire situation and my epiphany.

We ordered coffee and the blue plate special of meatloaf with mashed potatoes, butterbeans, squash casserole, and cornbread. Our waitress, Mabel, called my dad "Honey" and called me "Sugar." From my earliest teenaged years, my father had taught me always to be exceptionally polite to the ladies who waited tables, and I had learned from him to joke around with them and maybe even flirt a little bit, to set them at ease, so they would know off the bat we were not going to be persnickety or troublesome customers.

"They have a hard job," Dad would say. "They don't get paid much; they work long hours; they're on their feet for hours on end and carrying loads of food and dishes heavy enough some men couldn't carry. So don't take offense if they call you sweet names. They're just trying to be nice."

As soon as the waitress walked away, my father looked me dead in the eye and said, "This must be something really serious for you to come down just for lunch when we haven't seen you much at all since mid-summer. Are you in some kind of legal trouble?"

"No, Dad, nothing legal, but it is very serious. And there's no easy way to say any of this other than just putting the skunk on the table and talking about it. There's a pregnant girl who says the baby may be mine but she's getting an abortion."

"Oh, geez, Bern. I hope you can talk her out of that. I mean, whether you marry her or not, you need to take responsibility for helping raise the child. You know I've always taught you kids to take responsibility for your actions and decisions. Does she think you won't help? Why does she not want to keep it?"

"That's just it, Dad. It's Claire, and the baby could belong to me or two others. She's getting ready to marry husband #3, and since she doesn't really know who the father is, she doesn't want the baby complicating the new marriage."

"I see. But still, if it could be yours..."

I interrupted him mid-sentence. "I don't really believe it is, Dad. I really think I might be infertile."

"What? Where'd you get an idea like that?"

"Think about it, Dad. In all these years since I started dating, none of the girls have ever come up pregnant. Not one! Not even Shelley from college, after four years with her. None. When this came up with Claire, it just suddenly hit me. So I went to see a doctor."

"Well, that's good that you sought medical advice. You certainly don't want to get tangled up in a marriage if the child isn't yours, even if it is with Claire. I know you have always had some very deep feelings for Claire. Every guy has that one woman he can never say no to, and Claire always seemed to be that woman for you."

"Especially if it is with Claire!" I said. "You just have no idea, Dad, how crazy she can make you, madly in love with you one day and off with some other guy the next day. Yes, I loved her dearly and in high school we even talked about marriage, but that was long ago. I know what she is really like – always chasing after the next guy that she thinks can offer something more than the one she's with. And honestly, she hasn't made many good choices, me included."

"I don't know so much about that, Son. I know what kind of man I raised you to be so I know you were always good to her."

"Yeah, well. She wasn't always good to me or good for me. And I've grown to distrust everything about her, and even sometimes hate her for what she has become."

"So you're telling me even if the baby is yours, you would willingly support her and the child but you wouldn't want to marry her? I understand that. So what is it you want from me?" he asked.

"Tell me about that time I had the mumps, when I was about eight and got so sick y'all had to take me to the emergency room and I spent like two weeks in the hospital."

"What? Why are you asking about that?"

"Because Dr. Fleischman asked about it. He asked if I had had the mumps when I was a kid and out of the blue asked if I remembered whether my nuts swelled up. I told him I was sure I'd had the mumps and was in the hospital, but I honestly couldn't tell him anything else about that time. He said mumps can cause problems with fertility, though he did say it was rare. So if my tests confirm what I suspect, that may have something to do with it."

"Oh, son. I hope you are wrong. You will be an awesome dad one day; I just know it. Men like you are born to be great fathers, great role models, great protectors. I hope you're wrong."

"But if I'm right, then being a father is most likely out of the question. What if the only children I ever have are the ones who sit in my classroom?"

"Then you pour all of your fatherly love and advice into them. You nurture them and guide them. You know most of them come from homes with just their mothers. Not many have fathers around the house. You be the father as well as the teacher. I know you will make a difference either way."

"But if I'm right, I need to know what has caused it and if there is a way to reverse it. So the more information I have about childhood diseases and injuries and such, the better my chances will be for Dr. Fleischman to find a solution if it turns out to be true."

"Yes, yes, of course. You're right. So about that hospital stay. I remember you ran a fever of about 105, and you woke us up in the middle of the night because you had thrown up on yourself and all over the bed. You were delirious with the fever and babbling stuff that made no sense. When your mom was helping you clean up, she noticed the horrendous swelling in your groin area. That's when we rushed you to the ER."

"So, even though it's rare, the mumps could be the cause?"

"Yes, I guess it could. You were a very sick little boy, Bern, very sick. But let's not get ahead of ourselves. Let's just wait and see what the tests tell us. But either way, Bern, you know it doesn't change who you are as a man inside."

"Doesn't it? I mean, if I ever find the right woman to marry, it WILL make a difference. Most women want children and expect to have them when they marry. What if this is a deal breaker for the woman I want? What then?"

"Then she won't be the right woman for you, and you need to keep looking for the one who is."

I took great comfort from his words, much comfort. My father had always had a way of telling me what I needed to hear to ease my mind on a matter, even if the truth was a hard one. There was still the question of marrying Claire if the tests were negative and the baby possibly mine. "She won't stay with me, Dad. She never stays long with any man. She's always looking for a better situation, a man with more money, or one who is more settled even though she can't settle very long herself. We'd have a great sex life, for sure; but it would seem futile to marry her, and I'd be miserable the whole time knowing I could never trust her."

"Sex is a wonderful thing between a man and his wife. But you don't build your entire marriage on it. It's built on trust and support and compromises, knowing you have that perfect partner beside you and that you will take care of each other even in rough times."

His words breathed life into the monster inside me that had been waiting to surface. "Oh, like you took care of Mom during her really rough patch, huh?" The sarcasm in my tone of voice was scalding.

I could tell he wanted to double up his fist and hit me. I could tell he was raging inside. I could tell I had hit the one nerve that stung him in the core. He started to get up and walk out, then turned and sat back down.

"Look, Bern. I know you are hurting right now from several things, and when we hurt, we want others to hurt, too. So, ok, you've done it. You've hurt me, hurt me deeply, but there are things you know nothing about between your mother and me, so don't presume to be my judge. I have judged myself far more harshly that you ever will. But I warn you, Son. Don't you EVER again insinuate I was culpable in your mom's suicide. I'll break you in half like the wishbone of a turkey. I mean it!"

I knew I crossed a line that was sacred. Sacred because it damaged the love between a father and son, and sacred because I stepped into their marriage, knowing full well how devoted they had been to one another before that horrible night. You just don't mess with a man and his wife, even if they are your parents.

"You're right, Dad, and I'm sorry. I knew I shouldn't have said it as soon as it came out, but it's been boiling a long time. I've been angry with you for so long now."

"I know, son. I know. I've been angry with myself. But I couldn't change things when it was happening, and I can't change things now. And I've missed the way we used to be able to talk with each other. I've been hoping you would find a way to let me off the hook, but I guess not; and I guess this will always be the one wall standing between us from now on."

"Then just tell me WHY, dammit. Why did you do nothing to help her overcome her grief, to get her help for her depression like I told you so many times?"

"You think I didn't try?? I DID try! I tried until I was blue in the face! She refused every time I brought up the subject of getting some help. I couldn't just pack her up in the car and take her to Whitfield and drop her off at the front door. She would never agree to it. I tried!"

"Then you should have tried harder!"

"Dammit, I did! I even went to see Sister Rupert who is head of the psychiatric ward at St. Dominic's. I've known her for years, and I knew she could advise me on what to do. But you just don't understand how difficult it is to commit someone who does not agree to be committed. If they agree, the insurance won't pay because they say they aren't crazy enough if they know they need help. If they don't agree to admittance, they require a court order, and you know how slowly the courts turn and how painfully invasive an inquisition like that can be. I couldn't put your mother through that. I just couldn't."

"I just still can't believe there was nothing else to do but sit and watch her slide into deeper and deeper darkness."

He let out an exasperated sigh and tried once more. "Let me tell you something, Bern; something you will need to recall from time to time in the future, I'm sure. There is no clear plan for anything in life; what works in one situation will not work in another even though they look the same. You do what you can do, but then you have to quit when you get to the end of a rope."

"Quit? QUIT!! How do you quit something like that?"

"It's called self-preservation!" he thundered, and then looked around embarrassed he had raised his voice for all to hear.

"Remember that story I told you several years ago about having to let a drowning person drown alone? When you realize the distance and water conditions are so bad that you cannot save them, even if you are the strongest swimmer in the world, you might have to let them drown?"

"Yes, I remember it well. I just couldn't believe it came from you."

"Well, it's ugly and it's brutal, but you can't save everyone, Bern. That is one of the hardest lessons we learn as we age. Your mom and I both had to learn that in trying to prosecute murderers when we knew all-white juries would turn them loose. We had to try, but in the end, we had to quit when there was no further recourse. We beat ourselves up over each Not Guilty verdict, until we had to face the fact that justice is not always served, and we could not always win. We could drown ourselves in our anguish and sorrow for losing and blame ourselves for not doing more, even though at the time of trial we believed we were doing everything we could, we still had to watch killers like De Lay Beckwith walk out the door as free men. We had to quit obsessing over each case like that in order to maintain our sanity. When your mom went down, I tried to save her. I tried everything I knew to do, but in the end, I had to let her go on her own or go down into that black hole with her. I wasn't ready to give up on the world, but she was; and I couldn't pull her back to the shore where there was safety. So yes, sometimes you have to let them drown or they will drown you with them. Those are the facts, son. They will drown you, too."

"But didn't you always tell me, Dad, that success is not always about winning? That it has more to do with trying? And now you're telling me sometimes success is about quitting?"

"As a boy you needed a hopeful vision of the world we were living in. We were surrounded by hate and violence, murder and terror; we still are. But I wanted you to see the world differently from what was around us. I wanted you—all three of my children-- to have hope, when really your mother and I had long come to realize there was little hope for the justice we were working for."

"But you still tried."

"Yes, we did. We tried. Until the reality of it all, the senselessness of it all, was so overwhelming we had to trade our ideals for a more sensible approach to prosecution. Life forces you to make compromises like that sometimes. I hated myself for it, but your mom and I had you three kids to shelter and guard; so we chose YOU over the world. That's what you mean to us, meant to her. That's why she couldn't come back from that darkness that ate up her soul when Will was taken from her."

"I understand that darkness, Dad. I almost didn't want to live after that either. If it hadn't been for last summer with Claire, I might not have found my way out of it. The only light I saw most days was in the crystal clear bottom of a vodka bottle."

"We all lost a great deal. We all suffered the deepest of wounds. The three of us left here are carrying a heavy burden of living through it. But we have come out on the other side; we've gotten our heads above water. We just have to keep swimming until we wash up on some sandy, sunny shore without crashing head first into the rocks of the outer shelf."

"So we really don't quit, do we?"

"Not just yet, son. Not just yet."

We finished our third cup of coffee, left Mabel a good tip, and paid the check. I hugged him goodbye there on Capitol Street where I had first contemplated marrying Claire. It seemed fitting that I found some direction there. I knew there were some hard facts to face, but I felt better prepared to make those decisions after talking with my father. I made the hard decisions and committed them to paper.

1. I will not marry Claire regardless of the outcome of my tests.
2. I will reconcile fully with my father and my sister.
3. I will be the father God intends for me to be, whatever that means.
4. The test results will not be my only truth.

I folded the sheet of scrap paper and put it in my wallet. I looked at it almost every day after Dr. Fleischman called me to tell me the tests were conclusive. I was definitely infertile and from all indications of the tests, irreversible. I would never be able to father a child. I wept for that loss.

So I let November pass without a call to Claire. I left her to map out her life as she felt she needed. I prayed for her and Little Bern to have a safe, happy life. I prayed for my future wife, whoever she might be, that I might be enough to make us happy all on our own. I went to confession for the first time since Will's death. Then I sent Coleman a Thanksgiving card on which I wrote, "Next to my salvation, you have been God's greatest gift to me, and I give thanks for you every day. Love, Bern."

22 Friends and Lovers

Greenwood, MS   January 1978

Once again John Sylvester, Marin, and I were out for a night of drinking and dancing. We had been out at the lounge almost every night that "the girls" were playing at the Ramada Inn, and over the weeks of their gig there, we had become fast friends with them. It was not unusual for them to dedicate certain songs for each of us three or certain slow dance songs for Marin and me. During their breaks, they would often sit with us at our table, and we had the best time joking around with them and making fun of the way other people danced, but especially Marin's "style." She was always a great sport about it and could dish it out as well as take it, so there were never any hurt feelings.

As they say though, "all good things come to an end," so it wasn't surprising when the band girls told us they were leaving Greenwood the upcoming Sunday, headed for a long stint in Memphis, their hometown. Since they had been on the road for the past eight months, they were really excited that they would soon be living in their own homes and sleeping in their own beds again. They would even get to be home for Christmas. So while Saturday night would be a goodbye party, it would also be a homecoming party, a double reason to celebrate.

The next night John Sylvester showed up without Marin and said they had decided not to date anymore, to just be friends. They had known all along that they weren't really cut out to be a steady couple; they just hung out together all the time because they enjoyed each other's company so much and always had fun together. They had always been more friends with one another than anything else, and they were just tired of playing the couples game. He told me they had tried making out once but had ended up just rolling in the floor in hysterical laughter over the ridiculousness of themselves as lovers. I had seen them hold hands and put their arms around each other's shoulders. I had seen them exchange those small little kisses that could mean a little or a lot, depending on the couple. They got along so well I just never figured they would "break up."

"She asked about seeing you, asked if it would upset me," he revealed. "I told her nothing would make me happier than for my two best friends to give it a go."

"Whoa! Where did that come from? I have to say, John, I'm not sure about that. I mean, I really like her, liked her from the very moment I met her. I think she's great, but I've just always thought of her as your girlfriend, not just your friend."

"So you don't want to date her?" he asked, with a confused, questioning look on his face. "Why not?"

"Because she's YOUR girlfriend."

"She's NOT my GIRL friend. I mean, yes, she's a girl and she's a friend, but honestly, we've never been more than just really good, close friends. It's ok. It's no big deal if you think you might want to date her. Frankly, I can't think of a better girlfriend for you, to tell you the truth."

I was quite conflicted. I had had a thought or two about what it would be like to date Marin, to be something more than just someone she liked to dance with, but I had always immediately dismissed the idea because of her relationship to John Sylvester. We were now all three moving into a new arena with new dynamics, and it just seemed too weird somehow.

"So if you two have decided to be just friends, how come she didn't come with you tonight?" I asked.

"Because she and I both wanted a chance for me to talk to you first. Look, Buddy Boy, I've noticed a time or two the way she would smile when she was slow dancing with you. You couldn't see it because she's shorter and you just see the top of her head unless she looks up at you, but I've known for a while that she has feelings for you."

"What kind of feelings? Did she say she had feelings?"

"No, because I don't think she knows for sure what her feelings are, but I think that is something the two of you should figure out together."

Deep inside I was excited to think about dating Marin, but I didn't want to appear too eager in case John Sylvester had feelings for her that he didn't want to admit. "Well, for now, let's just let things rock along as they've been doing. With the girls leaving town Saturday, though, she needs to be here with us every night this week. So tell her she does not have to separate company just because you two aren't coming in as 'dates' anymore. Ok?"

So the reminder of time we had with the band, the three of us helped them retire their stay in Greenwood, at the Ramada Inn that we had dubbed "the HaHa Hotel" because we had all had so many laughs there together. Those last few nights were my litmus test in adjusting to life as a man with a gun but no bullets. I was at a loss as to what to really think about myself. I had often thought that I'd make a decent husband one day and that I'd be a good father, but now? I was unsure I'd be a good catch for any woman, including Marin, but I knew I couldn't let that stop me from living a life of joy and purpose.

Marin was the absolute, smartest woman I'd ever met. She could talk on virtually any subject from religion to politics, to social justice and the economic policies that impact indigenous people, to environmental advances and drawbacks, world trade and global expansion. She loved being outdoors to hike the woods or fish the river. She wasn't afraid of wasps and would kill them for me when she saw me about to kill myself trying to get away from one! She had the sharpest of wit and was amazingly funny with her brand of intellectual humor. She didn't take herself too seriously, but she was deadly serious about the need to improve the public education system so black children would truly have equal opportunities for economic success. Aside from our shared occupations as teachers, we had a ton of things in common, and like she and John Sylvester, Marin and I genuinely, genuinely enjoyed each other's company as well.

With my most recent medical news that cut so deeply into my psyche and confidence level, I thought perhaps dating Marin might be a good thing. We knew each other well enough that getting started wouldn't be very complicated like it is with most new relationships. Being around Marin was always easy and relaxing. I couldn't ignore the potential drawbacks though. What if it didn't work out and we ended up destroying a really great friendship? Or worse, what if we got really serious about each other and marriage became part of our conversation and plans? How would I tell her my secret? How would I tell any woman with whom I considered marriage? I had no clue, but for now I didn't have to have an answer.

So I just kept my secret to myself and moved forward as best I could. Shortly after the band left town, I asked Marin to dinner, and we were together every night after that. Marin and I slipped into a warmer and more familiar relationship over the cold days of December, and John Sylvester started dating a good friend of Marin's who lived in Winona. The four of us went out together often, and holidays approached quickly. I was not the least bit sad to see 1977 end! It had been one hellacious twelve months, so I was looking forward to a new year.

The band girls sent John Sylvester and me a flyer about a huge gig they had landed for New Year's Eve in New Orleans. They invited us to come down and stay with friends of theirs in Thibodeaux. Tickets to the NYE party were $100 a pop, an outrageous amount for that time, but the girls said they were each allowed one guest for free, meaning the four of us in Greenwood just needed gas money to get down there. So Marin and I, and John Sylvester and Hannah, all four headed to Thibodeaux and New Orleans to start a new year.

That New Year's Eve party was a turning point for Marin and me. Maybe it was all the free champagne. Maybe it was being among 400 other party goers ringing in a new year with new hopes. Maybe it was just the kind of "love in the air" that makes you joyous enough to kiss strangers at midnight. Whatever it was, I suddenly saw Marin in a different light. I looked at Marin and realized how special she had become. In a very short time, she had managed to run her finger along the cragged wall of my heart where she found a crevice and crawled inside. I knew then--one day I would ask her to marry me. We were just too perfect together not to marry. The secret would come out soon enough, but for New Year's Eve in New Orleans, there was only love and laughter, fun and friendships, hope and happiness. So before the night ended, I did what I normally do during critical times. I drank hard and wrote another poem.

For Marin

Never will I forget

an evening in New Orleans

spent with you--- a new year

to roll in

and take its toll

on young looks, filled pocketbooks, and
dreams.

The music, the champagne,

The New Year's kisses

All gave whispered promises,

but none so dear

as the promise made by you

when you danced in my arms...

The lights low, the song soft and ethereal

as Easter weddings by candlelight---

and you--- smooth as a mirrored lake---

precious as a quiet prayer in a war zone.

I don't believe you knew the memory of you

I was creating while we danced---

It's just as well, though, for now.

All that matters is that you were with me---

and that means more to me

than all the glory and heritage of the French
Quarter

and the centuries of drunken lovers

who walked these narrow streets.

23 Discovery

Sunnyside, MS   1978

Before going off to New Orleans, I mailed Coleman a Christmas card, the first of 25-30 I would send as years rolled in and out. Occasionally I received one in return, which made Christmas even more special. As much as I knew things were definitely over with Coleman, I still wanted to maintain a connection to her, to remind her she could still call me if she ever needed anything, anything at all. I knew inside I would always love her in some deeply affectionate way just because she was brave enough to kiss me first there in the broad daylight of Memphis.

In January we finally got Mom's will probated, and while she naturally left everything to Dad, she had stipulated that certain money market accounts and some stocks were to be cashed out and given to us three kids. Only now they would be divided between just two of us.

We did not grow up as "rich" kids. We were "well off," but our family was far from what in the South is considered "wealthy," at least as far as Connie and I knew. So it came as a thundering surprise when Connie and I each received a small fortune of $350,000, a staggering amount that neither of us ever realized our mother had amassed in her short life time. Most of it was earned through very savvy investments, meaning our mother was evidently as much a genius in the financial market as she was in the courtroom. I missed that genius of her probably more than anything else about her.

Admittedly that was a great deal of the appeal Marin had. The genius of her wit, the intellectual edge of it, was completely enamoring. Case in point: She told us about getting an obscene phone call very early one Sunday morning. With morning fog on the brain and eyes barely open, she had picked up the phone to hear a raspy male voice ask, "How about some pussy?" Ever the quick wit she had responded, "No thanks. I already have one." We had just howled with laughter!

On a flip side, she could also be quite stubborn to a fault. Her self-confidence denied she could ever be wrong having examined a problem from every angle. It became a standard joke with us to say I was "wrong again" whenever a plan didn't work out, and no matter what the reason, she would always say, "It's your fault." As she explained to me one day, "The game is not designed for you to win. If you make up the bed, you get 100 points, but if you put the pillows on wrong, you get 5,000 points deducted." Those fun kind of jabs were just part of everyday life with Marin Louise Walters.

From January to April, we spent almost all of our free time together, hanging out at her place in Greenwood or my place in Sunnyside, doing the most ordinary of things such as reading books, watching TV, cooking at home, washing dishes together. Even the most mundane things were enjoyable with Marin. So in late spring, we decided to live together at the Sunnyside farmhouse where she could have a vegetable garden and all our animals would have room to roam and enjoy the fresh air and outdoors.

She moved in May 1st with her two dogs, Janet and Ann, although most of the time one dog was called Dammit Ann because she would not come to you until you cussed her. I still had Mildred and Maxine to keep the rats away, but I had also acquired three dogs of my own that just showed up when some asshole put them out on the dirt road near my house. There was a black lab mix named Spooky Dog who had come up just before Halloween last year. There was a little beagle cur mix named Fuzz Lee, and then there was a black cocker mix named Sisyphus. As these names indicated, I was much more creative in naming my pets than Marin was, although I did think Dammit Ann was a great name for a stubborn dog! So there in Sunnyside, we two human beings with our two cats and five dogs made quite a troop.

Marin was an unbelievable companion in every way although we were very different. I was an English teacher; she taught math, geometry even. I taught middle school, and she worked at the high school. I was in the county school system; she was in the city schools. She was an untiringly hard worker who liked to work outdoors even in the Delta's brutal heat and humidity of spring and summer when I preferred napping under the fan. She loved to go fishing and had no qualms about baiting her own hook with worms, minnows, or crickets and handling her own fish once caught. I was the wimp who used a towel to hold my catfish, having been finned and cut one time too many. Beyond scrambled eggs and weenies, I wasn't much of a cook, but Marin could bake, broil, grill, or fry any kind of meat. She was a master at seasoning any dish, but what she did to a ribeye or filet could compete with Lusco's high dollar steaks for tenderness, juiciness, and flavor. She could cook anything, and I knew I was destined to add some pounds around the middle.

The thing I liked most about Marin though was the way she viewed herself. She was a thinker, always rolling those marbles around inside her head to consider every angle. Marin Walters was analytical in her approach to every problem or situation and delighted in weighing the pros and cons. The woman was also a total master at playing Devil's Advocate in any debate, whether she agreed with you or not. Her primary goal in any conversation was making other people think, which made her a fabulous teacher, well respected by all her colleagues who often chose her as the team leader during staff development. I learned early that it would be rare to win an argument with her, like so many lawyers learned about Nan Gresham in the courtroom, and indeed Marin was much like my mother in personality.

In getting to know each other we discovered that we both had attended Delta State at the same time! She was a sorority girl, which explained why we never crossed paths even though Delta State was small, comparatively speaking. She also played flute in the band and casually knew Shelley whom I had dated. So yes, she was very familiar with my evening song, "Darkness on the Delta." We'd often sit on the front porch near sunset, hold hands and sing it together, though as Coleman had told me....I was not that good at singing. I never let that stop me though, kind of like Marin didn't let her awkward dance skills keep her off a dance floor.

She told me she was born in "the hills" of Lexington, Mississippi, and had been raised in the Baptist church, which was most common in the Delta. As an adult she was not an active church attendee though because her personal beliefs conflicted so much with what she was taught in the Baptist church. She got so disgusted with all of their exclusionary tenets that she just quit them when she went off to college, something that greatly displeased her parents. When I asked her about going to church with me, she agreed to "try" the Episcopal Church and went with me the first Sunday after moving into the farmhouse. On the way home afterwards she said she would "love" to go back!

"What was it that piqued your interest in the church then?" I asked.

"No doubt the liturgy is beautiful, and the music is out-of –this-world reverent and inspiringly sacred. But the fact that it's ok to ask questions about God or the Bible? That is pretty much unheard of in the Baptist church. Matter of fact, they look at you like you're a two- headed heathen if you question anything in the Bible!"

"Seriously? You can't ask questions?"

"Put it this way. I asked my mother once when I was maybe in third grade how we knew our God was the real God if other people had a different one. She told me I must not have any faith if I could ask something like that, and she told me I could go to hell for it. Well, I learned very quickly to keep my questions and thoughts to myself!"

"Well, in the Episcopal Church you can ask all the questions you want, and they will love you in a group when you start playing Devil's Advocate like you always do. We love to agree to disagree and argue and debate our faith and how it applies to our modern world. So you will fit right in! Who knows? You just might have been an Episcopalian all along!"

My introducing Marin into the Episcopal Church was just one of several reasons her parents, Agnes and Hardy, took an immediate disliking toward me. At least, Hardy did and Agnes just went along with whatever he said like a good little Baptist wife who submits herself to her husband in all things. Aside from the fact I was not Baptist, I was also deemed to be far too liberal toward the blacks. Hardy even asked me once, "How can you call them equal and say they are as deserving as we are when they only spend their time in criminal activity or sucking off the tit of this state?"

Oh, Lord! My first crisis with her family was deciding to stay quiet, subdue my ethics, and not get into an all-out verbal brawl. It felt like I was "going along to get along," but I think my silence spoke as loudly as anything I might have said in defense. I believe Hardy knew then and there that we were unconditionally on opposite sides and there would be no compromise other than agreeing not to talk about race relations or religion. Like good southern gentlemen, we were civil and polite; but beneath the surface, we each had a tremendous disdain for one another. Take all of that and add the fact that his daughter was sleeping unmarried in my bed, and it practically made me his sworn enemy. I hoped it would diminish over time and that we would find commonalities over which we could bond, and I knew it had to begin in my heart first. It was something I prayed about regularly as marriage to Marin slipped into my thoughts almost daily.

As worried as I was though about how to build a bridge with Hardy, I was far more concerned about my students. All through the spring semester there was talk of closing the Wilkes School at the end of next year. Enrollment was down considerably in that part of the county with more and more families leaving the farm areas and moving into Greenwood and other larger (though still small) neighboring towns. I was told I would be placed in another county school, most likely the one into which Wilkes would be folded. Staff morale took a tremendous nose dive, and the students were concerned about being separated from their friends and going someplace away from their hometown of Money, to some town where they had never been. I learned the majority of my students had never been out of Leflore County, so going to a school in a town other than Money, even though it was still in the same county, was a scary idea to them.

When I discovered just how limited their physical boundaries really were, I decided it was time to break down some fears—by going to the movies. A decade ago Franco Zeffirelli made one of the best film adaptations of ROMEO AND JULIET ever made, the one starring Olivia Hussey and Leonard Whiting. That film was being brought back into a limited number of theaters specifically for school field trips, and it was going to play at a theater in

Greenville, Mississippi, about 50 miles away. I decided it was time the Wilkes "chirren" went across the county line!

When I presented this idea of going to the movie in Greenville to see ROMEO AND JULIET, I discovered another astonishing fact. None of my ninth graders had ever set foot in a movie theater! They had little concept of what I was proposing and no idea what to expect. So there I went again, off to see Mrs. Lucas to get an appointment with No Money Meredith. I would have to pay a bus driver to take us over and back and to pay for the gasoline and mileage as well as the $2.00 ticket per student. I walked in and told Mr. Meredith I wanted to take the ninth graders to Greenville to see ROMEO AND JULIET in the movie theater there. I had figured up the cost of bus, gas, tickets, etc. and placed the tally on his desk. I thought he would blow a gasket! I felt pretty sure he was blood red in the face from anger, but his beautiful brown ebony skin masked it.

"You cain't come up in her and ax for dat kine o'money!" he bellowed.

"I ain't axing," I sassed. "I'm just telling you we are going. I don't need any money from you. I just need for you to sign the paperwork for the bus and driver request." I then handed him my personal check for the full amount needed (Thank you, Mom). "Deposit it and let's make this happen. Do you know that none of our freshmen have ever even been in a theater?" I said. "You can't deny that is something they definitely need to experience. So I'm taking them. Oh, and by the way, there is a brief nude scene in the movie, so I need for you to write the parents a letter and tell them you approve for their children to go see this movie anyway."

"Da hell, you say!"

"It's nothing to freak out over, sir. If you blink, you would miss Romeo's naked butt, that's all."

"No hankity-pankity rompin' around 'tweenum?"

"No, sir. Just a one second glimpse of a bare behind."

"You wouldn't lie to me bout sumpin that surrus, wouldchoo? I can trust you won't be gettin' the school board on my ass, right? I don't wanna trade my black ass just for des kids to see a white one!"

"Mr. Meredith, if you trust me to teach your chirren every day, I think you can trust I won't betray you in this. It's all about expanding the world for these kids, not about setting you up to be fired or anything like that."

"Well, since you be payin' fur erry thing, I guess I can hep you hep dem kids. Tell Mrs. Lucas what all you needs and tell her to get it togedder for me to sign."

"Thank you, sir. Shakespeare would be proud of you!"

"Who?" he asked, joking of course, but just to let me know he really appreciated what I was trying to do for the students. I was thankful we had that kind of relationship, where we could be brutally honest, call each other out if we thought the other was wrong, and still get along well, without any hidden agenda or backstabbing vengeance later.

So the wheels were set in motion, and I spent time teaching them theater etiquette. On movie day, Mr. Perkins, the bus driver, and I, along with Miss Vassar, the world history teacher, took seventeen freshmen to the movie that spring. Traveling to Greenville gave them their first look at new fields of crops outside Leflore County and their first look inside a movie theater, their bugged-out eyes that saw for the first time a fully loaded candy counter that stretched from one end of the lobby to the other and a popcorn making machine that spit out popcorn by the bucket loads.

They giggled with delight when the lights went out for the start of the movie, and they giggled when the white butt flashed across the screen. Several of them cried over the tragic set of failed plans that led to the lovers' deaths. But they came away with a far greater understanding of Shakespeare and his ill-fated lovers when we started studying the play two weeks later. It was one of my finest moments of teaching, and oh, how I wished Coleman could have been there to see it all come together for her migrant students who struggled so much with reading.

24 Walls Come Tumblin' Down

Sunnyside and Money, MS   1978-79 school year

In early spring of '78 there was a great deal of anxiety in the air among our students and us faculty. Rumors began circulating that the school board had a plan to save some big money by closing down Wilkes and combining it with Sunnyside Elementary. No one had any specifics about how that might work; I mean, how does one go about closing the doors on a school that is the hub of a community? Where do you even begin packing?

There were a couple of teachers who had friends on the school board, and from what they were told, it was going to happen pretty soon. We held our collective breath that it was just gossip and a possible money-saving plan, and we tried our best to stay focused on helping the students get as good an education as we could provide. When school ended in May we still had no answer as to our futures.

Throughout the summer Marin and I lived out our idyllic farm life although the grasshoppers chewed up much of our garden greens and the mockingbirds developed a connoisseur's taste for our tomatoes. We fished the Tallahatchie River during early mornings for channel cat, using tractor spark plugs for our line weight because of the strong current. We hung baskets of citronella plants all around the front porch to keep mosquitoes at bay in the evening when we liked to sit and watch the sun go down on the Delta while we sat in the glider and shared a bottle of wine or turned up the stereo to dance in the front yard. We talked a lot about our futures and the possibility that maybe one day we might decide to get married, but now we were happy as things were.

In early July the school board met and by unanimous vote decided the Wilkes School would be shut down at the end of the upcoming school year. Classes had grown continuously smaller each year I was there, and it was no longer financially feasible to keep it open when another small but newer campus a few miles away could house both student populations. Despite the matter of busing the Wilkes kids across the county to Sunnyside, the good news was that for the first time the Wilkes students would be attending an integrated school. The white student population at Sunnyside was small but significant enough to create a reasonable ratio.

In the five years I had been teaching at the Wilkes School, we had had less than a handful of white students, literally less than five, and none of them had been old enough to be in any of my classes. I received a letter from the superintendent and was told I would be assigned to go with our students to Sunnyside. I looked forward to teaching an integrated class and helping them find more commonality than difference. I just hoped the Sunnyside kids were not far more "worldly" than the ones coming from Wilkes since a wide disparity of experience and exposure would surely prove problematic.

I was also excited about going to Sunnyside because it was just a couple of miles from the farm house; a much shorter drive to work meant an extra half hour of sleep. So while there were some benefits for us all in seeing the two schools combined, still it was disheartening to see another killing in Money, to see the Wilkes School in its death throes. I would need to plan early to make this year's Eighth Grade Graduation extra special since it would be the last ever for Wilkes and the Money community.

One major blow in the closing process was that Mr. Meredith was reassigned to another school, and for our last year at Wilkes we would have no principal, just a lead teacher capable of handling administrative tasks as well as running a classroom. It reminded me of old Mrs. Bird Hawk, (that's the nickname I had given my student teacher supervisor, Mrs. Burkhalter) who served as both assistant principal and English teacher and left me alone with her classes after just two days of observation. I had confidence in Mrs. Whitker who would step into that role vacated by Mr. Meredith, but I also knew she would need a great deal of support. I knew it would be hard on her, being a colleague with everyone on staff one day and then their boss the next. Some would be happy, but some would resent her for it. We would all need a lengthy adjustment time to resolve all the conflicting emotions we had swirling around the school closing, and we would need to prop each other up daily, encouraging one another not to give up on the school's mission, but to press forward as though we were competing for a prize, even though we were working toward an ending. At least Mrs. Whitker approved my request for another year's subscription of newspapers for the school so our kids could still keep up with the country and the world while theirs slowly ceased to breathe.

As we approached the start of a new school year, with the subject of marriage entering our conversations more frequently, Marin and I decided to spend our last week of summer in Jackson with my dad and Connie. Since I had never taken a girl home to meet my family, other than Claire and not even Shelley, they would know immediately what was on our minds. Marin was nervous about the trip, but I knew in no way would my family find any fault with her. She was too personable and likeable, too much like Mom in the Smarts Department, too fun loving and resourceful to garner any kind of dislike.

Dad and Connie both developed an immediate affinity for Marin within the first twenty four hours of arrival despite the fact that she whipped both their butts at canasta after dinner that evening. She also gave them a good run for their money several nights that week at a new game called Trivial Pursuit that had recently come out on the market. Like me, they appreciated her savvy in current events and her humor with politics. When Connie found out about Marin's affection of U.S. history, she planned a girls' day and took Marin downtown to the Old Capital Museum and lunch at Primo's on Capitol Street while Dad and I spent the day at the minor league ball park watching the Jackson Mets play the Shreveport Captains.

"So how long have you known you were going to marry this girl?" Dad asked.

"Since I danced with her by candlelight at a New Year's Eve party in New Orleans," I replied.

"Well, candlelight will do it every time," he joked. "I'm happy for you, Son. Really happy. I think you have found a fabulous woman in Marin. She's seems just the right blend to settle you down but still keep you lively and energized."

"She is, Dad. She is totally amazing, just incredible and beyond anything I ever thought my wife would or could be."

"That's as it should be. A good wife will always be a surprise and a mystery. And I hesitate to ask, but have you told her yet about your medical issue?"

"Not just yet. Matter of fact, I haven't even actually asked her to marry me yet. We're just talking about the possibility."

"Well, I'm sure it'll work out," he assured me. "Have a little faith. I just have this feeling she really is the one just for you."

As it happened during that same week, Connie and Walt set their wedding date for Valentine's Day and planned a honeymoon at the Peabody in Memphis. A pained zinger like an electric shock swept through me, thinking of Coleman in Memphis that first visit when she said she wanted to go to the Peabody instead of the La Quinta. Coleman-- sweet, warm Coleman-- and the way she would lean into me and touch my arm when she laughed, those memories would always bring electric twinges of regret and pain, the kind usually reserved only for our very First Loves. I knew I was no longer in love with her, but I also knew on some level Coleman would always be especially dear to me, that I would always love her in some distant tender way. I hoped she thought of me the same way.

As we moved on into deep fall, Marin and I began talking very seriously about marriage. There were many questions to explore and answer with brutal truthfulness though. Were we really ready for a lifetime together, or should we just keep "shacking up" a while longer? I asked if she thought her parents would ever "come around" in accepting me as a non-Baptist son-in-law. Should we stay at the rented farm house or look at buying a house of our own? How much debt was each of us carrying? And the inevitable question – what about children?

Marin brought it up first, asking me, "Are children important to you?"

I thought it was a strange way to phrase the question rather that asking how many kids I wanted, but my mind also went haywire trying to think of the right thing to say, the right way to break my secret news to her. I knew the question would eventually come up, but I didn't expect it to enter our conversation so quickly. I stammered and hem-hawed around without really revealing what I should. I just wasn't ready to tell her my secret yet. Evidently though, she was ready to tell me hers.

"Look, Bern, we need to get real about a few things, a couple of things from my past that just might change your mind about this marriage thing."

"We all have a past, Marin," I said. "Everyone who has ever married has had to deal with each other's past. I have one of my own that might make you reconsider as well."

"Oh, I doubt that," she said with a sad kind of smile. It hurt me to see her smile like that, a smile that told me there was a lot of damage in her past that she preferred never to share unless she absolutely had to. I took her hand, looked her full in the face, and then told her, "I don't care about it, whatever it is."

"Well, you say that now, but only because you're hoping it'll make me throw you on the floor and have my way with you," she joked. She was like me that way, joking around to dispel some serious situation, to lighten a mood.

"Well, maybe so," I played along. "But if it's that important that you tell me, then let's just get it out of the way here and now. I'm all ears."

We settled back on the couch, her arm through mine and holding hands. The dogs settled around the living room, in the corners or in their favorite chairs, and they seemed to know something really serious was going on. "I've been married before," she confessed, "and the divorce was brutal. He was having an affair, and the divorce almost did me in because I was also pregnant at the time I found out about the cheating. I know I don't really act like it, but I have major, MAJOR trust issues with people because of it all."

"Do you mean to say you don't trust me?" I asked.

"No, not at all. I'm just saying there are things in my past that make me extremely distrustful sometimes of other people and of my own judgment. Because of that I might get cold feet at the last minute. I wouldn't want to hurt you like that. And I trust you enough that I don't really think that will happen; but if it does, you just need to know why and give me time to come back around."

"Well, as long as I know you WILL come back around, I'm not locked down on a timetable."

"It wasn't just the divorce itself though. It was very contentious, but the result of that is what we need to talk about. The stress of it all caused me to have a really bad miscarriage, Bern, and they had to do an emergency hysterectomy." She paused and took a deep breath. "You hear what I'm saying? I can't have any children because of that. So there it is. That's me. That's the woman sitting here with you that you think you might want to marry. So you really should...think twice."

I looked at her, my heart breaking for her, but I realized she was not the least bit tearful, having both the strength not to pity herself and probably having already cried all the tears she had in her, tears cried out to sand dryness back then when it all happened. I pulled her close and whispered to her, "I'm just like you. I am the same."

She jerked away from me and looked me in the face and with angry, flaring eyes said, "Don't. You. Dare, Bern! Don't you dare to lie to me about this!"

"I wouldn't do that, Marin. I've been trying to figure out how to tell you for a long time now that I can't have children. I've been dragging that weight around, groaning over a way to find the right words. I found out about it just right before we started dating."

The look on my face convinced her that I was not patronizing her or being cruelly playful. "I don't know what to say, Bern, other than I'm sorry. I know you would have been a great father, that's why I hated so much telling you about my hysterectomy. When we first joked around about maybe getting married one day, I thought to myself, 'It'll never happened once he knows.' When we started talking about this for real, I knew it was better to tell you sooner rather than later, before everything went to hell and you walked out on me."

"Walked out? You really thought that is how I'd react?"

"I thought it was a very real possibility, yes. Haven't you been thinking the same thing about me, knowing what you needed to tell me?"

"I see your point," I admitted. "But now the secrets are out and I guess....."

She interrupted...."And we have to decide now if we are really going to get married, we have to decide we are not going to cry about this, we're not going to live with regrets from day one of our marriage. We need to promise to be enough together, just us, or we don't marry at all."
"I can do that," I said. "With you, I can do that."

"Good!" she said in her matter-of-fact voice as if that settled everything. "Because I won't accept less from you. If I'm going to marry you, I have to trust you know upfront that you can be happy with me, just me....and some dogs, of course."

"Of course! But I haven't exactly asked you to marry me yet. Any instructions on how I should do that, Teacher Lady?"

"Nope. Just be damn sure you mean it when you do. There will be no kidding around about it after that."

"What do you think your daddy will say when I go ask him for your hand?"

"He'll probably tell you to go straight to hell, do not pass Go, do not collect $200."

"Yep, I figured as much. But I'll ask anyway." Then for no other reason than because we were happy, we opened a bottle of champagne and turned the dogs loose to chase some squirrels and rabbits. We sat on the porch and watched the light dissipate into red, then orange, then pink, gray, and darkness. We held hands and smiled because of our simple life and the one in the future we knew would be absolutely grand.

25 Letting Go and Taking Hold
Greenwood and Jackson

November 1978 to March 1979

At Thanksgiving Marin and I decided it was time to finalize some wedding plans, so I called her father and asked him to join me for lunch at the Crystal Grill in Greenwood. I chose that restaurant because the food was always good and the place was always quite noisy. If Hardy got irate, the usual commotion of the multi-roomed café would prevent drawing attention to our argument.

Needless to say, there was one. Hardy was not at all pleased that his daughter and I wanted to marry. While I did not need his permission to marry, I thought the gesture of asking him for Marin's hand would somewhat assuage his dislike for me and earn me a point or two at least for being a gentleman about it.

"That's what you brought me here to talk about? Permission to marry my girl? Well, let's just make this a short conversation then. No!"

"Excuse me?"

"You asked, and I'm saying no.   End of conversation."

The waitress brought our sweet tea, and when she asked if we were ready to order, Hardy rudely told her that the tea was all we would be having and to bring our check. I thought to myself, "There's one more reason to dislike the arrogant bastard. Can't stand people who are rude and dismissive toward waitresses."

I took a deep breath and tried to restart the conversation. "Look, Mr. Walters, we both know we have our differences on things, and you make no secret of the fact that I would not be your first choice as Marin's husband.   Nevertheless, I am Marin's first choice."

"Well, actually, no, you aren't. She's already been married. Did she tell you that?"

"Of course, she did.   Do you really think Marin would hide something like that, that she would be devious like that? You must not know your daughter very well at all if that's what you think."

Yes, I knew I shouldn't have been confrontational at that moment, but I thought it was so disrespectful of Marin, and I was not about to let him disparage her in any way. I got the impression he partially blamed Marin for that divorce, judging from the tone of his voice when he said it.

"Well, we don't approve of divorce in this family..."

"So you blame her? How can you do that when you know he was unfaithful to her and trashed their marriage vows?"

"Aw, shit like that happens in a lot of marriages, and manage to last. She didn't even try to reconcile with him, just tossed him out on a first offense," he stated adamantly.

"So you do blame her for the divorce," I accused.

"I'm just telling you there has never been a divorce in this family in over five generations until Marin got too high and mighty to forgive an indiscretion and went straight to a lawyer. I'm telling you divorce is just not acceptable in this family, but what's done is done and can't be fixed now. But I don't condone a second marriage to make up for it. I won't have anything to do with that!"

"Ok. Fine. I can see this is going nowhere. I was hoping you would be happy at least for Marin, even if you don't like me. But I see it's more than just that. You obviously have some religious objections that we can't agree on and never will. But I'm telling you right now, Mr. Walters, we ARE getting married. I hope you will reconsider in the next few months and that you will attend to walk her down the aisle; but if not, we will have a Plan B of some sort. You're not being there will not stop us from making these vows to one another."

"Is she going to get married in the Baptist church like we raised her?" he asked.

"We haven't gotten that far in the planning yet, but if I were to make an educated guess, I'd say no."

"Then you can count me out on everything. I won't attend and I won't pay a single dime. You tell her that."

"No, sir! If that's your stance, you need to be man enough to tell her yourself. I won't do your dirty work for you."

"Listen here, you smartass sonofabitch! Don't you sass me like that! I'll whip your ass all the way back to Sunnyside!"

"Yeah, well, once you get liquored up enough to really believe that, you come on out to the farm house, but bring your lunch with you when you do because it's going to take you all day." I threw a couple of dollars on the table to cover my tea and a tip and walked out.

THAT was not how I wanted the conversation to go, but sometimes you just have to stand up to a bully and call him out. I was appalled that he would even dream of trying to blackmail Marin in this situation. I didn't know how she was going to react to my talk with her father, whether she'd be mad and blame me for escalating the situation, or whether she'd know that Hardy was just being his usual jackass self. Either way, it was a hurdle we would have to overcome.

When I got home from that lunch, I told her that Hardy had said no, that he would not give his blessing, and that I told him we were marrying anyway. I told her it was very confrontational and did not end well, but I did not tell her he had no plans to attend or why. "It was a short conversation," I said. "We didn't even finish our tea before I had to leave to keep from choking the shit out of him!"

"Why am I not surprised?" she asked. "You're both pretty hard headed, and both of you speak your minds. I'll call him in a day or two, after he has had some time to cool off and talk to Mom, and see if I can't get him to come around. He just needs a little while to get used to the idea."

"You do need to talk to him. It's a good idea to give him some think time; but I have to warn you, Sug, not to get your hopes up too high. He was pretty riled up about the idea."

"Well, I can get pretty riled up myself. It won't be the first time he and I have gone head to head."

I crossed my fingers, said some prayers, rubbed some juju beads, and patted a Buddha head—all in hopes things would go better when Marin talked to him. All to no avail. She was devastated when he told her he had no intention of coming to the wedding, walking her down the aisle, or paying for it. She cried for days. It was almost as if she were grieving for the death of a loved one, and I guess in a way she was.

I didn't know what to do to comfort her, other than to give her the space she needed to work it all out in her head and in her heart. That was just part of her strength she conjured up within herself to overcome disappointments and heartaches. She would grieve for a few days, and then she would rally herself. She didn't want to be coddled in the process, just give her room.

A week after she talked to Hardy, she came home after school and said, "That's it. I'm done crying. I won't shed not even one more tear over this. It won't change anything, and it's simply not worth the cost. If my daddy wants to miss one of the best days of my life, it's his loss, and he WILL live to regret it."

And damn if that wasn't the way it happened. I never saw her cry another tear. She didn't call him and plead with him. She didn't call and try to guilt him into changing his mind. She didn't play the Daddy's-little-girl card and beg him. She just let him go.

It reminded me of that hard truth my father told me about sometimes having to let a drowning person drown to save yourself. Marin had evidently learned that lesson some time in her past because that is exactly what she did. She let it go and moved on with her life, her future, her wedding, her marriage.

Since Marin and Connie both had weddings to plan now, they were on the phone together almost daily, comparing notes and asking advice. When Connie found out that Marin's father was refusing to have anything to do with her wedding, Connie hatched a brilliant plan of her own that showed just how much she had grown to love Marin as her sister-to-be. She talked with Dad about the plan since he would play a major role in it, and he instantly agreed to the plan in full. She talked to Walt, who also thought it a very logical solution to a difficult problem.

Since Dad had a wedding to pay for anyway, why not have a double wedding? So Connie and Walt changed their wedding plans to include Marin and me. It meant cancelling previous arrangements Connie had already made, but she was happy to start over with Marin to help. As wedding plans go, the process could not have gone more smoothly. After some discussion about the guest list, it was decided there would be a small group invited to the wedding and a much larger group to the reception.

Rather than marry at St. Andrew's Cathedral in Jackson where we had sat through the two funerals of our mother and brother, we chose to marry in a small, beautiful Episcopal church half way between Jackson and Greenwood. It was a brilliantly white clapboard church with a bright red roof and red door, all situated in a pastoral setting. On March 15, our mother's birthdate, my father walked both brides down the aisle of St. Mary's Episcopal Church in Marin's hometown of Lexington, Mississippi. Connie became Mrs. Walt Hutchins, and Marin Louise Walters married a man her father hated because the two of us were enough by ourselves. But when we turned to leave the church as man and wife, there on the very last pew in the back sat Mr. and Mrs. Hardy Walters, smiling and crying at the same time.

26 Back Stories

Sunnyside, MS   December 1978 to March 1979

Wednesday at supper Marin said, "I'm taking the day off Friday. Connie is coming up, and we're going to Memphis to shop for wedding dresses and some fabric we will need. We will spend the night, and I'll be back Saturday sometime around lunch."

"Oh, so it's about to get really serious!" I joked.

"You bet it is, Mister! We have a lot to do in a short amount of time if we are going to pull this off by mid-March. Thank goodness we at least have an idea about our colors and bouquets."

"Oh, yeah? What did you two decide?"

"I'm going to carry a bouquet of white tulips backed with magnolia leaves for the emerald color and hand tied with an apricot colored ribbon. It's a really unique choice and I think it's going to look really pretty."

"Sounds pretty. What did Connie choose?"

"She's going to carry a bouquet of white calla lilies laced with an emerald colored ribbon since our colors are emerald and apricot. So at least we have a start."

"Well, I'm just glad I don't have to go along on that shopping trip. I don't understand how a woman ever picks a wedding dress. I mean, they're all white and look pretty much all the same to me."

"Well, maybe to you they look that way on a hanger, but believe me, Buddy Boy, as John Sylvester would say, just wait until you see me in one!"

"Do they make wedding dresses small enough for a 110 pounder?"

"Oh, hush! You know they do! And I'm going to find the perfect one to set off this amazing 110 pounds!"

"So any ideas what you're going to do about that old saying...something about a new thing, an old thing, a blue thing, and seems like there's one more thing."

"Something borrowed."

"Yeah, that's it. You need to think about those things. They sound pretty important since they go back ages and ages."

"Connie has some ideas she wants to talk about along those lines. She's quite creative, you know, and I know she'll help me figure it all out."

"Yep, we've had our differences, but she's pretty special. And she is almost as crazy about you as I am! I'm beginning to think she likes you better than she likes me," I teased. "But don't let her talk you into something for the new thing. I've got my own idea about that for you."

"Ah, a surprise! You HAVE been thinking about this wedding!"

"As a matter of fact, I have. I've even made some decisions about my tux. I don't want to look like the ugly duckling beside the beautiful swan that day!"

"Well, don't be too set on your choice. You need to coordinate with Walt, you know. He might have a different idea."

"Naw, Connie will tell him what to wear, so I just need to sell her on the idea and cut out the middle man!"

"And you need to be sure the color will match the wedding colors. Don't come up thinking you're going to wear a purple velvet tux or some such like the style these days. Have you looked at the tuxedo styles lately? They're insane!"

"I know. I looked. All those strange colors and ruffled shirts the same color with matching tie. I don't like everything being the same color. So rest assured, I'm going pretty traditional with a dove gray one button coat with a pleated white shirt, no ruffles."

"I love it! A gray tux will look fabulous with an apricot colored tie and pocket square. Classy!"

"The trick will be finding a tie that color. Did I tell you when Connie told Dad about the wedding colors he offered me his emerald cufflinks that Mom gave him for his birthday one year?"

"No! That's great! That will tie in both colors if we can find an apricot tie. I really don't want you to end up wearing a green tie."

"Well, maybe when you two are looking at material, you can find something along that line we can use to have the ties made for us guys. I'm sure there's a tailor in Jackson who could do that if we need to."

"Good idea. Add just one more thing to the to-do list!"

"Aw, you know you're having fun."

And that was how our conversations at supper usually went as plans and final decisions were made and the wedding date drew nearer. It took four trips to Memphis to decide on the dresses; but frankly, I think Connie and Marin just enjoyed the fun of shopping and hanging out together. They really were like two sisters, and Connie's acceptance of Marin certainly helped me forgive her for the insensitive remarks she had made when she found out I was dating Coleman. I wondered if Connie told Marin about that.

I decided I needed to tell Marin, given that I would always have special feelings for Coleman, and I needed to tell Marin about Claire as well. I didn't want there to be any secrets, and if it came up later, I didn't want any surprises for Marin about my past. So I told her everything, including the fact that I wanted to maintain some contact with Coleman, though distant, by sending Coleman a Christmas card each year.

Marin, not being the jealous, clingy, or possessive type, said she wasn't concerned about any of that stuff in the past. After all, I chose to marry her, not either of them. That reaction told me just how much she did trust me, even with her deep reservations about trusting anyone.

Christmas and New Year's came and went in a whirlwind we hardly noticed. Then one afternoon in late January, Marin came home extremely upset, angry, and frightened. She was so mad she was crying and shaking and could hardly tell me why.

"He's found me! I thought I had gotten away from him, but when I came out of the building this afternoon, he was driving through the school parking lot."

"Who, Baby? Who are you talking about?"

"This nut job named Pete Mossberg who stalked me at Delta State. He was in the band, too, so he was around me daily, but then he started turning up everywhere I went, day and night-- the grocery store, the movies, Pasqual's Pizza. You name it! And then he started making threats to blow up my car and all kinds of other ugly things."

"Wait! What the hell? You went to the police, right?"

"I did. But they said until he actually did something illegal to me, they couldn't do anything to him. Making threats was not actually illegal. Is that insane or what? I was scared to death of him. You could just look at him and tell he was crazy. He had this kind of Rasputin look to him where you could just see evil in his eyes."

"Did he ever do anything other than threaten you?"

"Yes, he grabbed me in a parking lot and kidnapped me for twelve hours, holding me in an abandoned warehouse just off campus."

"Aw, shit, Marin! He kidnapped you? Why have I not heard this before now? Did he hurt you?"

"Not really, not physically anyway, but he sure did a number on my head. I thought surely he was going to kill me because he kept saying he was going to, but he just sat and looked at me with a big knife in his hand, running his finger along the blade. He kissed me one time, and even though I knew it was dangerous to provoke him, I was so angry and disgusted I spit on him and he backed away. Mid-morning the next day, he just turned me loose. He told me he just wanted to prove to me that he could get me anytime he wanted to."

"What did the police do after that?"

"He was arrested and given a three year jail sentence. It was a light sentence because he didn't really do anything to hurt me other than kidnapping. That was in spring of my senior year at Delta State, so while he was in jail I took the opportunity to disappear from Cleveland, which was his hometown."

"And you're sure it was this same guy in the parking lot at your school?"

"100% sure. There is no mistaking him."

"Did he see you?"

"I don't think he did, but I'm not sure. But he evidently knows now I work there, or he wouldn't have been cruising the parking lot. I'm scared to even go back to work. What am I going to do, Bern? I can't live in fear of him watching my every move again and turning up everywhere I go. I swear if he ever comes near me again, I'm going to kill him. I don't know how, but I will. I'm not going through all that terror again."

"Well, obviously you need to report this to the police. Even though he hasn't done anything, they need to be aware of his past actions and the danger he poses to you. You need to tell your principal, too, so they can be on the lookout in case he ever comes into the building. And it's time you learn to shoot my 9mm."

"I just don't think that will help anything. It's not like I can take a gun into the school with me. If I needed to use it, it would be in the parking lot most likely. So it won't do any good to have it in the car."

"But at least you could defend yourself here at home if he were to ever come around the house when you're here alone."

"You're right. I hadn't thought of that. I can hardly think straight now after seeing him. I am so livid!!"

"Well, planning ahead is the best defense. Let's just not panic. You'll need to get yourself together and keep a clear head and sharp eye out anytime you're on foot. But I just can't believe you weren't even going to tell me about this."

"I know I should have, Bern. But you know how Southern culture works when it comes to really nasty things in life. We never talk about it. We put it in the past and leave it there. Talking about it gives it life and makes it real again. And after a jail sentence for him, I just thought I'd never have to deal with him again. I wanted him to be a non-issue, so I made him one."

"Still, keeping something like that a secret..."

She cut me off midsentence. "Bern, please don't be angry with me right now. You know I would have told you all about it sooner or later at some point in all these years ahead we are planning together. But honestly, honey, I really thought he was gone forever from my life."

"Well, it certainly explains a lot about your problems with trust and being so suspicious of strangers."

"And really, not telling you is not a reflection of my trust for you in any way. I trust you more than anyone on this earth. I just put him in a locked box in the back of my mental closet and wanted him to stay there. To tell you that whole story I would have to get that box out and go through it again, and I just didn't want to think about it ever again. I'm sorry I didn't tell you, Bern. I should have."

So while planning the wedding, we made protective plans as well in case he showed up in the parking lot of Greenwood High School again. As it happened, Marin never saw Mossberg again anywhere around the school. As each day passed without seeing him, and seeing the Greenwood police drive through the parking lot each morning and afternoon as she went in and out of the building, Marin grew more and more at ease. Suddenly, wedding day was upon us.

St. Mary's Episcopal Church in Lexington gave us a small, intimate setting for the wedding we all four wanted. We had decided together we wanted a simple wedding with a guest list of about twenty-five each, only the closest friends and relatives. We wanted to spend more money on the reception than on the wedding, to celebrate big time this significant event in our lives.

Dad had his hands full escorting two brides; John Sylvester stood as my Best Man, and Hannah was Marin's Maid of Honor. Just as Episcopal funerals are lengthy and liturgy driven, Episcopal weddings are the same and nothing like what Baptists are accustomed to witnessing. We frequently joked that at a couple of Baptist weddings we had attended, it took longer to get the wedding party down the aisle than it did for the couple to say their vows.

Dad, Walt, John Sylvester and I wore our dove gray tuxedos with satin notched lapels, and Marin had found the perfect fabric for our apricot colored ties and pocket squares. It was an apricot color with a faint peach colored paisley pattern on it. We were all four quite dapper looking and bursting with joy.

After Dad escorted Connie down the aisle to the altar, there was some special music while he returned to the back to walk Marin in. I was facing the altar when our processional music started and John Sylvester put his hand on my shoulder and whispered, "Here she comes."

I turned to see the most gorgeous Marin Louise Walters I had ever seen. She wore her hair swept up and back with a chignon bun in the back, pinned with a lace and pearl comb that had belonged to her grandmother, her something old. She wore a set of pear shaped diamond and emerald earrings that I gave her as a wedding present, her something new. Hannah provided a cross necklace that she had gotten for her sixteenth birthday so Marin had something borrowed. The "something blue" was Connie's creation, a baby blue satin ribbon anklet with a single lapis lazuli bead. And yes, the dress was the perfect gown to set off those 110 pounds of curves and beauty.

Connie had described the dress to me, telling me it had a fitted, long sleeved bodice with a bateau neckline (which she had to explain meant a boat neck style). The top and back were covered in what wedding fashion called 'illusion and lace' that had a beaded Venetian lace pattern. Yep, she had to explain that, too! The rest of the dress, made of charmeuse and organdy, fit at the hips and then gradually flared to the floor. That all sounded great when Connie described it, but I had no idea a dress could be that beautiful and a bride even more so dressed in it.

It was absolutely stunning and fit her every curve! When I turned and saw her, I thought I would burst wide open with jubilance and overflowing love. The whole entire look of her from head to toe was completely breathtaking. She looked ravishingly delicious, and I could hardly contain myself, wanting to kiss her right then and there before the ceremony even began.

"Dearly beloved, we are gathered here..."

"Do you, Constance Amelia Gresham, take this man...?"

"Do you, Walter Ellis Hutchins, take this woman...?"

"Do you Marin Louise Walters, take this man...?"

"Do you Bernard Everett Gresham, take this woman...?"

We proclaimed our vows and patiently listened to four scripture readings: an Old Testament reading, a Psalm, a New Testament reading, and a Gospel reading. We had our rings blessed and exchanged, had our hands wrapped together in the stole of the priest, and we were promptly pronounced "husband and wife in the name of the Father, the Son, and the Holy Spirit." In other weddings, that would be where the bride and groom kiss and exit the church, but not at an Episcopal wedding! No, there are plenty more prayers to be said, prayers that not only bind the couple together in marriage but also bind them to the church and the Lord who created them.

"Give them wisdom and devotion in the ordering of their common life, that each may be to the other a strength in need, a counselor in perplexity, a comfort in sorrow, and a companion in joy." Amen.

"Make their life together a sign of Christ's love to this sinful and broken world, that unity may overcome estrangement, forgiveness heal guilt, and joy conquer despair." Amen.

After a few more short prayers were said, we knelt together, the four of us, on a special cushion before the altar and the priest pronounced a special blessing over our marriages.

"O God, you have so consecrated the covenant of marriage that in it is represented the spiritual unity between Christ and his Church. Send therefore your blessing upon these, your servants, that they may so love, honor, and cherish each other in faithfulness and patience, in wisdom and true godliness, that their home may be a haven of blessing and peace, through Jesus Christ our Lord, who lives and reigns with you and the Holy Spirit, One God, now and forever." Amen. It was then I was given permission to kiss my bride.

I thought we'd never get to that part!! I had kissed Marin probably more than a thousand times since we had started dating, but we had never kissed like we did then and there at St Mary's, a kiss both red hot but sweeter than any song of angels. But even then, the wedding was not over.

We still had the usual worship service with the Peace, the Eucharistic prayer and communion, after which we were all given a final blessing. We then turned to exit the church and saw Marin's parents sitting on the back pew. We all four stopped the recessional to hug one another.

"Thank you, sir, for coming," I whispered to Hardy when he reached to hug me, too. "It's a great wedding gift for us to have you both here."

We entertained about 200 guests with three open bars and a full sit down three course meal. We served prime rib or root beer glazed salmon, roasted garlic potatoes, a vegetable medley, carrot soufflé, French bread, and bread pudding.

It was a bigger, more formal affair than Marin and I really wanted, with the white linen table cloths and wait staff in white tuxedo dinner coats, but we did not protest as long as we got to choose the band. We chose a Sunday afternoon wedding so "The Girls" could come and be our dance band. Everyone loved them and filled the dance floor on almost every tune.

For the bride and groom's first dance, Marin and Connie had chosen the Anne Murray song, "I Just Fall in Love Again." Later when Connie and I danced together for the first time in years, she teased me and reminded me again, "Watch the toes! Watch the toes!" The evening could not have been more perfect.

27 Night of Honor and Memory

Money, Mississippi   May, 1979

After the wedding reception, Connie and Walt took off for the Peabody in Memphis as they had originally planned, and Marin and I headed to New Orleans for our honeymoon. It seemed the only fitting place since it was in that wonderful old-soul crescent city that I first realized one day I would take Marin as my wife if she would have me. We had to go back to New Orleans—to that New Year's Eve party when we were so new to each other, that midnight dance and kiss among hooting horns and cheers of strangers, that moment I first really looked at her in soft lights and slow music and knew she was made for me.

We spent a wonderful five days there wandering streets and shops, eating crawfish and oysters, riding through the narrow streets in a horse drawn carriage, and taking pictures at all the scenic spots. We took hundreds of photographs because we both wanted to recall years later every moment of that wonderful, magical time that all honeymooners have, to set the course of their marriages to make them endure with deep and abiding hope in each other.

Much too soon though our spring break honeymoon was over, and we were back at work designing lesson plans and developing our own ancillary materials, and spring gets really crazy really fast in the school business, trying to wrap up everything for the year. In addition to all my usual preparation and teaching, I also had that really important Eighth Grade Promotion Program to pull off. Everybody who was Anybody in the county school system was expected to attend, plus many of the civic leaders in the black and white surrounding communities. We were expecting a packed house with standing room only. I sent Coleman a special invitation and told her I hoped she would attend for the added reason of meeting my wife and my best friend. I had sent her one of our wedding pictures as well. Surprisingly, she had written a quick note in return to tell me how happy she was that I had found someone to love again and to tell me she would be there.

In preparation for the evening, I spent untold hours working with students, preparing each speech and special reading from the invocation to the benediction and everything in between. I pushed them harder than usual in their editing and rewriting about sentence structure and word choices; I coached them constantly about stage presence and posture, about volume, tone and voice inflection, all because of the importance of this one promotion. They would be part of a legacy, a part of history, being the very last class to process into that cafetorium and bid farewell to the Wilkes School, a major piece of Money's history destined to go down to dust as we all eventually will. We worked harder than ever to make this a most memorable evening filled with excellence and inspiration.

Having no band or orchestra program at the school, our promotion program music had always been on vinyl and played on a portable stereo system. We had always processed in to the usual Elgar tune of "Pomp and Circumstance," but we wanted something extra special for the end of this ceremony. I checked out several classical music LP's from the Greenwood-Leflore Library, and we listened to numerous recordings of classical music before choosing "War March of the Priests" by Mendelssohn as our recessional, the end of it all. It was a powerful musical statement on which to close out that phase of education in Leflore County.

When May 22 rolled around and we had our last rehearsal that morning, I knew they were ready, all twenty-one of them. They each arrived that evening spit shined in their Sunday Best clothes and polished shoes. They had chosen "Inheritors of Our Own Design" as their class motto, and they had built their speeches around that idea, that indeed they would inherit from their education and society only the things they were dedicated and strong enough to imagine and build. They knew if they wanted things to be different in the future, they would have to construct a different way of interacting with whites and the laws. They had such big hopes, such optimistic dreams.

Coleman arrived early enough that we had time for a quick visit and introductions. She hugged me and kissed my cheek, and she did the same with Marin, telling her how beautiful she was in the wedding photo I had sent and how happy she was to meet both my wife and my best friend. That was the first time we had seen each other since that last night in Greenville, and she was as gracious and classy and elegant as ever, that sweet smile and infectious laugh still very much a part of her. I hoped time never changed that. As usual though, there were a dozen last minute adjustments to be made and duty called, so I left her with Marin and John Sylvester to choose their seats.

The music began right on time, and when the last of the class members reached their seats on stage, Donnie Fisher, carrying the words of St. Ignatius' Prayer for Generosity, went to the lectern and said,

"Please stand and pray with us. Teach us, Good Lord, to give and not count the cost, to fight and not heed the wounds, to toil and not seek to rest, to labor and not ask reward—save that of knowing that we do Thy will. Amen."

On through the program we went, piece by piece, each speaker conscious of the importance of the moment and the part they were playing. Each student speaker did a superb job, speaking slowly and deliberately, with all the correct pronunciations and inflections, none shy or too soft spoken, none stumbling over any words or frozen with stage fright.

I was especially proud of Barnitta James when she read the class poem I had written for them. It had been difficult teaching her how to read poetry aloud, that one does not always pause at the end of a line but through to the next. I knew she must have practiced at home a good bit because she did a perfect reading, which was set to background music where certain words and phrases went with certain sections of music. How she managed to perfect her reading by practicing at home without the music was nothing short of amazing. She walked to the podium, her head high and shoulders straight, very much in command of the stage. She announced to the audience, "A dramatic reading for us all, not just for me and my classmates." We had not rehearsed that intro, and it came as a total surprise. It meant she was intent on delivering the message.

Let Us

And so we begin our new lives

With knowledge bright upon our foreheads

And so many dreams within our reach and

Courage to turn full face into the gale.

Let us not look back too long

But always forward to glory,

Let us keep our memories' perspective

And always carry

the words of hope in our hearts.

Yes, let us live in dignity

With pride to stand but not to trample.

We are the children, heirs to life,

Soon to be donors to all the world.

The path before us lies

Up the mountain to the stars.

What is past, is gone forever,

Leaving to us the duty to create

A world even brighter

And even more glorious.

We can bequeath to others

Only what we have the integrity to design.

Let us rise and be counted.

The class president was Jeanett Dickins, sister of the little eighth grade boy who couldn't read anything but "and" and "the" and had once tried to attack me with a baseball bat during my first year of teaching. I could not help but recall how much her older brother had struggled with reading and how unfortunate he had not been a migrant student whom Coleman could have helped. He was not in attendance with the rest of the family I learned, but was sitting in the county jail on drug charges. I said a silent, special prayer for him before turning my attention to Jeanett's speech.

"Fellow Classmates. This is our victorious day. We are seeing in what is a big way for us a mission accomplished, an achievement won, a goal reached. It has been difficult, but we have even greater challenges ahead because we are going out into one of the greatest and most mysterious ages in the history of mankind. It is an age of atomic energy, radar, rocket ships, interplanetary exploration with satellites, computers and mobile phones, as well as social and economic experimentation of all kinds. It is no day for the negative thinker. It is no day for the weak willed. It is no day for those who lack faith in God and in man.

Shakespeare said, 'All the world's a stage, and all men and women are merely actors.' He was not quite right, however, for on stage there are rehearsals, but with life there is no trial run, no dress rehearsal in the life we live day to day. So let us go out and arm ourselves with education, love, and faith, using our brains to learn more, think more, and plan more as we take our next steps into the journey of tomorrow. Let us believe deeply and reverently in God, in ourselves, and in our neighbors. Let us not stop here at this point in our education, but let's move on to learn more and more in order that we may help bring this world closer to the goal God had in mind when He first sent it whirling into space. Our education is the only real thing that will help us make such a difference."

I was so proud of her and proud for her family, for all the families who had pushed these kids to come to school every day, to work hard and make their grades, to hit this mark.

We broke up the speaking parts with various musical selections. The students sang two songs they had learned from the music teacher who came to Wilkes one day every two weeks and pulled students from PE class. They sang a song called "Somebody Bigger than You and I" and the new but highly popular Debbie Boone song "You Light Up My Life." The twenty-one of them did not make a great chorus, but they did a pretty decent job considering how little practice they had had together with the piano teacher.

Carnell Warren was given the honor of closing the ceremony with the benediction. He was nervous, but he liked to preach, so he agreed to lead the prayer. "Please stand and bow your heads. Our Heavenly Father, bless us all as we leave here tonight, and seal in our hearts the knowledge gained during our time here at Wilkes. Strengthen us each day with your love, and overpower us with the ability to love one another. Build us strong with your truth and wisdom that we may help create for one another a world that blooms daily with abundant human kindness---All for Your Glory. Amen."

As our recessional music began and the students were walking out, many tears were shed, not just in happiness for successful children, but in sadness for the end of the Wilkes School that would no longer have children like these walking in and out each day in the years ahead. It would be left vacant and empty, soon overgrown with kudzu and Johnson grass, an eye sore in a community already blighted with rundown, ramshackle houses, tractor sheds, and other out buildings, a new haven for graffiti artists and drug deals. It was indeed sad going back years later and seeing that it had come to such decay and ruin rather than being renovated into something useful to the community.

Darkness fell on the Delta again, and we all said our goodbyes to the school, to an era, to each other. In my years at the Wilkes School, I had grown so much as an educator, had learned in real life the average joys of daily living that poverty will rob from people. My years there were without doubt my hardest, partly because it was the time when I had the fewest resources to help my students, and partly because I was trying to change how those children, my chirren, saw the world and how they fit in it. I had never worked harder or tried to change such a big picture. I loved Wilkes. It was my starter wife, and I devoted myself to her and the children we cared for together. Putting her in a grave was almost as hard as putting my mother in her own.

28 Night of Horror

Money, MS   May 1979

So many people wanted to talk to me afterwards and ask about the plans for the school-- like I knew! Coleman left earlier than the three of us, so I did not get a chance to thank her for coming or to tell her goodbye. Marin, John Sylvester, and I were almost the last ones to leave that night, and we all three needed to unwind a little, so we headed to Greenwood to our usual watering hole. We parted company around midnight, and Marin and I headed to the farmhouse.

Around three in the morning the phone rang, startling us both, waking us from deep sleep. I answered it, and a voice said, "Miss Coleman needs you. Room 241 at the Ramada Inn. You should hurry."

"Who is this? What's wrong with Coleman?" But the line went dead.

I told Marin, "I don't know what's going on, but some guy just said Coleman is in some kind of trouble and I should hurry to the Ramada Inn. Call John Sylvester and tell him to meet me in the hotel parking lot. You can come, too, if you want, but I have to go."

"No, you and John Sylvester can handle whatever it is, I'm sure. I'll stay here, but call me as soon as you can." I threw on some khakis and a tee shirt and headed to Greenwood.

John Sylvester was waiting for me when I arrived, and the two of us headed upstairs to the room number the man had given me on the phone. The door was slightly ajar, and I could see the room was mostly dark with just a little light coming from what I assumed was the bathroom. I knocked on the door and called out to Coleman, but got no answer. I called again. Nothing. I pushed open the door and saw Coleman lying on the bed, actually tied to the bed, wearing only her bra and panties. Her eyes were closed.

"Go downstairs to the lobby. Call an ambulance first, and then call the police," I said to John Sylvester. As he turned to go, I went inside, conscious to disturb things as little as possible to protect the crime scene. I was shaking and breathing hard as I went over to Coleman and checked her pulse. She was alive! "Thank you, Jesus!" I whispered. I didn't know whether to untie her or leave her as I found her; from all assessment I could make, she just seemed to be passed out but not unconscious. "Coleman! Coleman! Open your eyes!" I shouted.

I slap-patted her cheeks. "Coleman, it's Gresham. Open your eyes! Look at me! Coleman, wake up!! Come on, girl. Wake up!"

She opened her eyes, barely, and I could tell from the look in her eyes she was evidently heavily drugged. "Oh, hey, baby," she whispered slowly, barely able to speak and completely unaware she was tied up, and then she was out again. I decided to untie her and try to get her to sit up even though the police would probably rip me a new one for doing so. I couldn't just leave her that way though. I covered her with the duvet that lay across the foot of the bed. I heard a siren in the distance, so I just pulled her close to me and held her until help arrived, incredibly thankful she was alive at least.

I followed her ambulance to the hospital, gave them what information I could about her name, address, employment, etc. I had not thought to look around the hotel room for her purse or her wallet. I told the nurse at the ER reception desk to send the charges to me.

"Is she on your insurance policy? Our policies won't allow me to charge her bill to you if she isn't on your policy."

Her comment and insensitivity infuriated me. "Did I say file it on my insurance? No, I did not! I said. Send. Me. The bill. I don't give a shit about your damn policies. I want her treated and given the best care. So take down my information so we can clear up the payment. Please!"

"Are you related to her?"

"No, I am not. Why does that matter?"

"Because we have to know the next of kin in case something happens."

"Her next of kin lives in Jackson. I'm all you have to deal with right now. The police can fill in the rest later."

"Well, if you aren't her next of kin, we can't share any of her medical information with you."

"Are you not listening or are you just plain stupid, lady? I didn't ask for any special treatment. I didn't ask for you to tell me anything about her condition. I simply said I would pay the damn bill. So just take down my information and Send. Me. The Bill."

About that time John Sylvester walked into the ER followed by a detective who walked over to me and said, "We need to talk."

We stepped away from the desk to a corner where we could have some privacy. "Mr. Hamilton here tells me you got a strange phone call telling you this woman needed your help. Is that right?"

"Yes, it was a man who told me what room she was in and where and said I needed to get there in a hurry. So I called my friend here and the two of us went up to the room and found her tied to bed."

"Who called the ambulance? And who called us?"

"I asked John Sylvester to call while I went into the room. I tried not to bother things too much, but I did untie her and cover her up because she was wearing just her bra and panties."

"Were there any lights on in the room when you went in?"

"Just the bathroom light."

"Did you go in the bathroom to maybe get a wet washrag to wipe her face and help her wake up?'

"No, I never went in there. Why are you asking?"

"Because there was a message, Mr. Gresham. It was written on the mirror with Miss Coleman's lipstick."

"What did it say?" I asked.

"Just a single word. MOSSBERG in all capital letters."

29 Disappearance

Sunnyside, MS   May 23, 1979

"Oh, shit! Marin is home alone!" I exclaimed to the detective. "Mossberg is a guy that kidnapped my wife several years ago. I gotta go!"

As I spun around to race out the door, I called to John Sylvester, "While I'm on the road, call Marin. Tell her to get the pistol and hide in the pantry until I get there. She'll probably know it has something to do with Mossberg, but don't tell her anything else. Just hang up. I don't want her in a total panic. I need her to be as clear headed as possible."

"I'll get a patrol unit headed that way, too, but there's more you need to know," the detective said, "so I'll follow you with my lights on so any other patrol on the highway won't stop us. Drive as fast as you dare but be careful. We don't need any more damage tonight."

"It'll be a caravan then," said John Sylvester, "because I'll be right behind you guys as soon as I get in touch with Marin."

"Really, John, I need you here in case Coleman wakes up. I don't want her to wake up here in the hospital alone, not after what she has been through. And explain to her why I had to leave."

"Oh, yeah. Sure thing, Buddy Boy," he said. "I understand. Once things settle down here and they get her stable, I'll come on out to your place. You get going."

The detective and I raced to the city limits of Greenwood and headed out of town toward Hwy. 49. Once we hit 49, we really let the ponies run, racing down the road at 90 mph. Once I hit the gravel road headed to the farmhouse, I lost the detective in my dust and was just praying I didn't sling up any rocks to bust out his windshield. When I turned up the drive toward the house, I could see blue lights from the patrol that had been dispatched by the detective. The officer and detective had evidently been on the radio together, and the patrolman had been told to wait outside since Marin would have a gun. As I got out of the car, he told me he had been there about three minutes but had not seen any movement inside or outside the house, just dogs barking.

The detective sent the patrolman around back, and he and I briefly argued about who would go into the house first, so we decided we would go in together. I would draw out Marin while he checked each room. I tried the front door and found it locked. That was a good sign I thought. I unlocked it and stepped into the living room and called out to Marin. Nothing. My heart jumped into my throat, hearing that blaring silence. I called her name louder, and that is when I heard her opening the pantry door in the kitchen. "Don't shoot, Honey. It's me," I called out. She ran into the room and into my arms, shaking but seemingly still in relative control of herself. "Where's the gun?" I asked.

"I left it on a shelf in the pantry. John Sylvester told me that you and the police were racing to the house and for me to get the gun and hide. What's going on, Bern? John wouldn't tell me anything else; he just said he had to go and that I needed to hurry and hide, but I knew it had to be something to do with Mossberg. It's him, isn't it?""

I heard the detective call out an "all clear" to the patrolman. They had a brief discussion, and the detective told him he could clear the scene with dispatch and leave. I guided Marin to the couch, and the three of us sat down in the small, cramped living room. "Yes, baby, it's Mossberg. He's close around somewhere; we just don't know where. He kidnapped Coleman tonight and left her tied up in a room at the Ramada Inn. I figured that was his ploy to pull me away in the middle of the night so he could find you here alone. I'm so glad you're safe."

"Dammit to hell!" she screamed. "The bastard!! That asshole bastard!! Is Coleman ok? He didn't hurt her, did he?"

"I don't think so, but I really don't know the extent of what happened to her. When I found her she was totally out of it, drugged up with something and unable to really talk. We got her to the hospital, but that's when the detective here...I'm sorry, sir, but I can't remember your name."

"It's Hirt. Detective James Hirt," he said.

"Yeah, and that's when Detective Hirt showed up at the hospital with John Sylvester and told me Mossberg left his name written on the bathroom mirror."

"That's right, Mr. and Mrs. Gresham, and there's more I need to tell you about and ask you about. You see, we found what we thought was a pipe bomb in the bathroom as well."

"Oh, my God!" Marin said. "Back at Delta State he was always threatening to wire up a bomb to explode when I cranked my car! I didn't really think he knew how to make a bomb though."

"Well, of course, we had to do an immediate evac of everyone in the hotel and get the bomb squad out. Turns out it was a fake, but it sure caused a big commotion."

"What I don't understand," I said, "is why he took Coleman. She has nothing to do with any of this. This is all about Marin, and Coleman just met Marin tonight for the first time."

"Where did you meet Miss Coleman?" he asked.

"At Bern's school in Money for the Eighth Grade Promotion Program. The school district is closing the school at the end of this year, so this last promotion program was a big To-Do. Every big

362

wig in the county was there, and Coleman came because she used to work with Bern."

"Did you sit together during the ceremony?"

"Yes, Bern was on stage and in charge of the program, so Miss Coleman sat with me and John Sylvester."

"And tonight was the first time you two have had any contact?" he asked Marin.

"Yes, sir. Tonight was our first meeting."

"That must be it then. He must have been there in Money, too, and saw her with you and your husband. He may have assumed she was a good friend of yours if he saw her sitting beside you and talking with you."

"Geez, how creepy," I said, "to think he may have been right there in the room with us and we never saw him. Never saw him come in or leave or at any point during the program."

The police radio on his belt crackled to life. "A unit has found the Coleman car," a disconnected voice announced. "In the parking lot of Wilkes School in Money."

"Damn! He was there! He must have taken her from the parking lot when she left," Detective Hirt surmised.

"Just like he took me from a parking lot," Marin recalled.

"Hearing you talk about this, it seems I do remember reading a report a few months back about a kidnapper recently released from prison that we tried to locate when we heard he was prowling around Greenwood High School," he said. "I've been looking for this guy off and on ever since that report landed on my desk, which is why I vaguely recognized the name on the mirror."

"And we still don't know where he is," I mumbled in exasperation. "Or where he will turn up next."

"Well, I'm hoping Miss Coleman can give us a current description of him, can tell us what kind of vehicle he's using, and anything he might have said to her to clue us in on his plans or where he has set up his home base."

The radio blared again. "Your vic is awake now. Are you returning to the hospital?"

"On my way," he said. "Look, folks, until we get all of these puzzle pieces together to give us a full picture of what happened tonight, I need you both to lay low. Keep your doors and windows locked, your curtains and blinds drawn. Don't go out after dark, and don't go anywhere alone. Stay together. And keep that gun close by. I hope you won't need it, but just in case. After all, we ARE dealing with a dangerous guy here evidently."

"Yeah, a maniac loose in the wind."

30 Purpose and Profile

Sunnyside and Greenwood, MS May 23, 1979

As Detective Hirt stood to leave, we saw car lights coming up the driveway toward the house. Detective Hirt drew his pistol and ordered Marin and me to go hide in the pantry until he could determine who was showing up at our house in the black dark just before dawn. What a relief to find out it was John Sylvester and not Mossberg!

"Well, let me get on back to Greenwood and see if Miss Coleman can give us any good intel on this Mossberg character. I'd like you to come along, too, Mr. Gresham, in case she gives us something critical that we don't recognize as critical but which you might. And she is more likely to work with us if there is someone there with her that she trusts. You know the blacks are always reluctant to talk to us. Mrs. Gresham, you're welcome to come along as well if you don't feel safe staying here right now."

"I'd feel safer here than anywhere else," she said. "It's unlikely he knows where this house is, and he can't drive up out here without my knowing he's coming up the driveway."

"No, you can't stay here by yourself, Marin. Be sensible. I know you're mad. Maybe even a part of you hopes he will show up so you can shoot him. But let's be smart about this. Please go change your clothes and go with us."

"Really, Bern. I'm ok. I think his drama is over for tonight. That's his pattern. Scare the shit out of me and then disappear for days or weeks. Sometimes even months. He won't be within a hundred miles of here the rest of tonight," she said.

"I can stay here with you, Marin, if you want. You really shouldn't stay by yourself," John Sylvester offered.

"That's a good idea," I said. "You sure about this John? I mean, it really isn't your fight."

"If it involves a problem for my two best friends, it IS my fight, too. Go ahead, Buddy Boy. Marin and I will hold the fort until you get back. We'll just drink some coffee and have some breakfast and hang out. It'll be fine. You go ahead."

I would trust my life to John Sylvester, so I knew he would defend Marin to the death if need be. Like she said though, Mossberg would come and go like a ghost. He would pop into her life to threaten her in some way, and then he would go away and patiently wait, wait for her to grow casual in her habits again, and then BAM! There he was again. So chances were, kidnapping Coleman was his trick of the day, and we wouldn't see hide nor hair of him for a while.

At the hospital, Coleman was still woozy but awake enough to talk to Detective Hirt. I stood beside her bed and held her hand to assure her she was safe now.

"I'm sorry," she said, "but I can't really tell you much. I was in the parking lot to leave the program when this man I don't know grabbed me from behind in a kind of choke hold."

"Did he say anything to you at that point?"

"Yes. Don't fight me or I'll kill you right here where you stand."

"Did you see a weapon of any kind?"

"Yes, he had a knife, a big knife, kind of like a hunting knife."

"What happened when he threatened to kill you?"

"I stopped struggling, of course. That's when he stuck a needle in my arm and everything went black."

"Do you recall him putting you in a vehicle?"

"No, I don't know anything from the time he stuck me with the needle and waking up here."

"So there was no conversation between you two in the vehicle?"

"No. Not that I can remember. Who IS this guy? Do you know who he is?"

"Yes," I told her. "He's a stalker who has been terrorizing Marin since her senior year at Delta State. Evidently he was at Wilkes and assumed you were a good friend of Marin's since you sat together, so he took the opportunity to use you to terrorize her again."

"Oh, my god, Gresham! For real?"

"That's our theory on why he kidnapped you anyway," the detective said. "Unless there's something you aren't telling us."

"Like what? I told you I don't know this man. I've never seen him before. He just came up behind me out of nowhere with that damn big ass knife. What else could I do other than what he told me to do?"

"I'm sorry, Miss Coleman. I didn't mean to insinuate you were to blame in any way. I'm just trying to figure things out by looking at every angle."

"Well, look at another angle," I said angrily. "She had nothing to do with this stunt. Like I told you, she didn't even know Marin before tonight."

I was weary and worried and I needed sleep. I had been up almost 38 hours with only three hours of sleep, so I was punchy and easily agitated. Thankfully, I think Detective Hirt knew I was close to my crash-and-burn point and took no offense when I got smart with him.

"So you have no idea how you came to be in that hotel room?"

"What hotel room? What are you talking about? You found me in a hotel room? What did he do to me?"

"It's ok, Coleman," I said. "I'm the one who found you. He evidently has our phone number and he called me to tell me where you were. We called an ambulance and the cops as soon as I found you. You were pretty out of it."

"Yep, lab tests say it was heroin he used on you, ma'am. He shot you up with enough to knock you out cold and brought you to Greenwood to the Ramada Inn where he left you tied up in a room there. There is no evidence of a sexual assault, if you are worried about that, so that is good news."

I had been afraid to even think about that, let alone ask about it, so it was a relief to know Mossberg had not done any harm to Coleman physically. She would be alright once the heroin was fully dissipated from her system. Chances were good that Mossberg knew very little about her, but he did know her name now and probably got that from her driver's license, which meant he also knew her address. I insisted to Detective Hirt that she be given protective watch while in the hospital and when she went home, just in case Mossberg had more plans that involved her. I was scared for Marin, and I was scared for Coleman. In all actuality though I should have been more concerned for myself.

A couple of days after Coleman was released, Detective Hirt came to see me at the farmhouse.

"Look," he said. "I know you are concerned about your wife and your friend, Miss Coleman, but the FBI profiler helping us with this case says most likely if anyone gets hurt here, it will be you, Mr. Gresham."

"Me? What makes you think that?"

"Well, he obviously doesn't want to kill Marin. He had a chance to do that years ago and didn't do it. He had a chance to kill Miss Coleman, but he didn't kill her either. And he didn't rape either woman even though he had the opportunity, so we think he is most likely impotent. He didn't beat up either woman, and so we have no reason to think his goal is any kind of physical harm. We don't think his goal is ever to kill Marin, ever; his goal is just to terrorize her, for as long as he can get away with it. He knows if he kills her, he has no one over which to exercise that kind of control, and this IS all about control. So we are pretty certain he will not harm either lady physically other than kidnapping if he gets a chance. And he will kidnap her again only to scare her. But you, sir, are a problem to him. While we are pretty sure he is no killer when it comes to Marin, or even Miss Coleman, chances are he might direct that violence toward you."

"Well, I'll be honest with you, detective. I had a little brother murdered a few years ago, and it really changed me. He was only sixteen. Since then

I have carried a gun with me pretty much everywhere I go. I stood over his casket, looking at him, and I swore it would never be that easy to kill me. So if you run into Mossberg, tell him to be very careful. I might be bookish, but I've also got a black spot on my heart."

31 Photo Album

Sunnyside, MS   September 1979

Even though our eighth graders finished on May 22, the rest of us still had two more weeks of work for the school year. Our job was to focus on packing up everything that was to be moved out due to the Wilkes closing and junking everything else. Right after Coleman's kidnapping, though, Marin and I stayed home from work for three days as the detective had asked us to do, just in case Mossberg was anywhere near the schools, but that was our max. Neither of us was the kind to hide and cower in a corner, afraid to live our lives.

To be on the safe side though, I bought Marin her own gun, and a knife, and a taser. I also bought Coleman a gun, and I hired an off duty cop to teach both of them how to shoot with confidence and accuracy. I then hired a self-defense instructor to give them both a crash course, and I taught Marin a few boxing punches so she wouldn't shy away from using her fists too if necessary.

Aside from our focus on self-defense, we passed the summer by gardening, revamping lesson plans, and expanding our critter family. We bought some chickens, a couple of goats, and a donkey. The dogs had trouble adjusting to these new family members. They just could not understand why they were not allowed to chase them all over the place; after all, chasing them was the most fun ever! Sisyphus was the hardest to break from chasing, and Fuzz Lee became an egg thief.

Because of all the anxiety related to Mossberg, we also decided to make an offer to buy the little farmhouse because it gave us such comfort. The owners gladly accepted, and we became first time homeowners with our own little plot of earth. Meanwhile, we all sat on pins and needles, for days and weeks, Marin and I, John Sylvester, Coleman, and Detective Hirt. He thought it prudent to also inform the school administrators at each of our three schools about the potential threat, so they knew to be on the lookout for any sign of Mossberg even though we had no current picture of him. When Marin saw him cruising through the school parking lot back in January, she said he looked pretty much the same as he had when he attended Delta State, but it was anyone's guess as to whether or not he had changed his look to disguise himself now.

A sketch artist had drawn an educated guess of how he had probably aged and looked like now based on college pictures, but none of us knew for sure if he had long or short hair, whether he still wore a beard and mustache or not, whether he still dyed his black hair blonde or not. We just didn't know. So every stranger looked suspicious.

As for Coleman, John Sylvester and I helped her move to a new place immediately after the kidnapping since Mossberg now knew her name and address from her driver's license. He had also taken her clothes and shoes with him that night when he left the hotel, which was puzzling. The guy was just a total freak in every aspect, and none of us could get a handle on where he was or what he was planning. We just knew sooner or later he would crawl out of the woodwork again like the cockroach he was.

"I got two other officers working with me," Detective Hirt told me, "but we have precious little to go on since Miss Coleman couldn't tell us anything about his looks or his vehicle. The desk clerk who rented out the room to him that night said he barely remembered him, so he couldn't accurately describe him either. To make matters worse, the clerk was fired the next week for being drunk on the job, and we have not been able to locate him for any follow up interviews."

"So what is your next plan of action?" I asked.

"Well, we go out on all calls reporting any suspicious person or vehicles, and we sift through reports on the daily police blotter for any arrests of persons who match up in age. Truth be told though, until Mossberg is ready to pop up again, we are really just spinning their wheels and working blind."

The news was not encouraging. To keep our minds busy and try to reduce the stress and worry of Mossberg's return, Marin and I developed little story games we played in the evenings after supper. One of our favorite tricks was to sit on the couch and flip through our wedding album and the dozens of pictures we made in and around New Orleans on our honeymoon. We sometimes used our other photo albums too that contained childhood and family pictures, and pictures made on family vacations and other travels.

We would do this at least once a week, usually on Tuesday nights when TV was the most boring. To entertain ourselves, we would select a picture and make up a silly story behind it. One of us would start the story by giving two or three sentences, then the other had to embellish it with two or three more. We would go back and forth like that until one of us ran out of ideas, which usually took a while because we both possess a pretty creative bent.

School started up again, and still we waited for the cockroach, with no sign of him anywhere. Detective Hirt, however, had grown tired of the hunt that rendered no results.

"Look, man, I get it. I know you think you have reason to continue worrying; but honestly, I'm convinced Mossberg has left the area. Throughout the entire summer, we haven't found one shred of evidence he is still lurking anywhere around here in Greenwood. Some other cases have come up, too, that we need to work on just as hard as we've worked trying to find this invisible man, so I'm going to have to pull back my two guys from your case. We just don't believe he is around here anymore. We would have spotted him somewhere by now if he were anywhere near here. Hopefully, the FBI will find him, wherever he is, but I'm telling you he ain't here in Greenwood or anywhere else in Leflore County."

"So you're just going to write him off like a closed case? We all know better than that. We know his pattern is to show up and do something scary and outlandish and then disappear for a while. You know as well as we do that he is going to show up again. You're giving up the search now just about the time Mossberg is due to reappear. It's been three months, so he could pop up any day now!"

Detective Hirt assured me he would continue to work the case alone as much as he could, but I knew he was just trying to placate us and that very little attention would be given to locating Mossberg until he was involved in another incident.

So I began the new school year at Sunnyside Elementary, just a couple of miles down the road from the farmhouse. I could be at work within five minutes if I didn't end up behind a school bus stopping to load students, but I didn't like the idea of Marin's thirty minute drive to work alone. Marin was a little nervous about returning to work as well. We were pretty confident that Mossberg had not figured out where we were living, so it seemed logical to assume his only option would be hanging out near Marin's school.

Marin felt confident about her new skills with the gun and self-defense techniques, but she worried about the open spaces where she was most vulnerable. I had done everything I knew to do to protect her and help her protect herself if she was caught alone. I wanted her to be as safe as we could possibly make her. If she went somewhere that she couldn't legally take a gun, she had at least one of the other two weapon options, plus her fighting skill. This time at least, if Mossberg tried to take her, it would not be as easy as the first time.

One of the best defenses for her though, and my greatest comfort, was the plan we worked out with John Sylvester, a plan he created himself. "She just needs a twenty-four hour escort and body guard. Between the two of us, Buddy Boy, we can make sure the asshole has no chance of taking her again."

"What do you have in mind, John?"

"Look, I don't have to be at work until 9:00 each morning. I can just get up a bit earlier and meet Marin in the school parking lot when she drives in each morning. I'll make myself as invisible as possible and just watch to be sure Marin gets into the building safely. Easy peasy. No sweat," he said. "After school Marin can just stay in her building in areas where there were other people and wait for you to show up as her escort."

"It'll be about 4:15 before I can get there from Sunnyside because I have to wait until all the buses have left my campus," I explained. "I'm not sure my new principal at this new school will take to the idea of my leaving early every day."

"That's ok, Honey. I usually have some work I can do after school. That'll make less work for me to take home, too."

"Ok, then. So here's what I'll do. When I get there, I will park in the bus zone so you can see the Thunderbird from the office and then you'll know it's safe to leave and go to your car."

John Sylvester and I both were determined Marin would never be alone if at all possible. It drove her crazy at times, but it added to her confidence that odds were greatly diminished for any sneak attacks. Also, as long as John Sylvester and I kept low profiles in tailing Marin, perhaps Mossberg would be emboldened enough to show himself and maybe we could trap him. It was at least more of a plan than what the detective had for finding him.

Our safety plan worked like a charm the first four weeks of school, when there was still no outward signs that Mossberg was around. At least that is what we believed until a package arrived by mail one afternoon in early October with no return address.

"It has to be from Mossberg to come unaddressed like that," Marin cautioned. "It's a flat envelope though so it's not likely a pipe bomb," she said with intended gallows humor.

We briefly debated taking it straight to Detective Hirt in case it really was something from Mossberg. "But if it isn't from him," I said, "we'll look like two scaredy goobers making up ghost stories. I think we should open it first."

"Maybe so. Let's open it. If it's anything important, we'll take it to Hirt and maybe he'll reactivate the case."

I carefully ripped open the top of the big envelope. Inside were five photographs. The first one showed Marin and me from the back standing in front of St. Louis Cathedral in New Orleans. She drew a deep breath, and I turned burning red.

I flipped to the second photo. It was a picture of Marin and Coleman sitting side by side at Wilkes, looking at each other and smiling.

"Oh, God!! That's me at the Piggly Wiggly!" Marin said, as she stared at the third picture. It was a side profile of Marin standing in the produce section, smelling a cantaloupe.

The fourth was again a picture of the two of us from the back. We were holding hands and walking into church in Greenwood.

As unnerving as these four pictures were, though, it was the fifth that made our blood run cold. It was a photo of a man, definitely not me, from the shoulders down, his head cut off in the picture. He was sitting in our living room, on our couch, with our wedding album in his lap and his left hand on a sleeping Fuzz Lee beside him.

32 Quarrels and Reason

Greenwood, MS   October1979

"I am NOT going to my daddy's! I refuse to let that creepy asshole of a son-of-a-bitch run my life!"

"Marin. Baby, please, listen. He has been here. He knows we live here. It just is not safe for you to be here right now. If you won't go to your daddy's for a couple of weeks, then go to Jackson and stay with Connie and Walt. They'd love to have you stay with them a little while."

"Dammit to hell, Bern, you are not listening to me! I am not leaving our home! I'm not running!"

"Marin, dammit! You can't stay here right now!"

"I can stay wherever I damned well please, thank you very much, mister! You aren't my daddy, so stop acting like you are. I've made up my mind. Besides, you are in greater danger here than I am.

Or have you conveniently forgotten what Detective Hirt and that profiler said?"

"I can take care of myself, but it would be a whole lot easier if I knew you were safe somewhere else."

"I have a job! I can't just walk away for a mini vacation for a couple of weeks while you and John Sylvester play like you're Jim Rockford and Steve McGarrett," she said, referencing my two favorite TV shows.

"We're not playing around here, Marin. Stop minimizing this. He's been in our house, probably been through every drawer, looked through every photo album, learned what size bra you wear, what our bank statements look like. Who the hell knows what all he has learned about us from hanging around here! And he has obviously been here many times if Fuzz Lee lets that maniac pet him! Has any of that crossed your mind?"

Marin stopped short. "I just assumed the day the picture was taken was the only day he was here. But you're right. He's been here enough times to make friends with our most protective dog. Good Lord! I just want to scream I'm so mad!"

"I know; I know, love. I'm mad, too, but we have got to find a way to put a stop to all this. I'm not a murdering man, but given just one tiny reason, if we are ever face to face, I swear I will take him down and not bat an eye. But first we need to get these pictures to Hirt and get him and his guys back on the lookout. Mossberg is definitely around here and close by."

"I'll get my things. You lock up --for whatever good it does."

"Yeah, I know what you mean."

In Greenwood at the police station, Detective Hirt did not seem too interested in the pictures at first since they were taken in public places and some were months old. We could see him turn white though when he saw the last one. He had been in our house several times and had sat on that very couch in the picture. He knew immediately what he was seeing.

"That sonofabitch!! WHERE is he hiding that we can't find him?"

"I don't know but he's definitely in the area if he is hanging out at our house, looking at our picture albums, and making friends with our dogs. This has gone on long enough now. It's time to step up our game."

"I agree. I'm going to put in a requisition for some surveillance cameras around the perimeter of your home. If he returns, we'll get him on camera for a good look at him, and we will get a good look at whatever vehicle he is driving."

"That sounds good. Can you convince my wife to go stay with relatives for a few weeks?"

"Actually, if we really want to draw him out, we need for her to maintain her routines."

"You mean use her for bait? No! Absolutely not! No!"

"I'll do it," Marin immediately offered. "I'm not as afraid of him as I used to be. I have no problem going about my business and living my life. It'll probably piss him off real good that his pictures didn't scare me into running away somewhere. I hope it does anyway. I am sick of this bastard interfering in my life."

"Understood, ma'am. Y'all just sit tight and let me get things in gear around here. I hope we can get those cameras installed by early next week. Meanwhile, y'all just go to church tomorrow like usual, go to work Monday, do all your usual things."

At this point I knew there was no way Marin would ever agree to leave town for a while. She was a headstrong woman with plenty of grit as well as wit. It was one of the things I loved about her. She was no push over and was quick thinking.

I recalled the time she broke up a group of guys gambling in the stair well after school one day. She ordered them to follow her to the office when one smarted off and told her, "Lady, don't nobody give three fucks about you!" She simply told them, "You might be right, but we're going down there anyway." Believe it or not, every one of them got up and followed her. So I knew I could trust her to keep her head if anything went south, God forbid.

She could be hot headed, but she knew how to keep a situation from escalating.

On the drive back to Sunnyside Marin tried to ease my mind. "You know, honey, I'm a smart woman. I need you to trust my instincts, to trust me. This is all going to work out, I'm sure. Detective Hirt and his guys will find him, very soon. I'm convinced this is drawing to a close. But really, I am more concerned about you than I am for myself. You will be his target until he gets you out of the way somehow. I need you to take your role in all this more seriously."

"I do take it seriously, Marin. It's just easier for me to focus on taking care of myself if I don't have to focus on taking care of you, too. Do you know what I mean? It isn't that I don't trust you, or I don't trust what Hirt said. If I'm the primary target here, and not you right now, then why not leave and let me focus on that?"

"Because this involves both of us. Your safety is my safety. Your trouble is my trouble. Remember what your dad told us during our wedding reception. 'Marriage will bring double the joy and half the sorrow.' We are better off being together in our trials."

"I understand what you mean, and it's a nice thought during smooth sailing. But this is danger, and that makes it more than a trial."

"But I know you, Bern. You will get lax in the process if I'm not around because you are easy going. It's your nature. You will always be much more alert to things if I am around. It will also be a comfort to you to see me at home, in the kitchen, in the shower, in the yard. You said yourself I bring an ease to your life, that it comforts all the sore spots in your past to see me. So I need to stay. I want to stay."

"You're a hard headed woman, Marin Gresham."

"And you're a hard headed man, mister. So looks like we just need to call a truce on this argument. I'm staying. End of story. You take care of you. I'll be here for your comfort. And we will both be alright."

That night we showered together and took our comforts in each other's arms and eyes, in quietness and soft breathing after. Before falling asleep, I opened my prayer book to the page for The Blessing of the Marriage.

"By the power of your Holy Spirit, pour out the abundance of your blessing upon this man and this woman. Defend them from every enemy. Lead them into all peace. Let their love for each other be a seal upon their hearts, a mantle about their shoulders, and a crown upon their foreheads. Bless them in their work and in their companionship; in their sleeping and in their waking; in their joys and in their sorrows; in their life and in their death...that their home may be a haven of blessing and peace..."

33 Miscalculations

Greenwood, MS November 1979

The phone rang at 10:00 Sunday night. John Sylvester was on the line calling me.

"Look, man. I've had the twins all weekend, and I'll have to drop them off at school. So I won't be able to check on Marin in the morning at school. Can you cover it?"

"Oh, sure. I'll just let my team know I will run a bit late. That's all I'll need to do."

"Good deal. Sorry for springing this on you so late."

"John Sylvester, there's never any need to apologize for this. I can never thank you enough for the many, many times you have been there in that parking lot, rain or shine, giving both Marin and me great peace of mind. You're a friend of pure gold, and I love you, man," I said as he prepared to hang up.

"Stop it, you queer boy! I always knew you were a bit of a pansy," he teased.

"Yeah, well, you always liked hanging with me, so what's that say about you?" I jokingly retorted.

"Bye."

"Talk to you later."

The next morning, knowing my own lead foot and Marin's "granny driving," I decided to give Marin a ten minute head start. I knew I would catch up with her before she hit the Greenwood city limit sign. At least that was the original plan. John Sylvester called just as I was walking out the front door to say he would be "on patrol" after all.

As he drove into the high school parking lot, he saw a man pushing a limp woman into his car. Though he had no clear line of vision, there was no doubt Mossberg was taking Marin again, and he was about ten seconds too late to stop it. His forward progress was blocked by a school bus stopping to unload in the one way entry lane to the parking lot. Dozens of high schoolers were piling out in all directions around the bus, and there was nothing to do but watch the scene unfold like a slow motion nightmare.

John Sylvester jumped from his truck and began running and yelling toward the kidnapper's car. Everything suddenly blasted into high gear though, and the car was speeding away. The whole thing couldn't have taken more than a minute. Racing back to his own vehicle, he knew his only chance of helping was to follow, hopefully without being spotted. Thank God the bus had moved so he could round the circle and pull out through the back exit where he had seen Mossberg leave.

His heart and mind were racing as he sped along, desperate to spot the car ahead, finally catching sight of it just as they were heading into the morning rush hour. Traffic in Greenwood is always slow paced, but morning traffic was a crawl. For once he was thankful for slow, sleepy drivers that forced a slowdown once they hit the main highway. There were plenty of other vehicles he could use for concealment while still keeping his eyes on Marin's kidnapper.

"OK, man. Don't panic. Pay attention. Maroon Ford 500. Tag 3948 KM." He repeated this information, trying to commit it to memory, as he rummaged through the glove compartment for pen and scratch paper. "Don't know what year that model is," he thought to himself. "Doesn't matter. Just don't lose them and let him get away from you."

Traffic continued to move slowly, haltingly, as farm trucks, concrete mixers, school buses, mini vans, and sedans switched in and out of lanes. A cargo van cut him off, and for an instant the maroon Ford disappeared. Switching lanes when traffic pulled forward again, he was relieved to see the Ford five cars ahead of him.

"Now think, man!" he said to himself. "You need a plan other than just following this nut job wherever he's going with Marin." An old farm truck backfired somewhere behind him, and it was at that moment a chilling realization hit him. He had left his gun at the house.

"Fucking shit! Dammit to hell!" he cursed out loud. "Ok, take a deep breath. Damn, I wish I had one of those mobile phones! This is NOT going to be easy with no gun, no phone, and no help."

Mossberg turned off the main highway and headed toward the airport on the outskirts of town. It isn't a commercial airport, not particularly busy, but not totally isolated either. At this hour of the morning though the place was pretty deserted.

"What the hell is he planning to do at the airport?" Then it dawned on him Mossberg might have a pilot's license and a small plane, which would explain why it has been so hard for the police to find him. "Lord, please don't let him get her on a plane! Help me out here, will ya?"

He hung back as far as he dared where he could keep Mossberg in sight but keep himself from drawing any attention. Brake lights on the Ford glared an angry red as the kidnapper turned behind a row of small out buildings behind one of the large hangars. Mossberg stopped behind the second building, so John Sylvester parked at the end of the large hanger and crept around the corner to hide behind some shrubbery and watch. He watched as Mossberg carried Marin inside as she kicked at air and grabbed for his hair, evidently having roused from the drug that had knocked her out in the parking lot.

Getting his first really good look at Mossberg, John Sylvester couldn't help but draw a comparison. "Holy shit!" he thought, "that bastard looks just like Rasputin's twin!" Since Mossberg was taking her inside, John Sylvester decided to take the opportunity to try and find help or someplace open that early where he could use a phone to call Hirt, all without luck. There was no one around anywhere except Mossberg, Marin, and him.

Returning to his original hiding spot, he scouted the outside of Building #2 for closer concealment and made his way to the bushes closest to the building. When he was finally able to get a peek in the dirty window, he saw Mossberg was finishing up binding Marin to a straight chair.

"Holy shit! He really doesn't intend for her to escape!" he thought as he noticed all the rope. Mossberg had tied each of her ankles separately to each of the two front chair legs. Her hands, down by her side, were each tied separately to the two back legs. A very lengthy rope was wound around her waist and through the back slats of the chair, then crisscrossed over her chest, around under her arms and secured to the upper slat on the back of the chair. "Five separate pieces of rope! He really planned this to the last detail!"

John Sylvester could hardly hear what Mossberg was saying to Marin, or she to him, but it was obvious she was expressing her anger quite effectively, so Mossberg decided to gag her. He pulled a white handkerchief from his back pocket and stuffed the whole thing in her mouth. He then pulled out a roll of surgical gauze from his front pocket and began winding it around the lower part of her face so she couldn't spit out the handkerchief.

"That should hold you for a while and keep you quiet, Missy," he said. Mossberg laughed out loud as if he had just heard a great joke. "Otherwise, I'll have to pull out my quick and easy chloroform again. That stuff is really something, isn't it?"

Marin grunted something unintelligible, but he could see the profanity blazing in her eyes. Mossberg loved that angry look, loved to provoke it out of her. He loved the smell of her perspiration from all the struggling. There was great delight, evil and dark joy, in seeing her eyes and nostrils flare. "Well, I hate to leave such lovely company, but I've a piece of business before we can take off. So you sit here like a good little girl, and I'll be back in about five minutes. I gotta find someone to fuel the Cessna."

Mossberg picked up his car keys from the nearby table, which was a clue Marin might be left alone, at least briefly, for some reason. As Mossberg headed toward the door, John Sylvester scrambled around the far side of the building, hoping Mossberg would be leaving the same direction from which he had come in.

As soon as he heard the car tires on the gravel and the sound dissipating, he took his chance.

"Marin, it's me! I'm outside," he shouted. "I can't break the lock on the door, so I'm coming through the window. Just hold tight."

Finding a piece of brick and breaking the window pane, he reached in and unlocked the latch to open the window. Crawling through the small window proved more difficult and time consuming than expected. Under any other circumstances he was sure Marin would have laughed at him wiggling and shaking as he tried to squeeze through.

Finally he made it in and took off the gag and began cutting the ropes with his one weapon, his pocket knife. "We've got to hurry!" she said. "He'll be back any moment. He was only going around to the main terminal to get someone to fuel a plane for him."

As Mossberg approached the building on return, he immediately noticed the open window and knew someone must be inside with Marin. He stopped the car in the middle of the road, got out, and walked the rest of the way to the building, his rage mounting with every step. He reached in his pocket and pulled out the small revolver he had bought just ten days ago in Alabama. He had fired it only once, just to see what it felt like, since he was inexperienced and unfamiliar with handguns. He thought he might need one this time though, and true to form, his instincts were right.

Neither Marin nor her rescuer heard Mossberg approach or unlock the padlock on the door. Her savior was working frantically to cut the ropes with the small pocketknife that made the work difficult. He had managed to free the rope from her waist, chest, and shoulders. He was kneeling down in front of her, reaching over her, starting to cut her hands free when the door opened and a shot rang out at the same second.

"Surprise!" he said to Marin as John Sylvester slumped to the floor. "Aw, look at you all covered with blood. You're absolutely lovely when you're terrified. You're so pretty," he said in a congenial tone through a maniacal smile. Mossberg then turned immediately nasty. "Who is this fucking clown bleeding all over you and my floor?"

"You shot... him... in the back... you mother...fucking coward!"

"I said...WHO is he?"

"His name... is John... Sylvester Hamilton. He's a friend... of mine!"

"Why are you talking so funny, like you can hardly catch your breath? Did I scare you that bad?"

That was the moment Mossberg noticed there was more and more blood pooling around the chair, spirting from Marin's leg.

"Oh, Lord, Marin! Shit! That wasn't supposed to happen!" He knew in that instant that he had made a fatal mistake. The bullet must have gone through the man's chest and hit Marin also. Her head dropped forward, and she closed her eyes.

Mossberg went over to check her pulse and to see if indeed she had been struck by an exiting bullet. He felt a pulse in her neck, barely noticeable and growing fainter by the second. He saw the bullet wound in her leg, the spirting blood, and knew immediately he must have hit her femoral artery.

He leaned down to roll the man over. The man, dying but not yet dead, had just enough life left in him to grab Mossberg by the shirt and pull him close enough to plunge the pocketknife blade deep into Mossberg's throat, taking aim and hitting the jugular.

About this same time, Miss Malinda, the custodian at Sunnyside stepped into my classroom to let me know I had an important phone call in the office.

"Mr. Gresham, this is the principal at Greenwood High calling to check on Marin. She hasn't come into work this morning, and we wondered if she is sick."

"Call the police. I'm on my way."

During the ten minute head start, just before I walked out of the house, John Sylvester had called again. Dimple wanted to meet him half way to pick up the boys and their dirty clothes. She said she would take them to school, so John Sylvester was going to do his usual parking lot duty, but evidently something had gone terribly wrong.

By the time I got to Greenwood High School, several police cars were there, and Detective Hirt came running toward me. "Stay here and talk to the officers. Give them a description of Marin's outfit this morning and anything else you can tell them. We have a report of shots fired out at the airport. I need to go...."

"GO? Oh, hell no! What about Marin's kidnapping? I need you all over this right now. We're already at least an hour after the fact!"

"Look, Mr. Gresham. These two things might be related. I can't talk now, but I'll let you know something as soon as I get a handle on all of this going down right now."

"Let me go with you!"

"No, STAY HERE. Sergeant, take care of this guy for me, will ya?" Hirt sprinted away to his unmarked squad car.

At the airport, Detective Hirt and two squad cars pulled up to the main hanger. A crop duster pilot came out all agitated and yelled, "Y'all need to go behind here to Building #2. There's three injured people in there! We heard only one gunshot, but there's lots of blood. I think they all three might even be dead. Nobody's moving. An ambulance is on the way."

34 Shattered Lives

Greenwood, MS   November 1979

I sat outside Detective Hirt's office in a metal chair that was bolted to the floor. An hour passed. A female officer came by and unlocked his office door and told me I could wait inside. "There's a nice recliner in the corner. You'll be much more comfortable in there, Honey," she said.

I wanted to yell at her and berate her and tell I didn't give a damn about comfort. I wanted news of my wife! But I didn't. I just said, "Thank you, ma'am."

I waited almost three hours before Hirt returned. He was not surprised to find me in his locked office, so he must have sent word to the officer to put me there, knowing what he would have to tell me. When he saw me, he could only say he was sorry, over and over. I could not believe what he was saying.

"You told me he would never kill her! You told me I would be his target if there was any killing! How were you so off in this?"

"We don't believe from the look of the scene..."

"The scene?   The fucking scene!   This wasn't a goddamn play, you asshole!"

"I know, Mr. Gresham. Believe me, I know. But it looks like she was accidently shot. Mossberg, we think, was shooting at Mr. Hamilton, and the bullet went through and hit your wife. I am so sorry, but Mr. Hamilton was dead at the....was found deceased also."

"Don't you DARE fucking tell me Mossberg got away!"

"Oh, he's dead alright. Looks like even after being shot, Mr. Hamilton managed to dispatch him with a pocketknife.   He was dead at the....dead also when we found them."

****

The whole of Leflore County was aghast at the events at the airport. Murders like that just did not happen in Greenwood. This wasn't Jackson after all. From Greenwood to Money to Sunnyside to Itta Bena people were asking themselves how things could have gotten so out of hand with the police involved from the start.

Detective Hirt took the brunt of all the inquisitions from the mayor and police chief to the city council members, school board members, teachers, principals, parents of Marin's students, and even fellow officers. The questions were unending and unanswerable, and the daily barrage came from all angles. The detective was personally shaken at the loss of two good citizens whom he felt he had done his best to protect but had failed miserably in the end. Men die daily in on-the-job accidents, drunk driving wrecks late at night, in war and over poker games. It's much harder when a woman is killed, especially a young, vibrant, spitfire of a woman like Marin Gresham.

Agnes and Hardy Walters, though devastated, went around town with a stoicism typical of their generation. They may have cried at night, but they waited until the other was sleeping. They would slip off alone to the bathroom, sit on the side of the tub, and use a cold, wet washcloth to muffle the sounds of heaving sobs, and never letting the other know how broken they felt in this loss. When people at church or in the grocery store stopped them to ask how they were doing, their reply was always the same, "Gettin' by. We're gettin' by ok." They believed if they said it often enough, maybe one day it would be true.

Connie and Marin had grown so close in such a short period of time it seemed odd to some people that Connie could grieve so deeply for her sister-in-law who was more friend and sister than in-law. Marin had been there on the happiest day of her life—seeing her brother marry a woman perfectly suited for him and getting married herself to a man she loved implicitly but still did not quite fully trust after having been left at the altar once before. She didn't know if she would ever trust a man's love completely, but she was working on it every day because Marin had said she needed to let the past go. Marin had said giving fully was the only way to truly be alive. But Marin gave fully, and now she was dead. Connie could not seem to reconcile it all and struggled to talk about it to anyone, even to her husband.

Dimple Tate, John Sylvester's ex-wife and mother of his twin boys, was just mad as hell, mad with everyone involved in any way. Because she was so self-centered, she often was lacking in decorum in many situations, so I was not surprised when she accosted me after John Sylvester's funeral. "Well, I hope you're satisfied, getting John killed like that! You should have NEVER, I mean NEVER, let him watch over Marin like he did. THAT WAS YOUR FUCKING JOB, NOT HIS, you chicken shit little bastard!"

She was probably right, but being numb to the core, I stood there and just looked at her with no expression on my face. Not sadness, not anger, not shame, nothing. Not even pity, which would have been my usual response any other time a woman had lost her husband or the father of her children. It was good John Sylvester had always been a hard worker, one who never minded being sent to more training because he wanted to be one of the best at his job. His Social Security would provide for the boys plenty enough, but it would never be enough for the ever spoiled-rotten widow Dimple Tate. The real deep-seated cause of her anger was not that John was dead, but that she might have to actually go to work herself, which she had never had to do.

I had dealt with death plenty enough, but never did I ever expect to attend the funeral of my best friend without my wife at my side. I never expected to attend my wife's funeral without my best friend at my side. The past was littered with single deaths to grieve and process. Now there were two, double the agony of dark despair, double the pain deep in the gut that won't allow you to stand up straight, double the emptiness of laughter or even simple smiles in life.

I felt as though I had been holding on to one end of a long, sharp piece of razor wire, and I believed God held the other end. I knew if He ever let go, it was going to hurt in a way nothing ever had before. But I never really believed God would let go. I was wrong thinking He was on the other end. It was Mossberg who loosened the grip and sent the razor wire ripping through us three despite my best efforts. Had I known it was Mossberg on the other end, I would have turned loose and cut him to ribbons. I just didn't know.

Now I was cut into hundreds of pieces, like so many pieces of confetti, but the pieces aren't colored anything but black. I could blend perfectly into any night sky, fully camouflaged among the stars and planets, but having no purpose there. I could not bear to go back home to Sunnyside after the funerals, to even look upon those things that had been part of our life. I could not imagine even touching those things without a feeling of electrocution, the pain so intense.

I did not want to sit on the couch where she liked to lie down with her head in my lap. I didn't want to look across the table to the spot where she sat to eat her supper with me. I didn't want to put a fork in my mouth that might have some little essence left of her lips. I didn't want to wear the same clothes I had worn when we worked in the garden together, or a shirt she might have touched when she reached around me with her hands on my back to kiss me. I could not even fathom patting the fur of one of the dogs where she might have stroked its ears or muzzle. I just could not.....could not.....

I never set foot in the house after that. I put the little farmhouse up for sale for twenty cents on the dollar to get it sold quickly, and it sold within three days. The only stipulations were that they destroy any paperwork they found in the house and that they take the house as is---every stick of furniture, every dish in the cabinets, every curtain in the windows, every piece of clothing in the closets, every can of food in the pantry. I went to the house the day of the murders only to pick up our four dogs and two cats to take them to a colleague's house who had a place in the country nearby. He said he would take his trailer over the next day to pick up the goats and donkey, and his wife would gather the chickens. He agreed to keep them all and care for them as long as I needed him to do it. I gave him $500 for their food and told him I wasn't sure I could come back for them. He said he understood.

I immediately resigned from my teaching job at Sunnyside and walked away with the clothes on my back. I moved into the Hotel Irving on Howard Street, into a single room with a bath. I went to Gibson's and bought six new pair of underwear, some socks, and toiletries. I went next door to Phil's Squire Shoppe and bought four new shirts and three pair of pants. I went to Connelly's and bought a pair of tennis shoes and some dress shoes. I went to Kornfeld's and bought some jeans and tee shirts. Beyond that little bit, I didn't really think I'd need a wardrobe since I had no plans to be in public much.

I remembered the words of my poem..."Montana mountains speak to me..." I remembered the bare heart torn to pieces and turned to dust, covered with footprints of real bears. My plan was simply to hibernate.

35 Round Three After Five

Greenwood, MS   December 1979-1980

My room at the Hotel Irving had one floor lamp in a corner with a club chair, a double bed, a night stand, and a bureau with six drawers.   The bathroom had a sink, a toilet, and a shower. There was no TV, no radio. While I still had presence of mind to set up house in my one room hide-away, I went out and bought myself a large cooler so I could stock a few beers on ice. The housekeeper in charge of cleaning my room came on duty at noon each day. I paid her a salary and expense money to bring me lunch each day when she reported to work. Some days I ate. Most days I did not.

Most days I just lay in bed, amid the three dark corners and silence. I shaved and showered only when Helen, the housekeeper, told me I was stinky, which was about every four or five days. She would say to me, "Missa G, you cain't do this to yo sef. You is a yong man and needs sunshine and frush err. Lemme calls someone fodge jew, to hep chew."

"I'm doing ok, Helen. Thank you," I'd say, but very little else. I had no desire to speak aloud, to talk to anyone. Every once in a while, I would get up and sit in the lamp light for a few minutes, but then the darkness would overtake me again. I felt as if I lived beneath the waves of some mighty black water, that I was like some great ship taken down in a tidal wave that ripped apart my hull and riggings. I was the captain gone down with the ship, deeper into the black water where sea vipers sting, where the pressure grinds the bones to powder and turns flesh to jellied death. I was drowning in misery, pain, and grief, and I was reconciled to dying. I did not care if fish nibbled at parts of me. "Hello, Darkness, my old friend. I've come to talk to you again." Thank you, Paul Simon, for living in my head then.

I had been living in the hotel for a month when someone knocked on my door in mid-December. I had been lying in bed naked and did not want company, so I ignored it. I knew Helen's knock and knew it was not her. I didn't know who it was, and I did not care. Poe came to mind. "Suddenly there came a tapping, as of someone gently rapping, rapping at my chamber door."

"Go away!" I muttered, and nothing more.

"Honey, open the door. It's me. Claire. Let me in, please."

I wrapped the sheet around me and opened the door. I turned and walked back to the bed without saying a word to her. She closed the door, set down a suitcase, and sat down in the club chair in the lamp light. She said nothing. We just let the silence hang in the air.

After an hour of just hearing each other breathe, she said, "I won't let you do this."

"What?"

"Waste away."

"My life, my choice."

"We'll see," she said. And so it went for several days with minimal conversation. Each morning she dressed and went out to get us both breakfast.

"A bite or two is not enough. Eat some more."

She insisted I shower every day and shave at least every other day. She would strip and get in the shower with me when my hair needed washing.

"Turn around and get on your knees so I can reach your hair." I complied. She'd stand behind me and wash my hair. "Hold your head back so the soap doesn't get in your eyes, Honey." I complied. "Here, towel off." I complied.

She slept naked in the bed with me, and when I would turn away from her, she would spoon me and kiss my back between my shoulder blades. "You'll be ok, Sweetie," she'd say, and each morning after breakfast she'd lay out some clothes. "Put these on. It's time for our walk." She would wrap her arm through mine, and we'd walk up Howard Street to Barrett-Hodges Drug Store and back. We walked after each meal and at 10:00 at night. I didn't mind the bedtime walk. The street was dark and silent and empty, and it felt like my soulmate. Anyone seeing us probably thought she was the mate, seeing us walk arm in arm or hand in hand, but it all meant so little.

We spent an inordinate number of quiet hours together, just sitting in the room among the silence. She would lie in bed reading and stroking my hair while I slept away most the day and night. Her love was patient in waiting for life to return to me. Every night I would feel her roll in close to me. I felt her legs, her breasts against my back, her pubic hair against my buttocks. But it was feeling without sensation, like touching your nose when you're drunk. Your finger feels the nose in place, but your nose doesn't feel your finger.

This was a different Claire in her motives. She was not the hungry tiger ready for a good bang or some oral sex. She was patient in waiting. She had come because she wanted to be with me, because she was once again alone, having just divorced her fifth husband. She wanted us to try again but knew it would take a long time for me to heal, IF I could heal, and she was willing to invest the time. She believed a third time around would work this time between us.

Christmas came and went with no celebration or feasting or gifting. We were just there in the room, showering, walking, sleeping.

On New Year's Eve we crawled into bed after our bedtime walk. "Kiss me tonight, Bern," she asked. I turned away with a simple, "No, not tonight."

1980 rolled in with fireworks over the Yazoo River that we could see from the hotel window. Another week went by and another. Time just melted the days and nights into an oblivious river of wasting.

Then the night of reckoning came. She lay next me and moved her leg across my groin and I stiffened. She propped herself up on her elbow and took me in her hand. "AH! There's my man!" she said through a smile. She rolled over onto me, and I let her. We twisted and turned and groaned, hard and mean, soft and tender. But I never opened my eyes.

I did not want to see Claire in the dimness of that room. I didn't want to see Claire at all. I wanted only to see Marin in my mind's eye. When I could not look at her and still could not bring myself to kiss her, she knew a third time was not possible. I was too broken, and even Claire's wonderful, ecstatic sexual love could not heal me as she had always been able to do in the past.

Two days later, after having spent a little more than two months with me, she packed her suitcase to leave. "I shouldn't have come," she said.

"But you did."

"Yes. I did. I wanted to ... I don't know. Save you? Heal you? Love you? Start over. I don't know."

"Thank you, Claire, for coming." I kissed her right before the elevator door opened. She stepped inside and descended back into the world of real living people.

I mouthed the word "goodbye" just as the elevator door closed, and I never saw Claire again.

36 Miss Helen's Soul Music

Greenville, MS   1981

I stayed a little over a year at the hotel on Howard Street, and over the course of that year, my housekeeper Helen became a really close friend, almost like a mother figure even though she was old enough to be my granny. Her wisdom about pain and suffering from the late 1920's through the Civil Rights Era was a catalyst for raising me up from the living dead.

Miss Helen would come sit with me and visit an hour or so before starting her noon shift cleaning the hotel rooms. If I was doing reasonably well, we would talk about whatever was on her mind or heart, or on mine. If it was a dark day, she'd just sit in the room with me as I lay in bed, and she'd softly sing some of the Negro spirituals that gave strength to so many. I think she thought if those songs gave her people hope and courage to press on despite all the violence and indignities they suffered, perhaps they would stir the same hope and courage in me.

"You needs sum music in yo life," she'd say. "Music can soffens up the hardess heart and can mends the most broke. I'm tellin' you, Missa G, you gets some music up in her, and you will gets betta."

"I don't know that I want to get better, Helen. I'm broken down almost beyond repair. I'm not sure there is any more happiness in this life for me. I can eat and walk and breathe and sleep, but I can't seem to find my way to living."

"You hursh dat kine a talk. Dat ain't no way for no man to be talkin', speshly ah yong mans like you be. You's gone live til da Lord take you, and I believes He ain't quittah you yet. Dares more to come. Believe me, dares more."

"I tell you, Helen. I'm broken, utterly broken."

"Naw, you ain'ts broke, Missa G. I seen broke mens. Mens strung up and gutted like hogs wid day peckas cut off. Now dat be a broke man. You gots a huge crack in yo soul rat now, but you ain'ts broke until you is dead."

One day Helen came in much earlier and immediately made a demand. "Gives me qwenny dollas."

"What?"

"You heard me. Qwenny dollas. I needs qwenny dollas."

"OK. Why?"

"Nevva you minds dat. Just gives me da money and you kin fine out layda."

She came back an hour later with a Philco radio. "Her ya go, Missa G. Music time!" She plugged it in and tuned in to a Memphis station. "Now we's gone gets you back out in the wurl, likes it or not."

Every day after that she came to visit and turn on the radio. Sometimes she could get me out of bed for a little "booty shaking" as she called it. "It's good fada soul to shakes things 'round a bit." Half the time she'd holler from the doorway, "Put yo pants on, Missa G. I'm comin' to dance." And she'd laugh at herself with such joy. I loved her laughter. It was the one thing in life at that point I can say truly made me feel something good inside.

One day I asked her, "Why are you doing all this for me, Helen? What do you care about a broken down white man?"

"You ain'ts as broke as you might believe. I kin still sees dat spark in you. I knows who you is, Missa G. I knows what you done fa Woodrow's momma years ago, payin' her rent fa ova a yur after dat po' boy drownded. I know Miss Tiny tried to get you fiyard and runned off dat nice Miss Coleman. Miss Tiny was wrong 'bout chew. Thank Gawd she be dead now and not runnin' erry bodies bidness. You is a decent mans, a hurt mans with a broke heart, but suff'rin' builds us up fa bedda thangs to come if we can bees patient and not gives up."

Again she reminded me, "You's ain'ts broke til you's dead."

I thank God every day for Helen, dear Miss Helen who refused to let me give up. Her singing and dancing and preaching at me daily gave my mind some things to think about beyond just wanting to stop breathing. Late nights when blackness would wash over me from sobs like a wounded animal, her blackness would pop into my mind and the sound of her singing would stir my mind to sing along in a soft whisper to replace any whimper.

424

She was a strong woman who was not afraid to break rules for a good cause. Getting me out of bed to dance with her was something she considered a good cause. She truly believed I was worth saving.

I knew though after several months with Miss Helen that I could not hide out in the hotel forever. I would need to find myself another hide out, one more permanent if I was really going to survive this gigantic hole in my life. Moving out of the hotel though would mean leaving my only friend, Miss Helen, behind. I didn't know if I would have strength enough to walk away, and saying goodbye was the hardest day I lived since losing Marin and John Sylvester. I had been doing much better in keeping the darkness at bay, and it was Miss Helen who told me it was time to start thinking about leaving.

For the last two months I was there at the hotel, I had a realtor looking for me a new home. I could not stay any longer in Leflore County, so I told Aletha Abernathy it had to be a place in Greenville or Memphis. All of our conversations were conducted by phone; I never even actually met her face to face, but she found me a house in Greenville, with everything I had asked for in the way of style, space, and surroundings.

By phone I hired an interior decorator to furnish it in advance of my move in. I also hired an attorney to handle all the legal transactions on my behalf so all I had to do was walk out of the hotel, get in the car, and drive....home.

The house was typical Southern gentry, massive and spacious with large windows that measured almost floor to ceiling. It had a wrap-around porch where I could sit outside in the shade any time of day no matter where the sun hit the house. It sat on a ten acre plot of prime Delta land just outside the Greenville city limits, surrounded by a beautifully manicured, luscious lawn of what I called "golf course" grass. The driveway was flanked on each side by magnificent blooming forsythias, and the edges of the sprawling lawn were bordered on the front and both sides with redbud trees, dogwoods, silver leaf maples, and gingko trees. Eighty year old oaks stood strategically placed for shade in three different parts of the lawn. But it was the veranda on the back of the house that was my special place.

Standing on the veranda, looking at the backyard of lush green that had a gentle slope, it ran like a young girl down to the river's edge. Beyond "The Slope" was a white sandbar about the size of a football field, and lapping at its edges was the

Mighty Mississippi, rolling past, pushing time along, to help me push my time more and more each day toward healing.

It was a beautiful home, completely unlike the little farm house Marin and I had shared. I filled it with all types of rocking chairs, all my favorite books and records-- and a grand piano, even though I couldn't play. Perhaps one day someone would. I lived a solitary but pastoral life, at ease in the aloneness. Like J. Alfred Prufrock, I measured out my life in coffee spoons, but at least I was doing more than killing time and killing myself.

37 Night Music and River Dance

Greenville, MS 1985

After living just outside the city limits of Greenville a year, I got a dog from the pound, a two year old forty pounder that was a mix of border collie and lab. I named him Otto and had one hell of a time training him to stay out of the river, fearful he would one day be swept away in an undertow, suddenly gone like Marin. Like her, though, he was fearless, and he'd look at me like, "You act like an old man. C'mon and play with me in the water." Eventually though he learned to go no farther than the water's edge, even if Old Man River did call him.

Otto was good company, and he forced me into routines of getting up and dressing every day, doing chores around the house and yard, cooking and feeding us both. He loved riding along the levee in the Thunderbird. He was pretty good at conversation, too, and an even better listener. He loved music, and when I had the stereo on, he would just lie around like an old hog, relaxed and snoring in the sun. When the music played, he was off duty. He did have his own agenda though and tried his best to talk me into buying some pygmy goats for him to play with, but I just wasn't ready for that much company.

Two years after getting Otto, he told me one day he thought I needed to go back to work, to get back to living a real life. He had plenty to do on the place to stay busy during my work hours, chasing dragonflies and squirrels, and in truth, I had missed teaching—more than I wanted to admit. I missed the curiosity of kids and their juvenile sense of humor. So I brushed up on educational issues, made an appointment, got dressed up with a tie, and went to see the superintendent of the Greenville Public School System. School would start up in another month, and I was hoping I was not too late in my decision to return to work, hoping all the teaching positions weren't already filled.

"Why do you want to teach black children?" he asked me.

The question both startled me and appalled me. The look on my face must have taken him aback as well since I looked at him like he was some kind of idiot. So I answered his question with a question. "Why would I not want to teach them?"

"Look, Mr. Gresham, I'm just trying to figure out your motivation. We get a lot of people come through here thinking they want to teach little black kids and believing they can 'save' them. These kids don't need saving, and I don't need another white guy coming up in here for another social experiment who thinks he's a savior."

"Look," I said, "I just want to teach. I could barely save myself after my wife was k.....after my wife died five years ago. I surely am not here to save anyone else. I just want to teach, and I'll teach anything they want to learn."

"And what if they don't want to learn?" he asked.

"Then it becomes my job to figure out why and fix it if I can. If I can't ---and plenty of things interfere with a kid's learning, as you know---then it still won't be my job to judge them, but guide them as best I can in finding something they DO want to learn. They may not give two hoots in hell about Shakespeare and just want to learn how to raise chickens or fix a tractor engine. In that case, I'll teach myself some chicken farming and whatever I can learn about diesel engines, and I'll teach that."

"Are you for real? I mean most educators are so stuck on content and just want to teach a subject," he explained. Then he began to mock those types of teachers, using a prissy kind of voice. "I want to teach math. I want to teach reading. I want to teach home economics." Then backtracking, he asked, "So you don't care if your English class becomes part shop class?"

"I said I want to teach. I didn't say I only want to teach English. I said that was my major."

"SUZY!!" He bellowed to his secretary on the other side of the door. "Bring me a contract in here for Mr. Gresham. We're sending him over to the high school to work with the freshmen."

The school year began with the usual in service meetings, room preparations, and book hauling to our classrooms for distribution. I thought of that first day long ago when Theophilus bet I couldn't pronounce his name. What a great student he had been. I looked forward to more like him.

A month after school started, my principal, Mr. Lindsey, called me in for a conference—every teacher's dread, being called to the principal's office.

"I'm putting you on the district curriculum writing committee to work with some middle school reading and language arts teachers. Our kids are lagging farther and farther behind the rest of the country every year. We've got to figure out a way to get these kids ready for high school. They come in here barely reading above a fifth grade level. So we're going to start at the root and revamp our middle school language arts programs. You will be the head of the committee and the liaison to advise those teachers what they need to be teaching. You will be out one day a week for the next six weeks. You got six full working days to hammer out the plan; then those teachers can select the materials needed later."

"How do the middle school teachers in the district feel about this?"

"Who the hell cares? We have a problem to solve."

"I see," I replied. "Not how I would approach it with them, but we will find a way to fix it if possible."

"That's why I'm sending you, Mr. Gresham. You have the diplomatic skills many of us administrators don't have time for."

If I had been talking to Mr. Meredith, I would have argued with him and told him it was not diplomacy but simple respect for the job they do that gets teachers to work with you and for you. But I just thanked him for the opportunity and left.

When I reported in to the central office for the first curriculum meeting, I was given a list of teachers expected to attend. The fourth name of the list... was Essie Coleman. I instantly thought about leaving the building and never going back to work. I just didn't think I could see Coleman again, knowing it would pile a bunch of hurt on top of the fragile healing that I was working on so hard. As I stood there debating the escape, she tapped me on the shoulder from behind. I turned around to the biggest hug I had had in years. Her smile was as refreshing as I remembered. She then leaned in as if we were plotting a conspiracy and she said, "I'm so sorry, Gresham, about your wife. Marin was a special lady."

Once more, I could not find a voice for the moment. I just nodded. She put her hand on my arm like she always did when she laughed, and she said, "Dawn always breaks. Time is valuable with grief. Make it your friend."

And so began another chapter with my dear Miss Coleman, at once very much the same and yet very much different from the relationship we had had previously. We became the closest of friends with a special bond. We met at my house outside town on my ten acres once a month for dinner together. We cooked steaks on the fire pit and drank wine on the veranda as we watched barges float past on the river.

One night the conversation turned toward marriage, so I asked her, "Why have you never married, Coleman?"

"Well, you know what they say about brown sugar? Well, evidently it's the same with powdered sugar," she said, referencing our previous relationship. Then she reached over and touched my arm, laughing at her own joke. "No, seriously Gresham, I just never wanted kids, and every man interested in getting serious with me-- did. So I just figured marriage is not for me."

"But you would have married me back then though, wouldn't you?"

"Maybe. Under different circumstances than what Greenwood had to offer. It's nice now though that we can just be here together, alone and away from everyone else. I love this place you have here, Gresham. It's peaceful. Your heart needs this."

"Yes, it does. C'mon. Pick up your wine glass, and let's walk down closer to the river."

"Let me kick off these high heels so I don't sink in the grass."

"Good idea. I'll go barefoot, too."

We often walked down The Slope to the river, holding hands along the way. Sometimes she would lean into me and take my arm. Sometimes she would put her arm around my waist and slip her thumb through the back of my belt. We would star gaze, but mostly we just sat on the sandbar and listened to the sound of the Big River, rolling through miles of time.

One night, in late spring, on our walk back up The Slope, she stopped.

"What is it?" I asked.

"What if I wanted you to kiss me?"

"Then I would."

"But when you close your eyes, you'll always see Marin, won't you?"

"I don't know, Coleman. Probably tonight, but I don't know about always."

"Then kiss me anyway," she said.

Before she came for dinner the next month, I had some sparse lighting installed high in the trees and some wiring done so that we could have music outside when we walked to the river. We danced barefoot in the grass. It was both comforting and sensational to hold her close, to soak in the smell and warmth of her, to feel some twinge of uncomplicated, guiltless joy.

Every time she got ready to leave, the last thing we did was dance to a slow dance version I had found of "Darkness of the Delta." Sometimes we sang along, usually a loud and slightly inebriated version. But mostly our pleasure was in the fact we could laugh easily together in fun and tenderness. We could live and breathe freely on The Slope by The River.

Coleman was my solace and a healing poultice for the wreckage that nearly killed me. I was for her the friend who accepted her as a loving, giving woman without the expectation that she give me children. We both provided a comforting joy in each other's touch and kiss, a tenderness in living apart from the world of judgment and prejudice, if only in the dark of Delta nights in a world we created only for ourselves. In finding her again, I learned God had not forsaken me; He just waited for me to look up again for a resurrected life of my own. Sometimes we do entertain angels unaware, but like with Coleman, we know exactly who they are and why God has placed them on the crossroads, knowing eventually we would come again along that path.

I still love the Delta, despite all the darkness it brought into my life that cracked my soul by taking a jackhammer to it. I still love it despite all its murders and murderers set free, or worse, never brought to trial. I love it despite its dichotomy of culture where division and suspicion seem to be the hard and fast mainstays, and reconciliation is rarely ever the goal, or even the possibility of a goal. One cannot deny there is a wickedness among the beauty, an aversion to peaceful living among "the others," a fear that equality is like a pie, if someone else gets a piece that leaves less for me.

I love it despite its boundaries that do not allow for sharing space, where separation is expected and demanded, and fear is the wedge that is immovable. I love the Delta, too, despite its holding the bones of my wife and my friend. Like the sticky sweat of Delta humidity that pastes your clothes to your body, the Delta attaches itself to your heart and soul with an intense love that you cannot deny or leave behind or wash off. Coleman and I both knew all this, felt all this, and could not escape it. So we stayed and built a life despite it.

That Delta that smothered me in grief like the kudzu that kills everything it covers also mended the crevasse in my soul. With the flat land fatted with row upon row of cotton and soybeans, fresh in the ground, it can still stir a soul to look up and thank God Almighty for the beauty and smell of good dirt. But mostly I was healed by the sounds of Old Man River running at night, moving into tomorrow, washing over all my wounds and packing them with mud so I eventually could stop bleeding inside. The other half was resurrected by Coleman's return, healing the man in me to stand up and dance again, healing more at the core that Claire never could reach.

Often after dinner, in our walk back up The Slope from the river, we would just collapse in the cool grass, lying on our backs and looking up at the heavens. Back at the house, we often fell asleep side by side on the large chaise lounge on the veranda until early sun dragged us from dreaming. Other times she would intentionally stay, and we went to bed in a room with windows facing the river, where early sun made it look golden. Neither of us could say we were in love, not like we were when we first met and dated, but there was an easy love between us and a smooth sleep whenever she lay beside me.

There would always be darkness in our lives for the losses we have to endure and the cherished things we have to give up. I learned with Coleman we can also make peace in the dark night and find freedom and strength there, if we are willing to "just be" a part of it and unafraid of the role it plays in bringing us to new light. The darkness can indeed be terrifying at times, when it fills us up inside and refuses to let us see others, but for those who can cross barriers and sit at ease by the river, the darkness has a fulfilling joy if we will always be intentional about getting up and dancing when the river murmurs our favorite music.

When it's darkness on the delta
That's the time my heart is light
When it's darkness on the delta
Let me linger in the shelter of the night

Fields of cotton all around me
Voices singin' sweet and low
Lord, I'm lucky that you found me
Where the muddy Mississippi waters flow

Lounging on the levee
Listenin' to the nightingales way up above
Laughter on the levee
No one's heart is heavy
All God's children got someone to love

When it's darkness on the delta
Only heaven is in sight
When it's darkness on the delta
Let me linger in the shelter of the night

Lyrics by Marty Symes and Al J. Neibur

CPSIA information can be obtained
at www.ICGtesting.com
Printed in the USA
LVHW100935241218
601529LV00050B/1415/P